The Government of London

The Government of London

THE STRUGGLE FOR REFORM

GERALD RHODES

with a Preface by
Professor W. A. Robson

University of Toronto Press

72256

Printed in England

Contents

72256

APPENDICES

Maps

Preface

The government, planning and functioning of giant cities, or metropolitan areas as they are often called, present problems of worldwide significance. They are found in the developed and in the underdeveloped countries; in those with a market economy and in the communist régimes; in the East and in the West; in the richest and in the poorest nations. The problems facing the giant cities have sprung from similar causes which have produced similar results everywhere.

What are these problems? They are those arising from the difficulty of providing basic services at an adequate standard on so vast a scale; of controlling the growth of population and the extension of the great metropolis without curtailing its vitality or reducing its standard of living; of coping with the ever-growing numbers of commuters who make the daily journey to work at an increasing cost in terms of money, time and nervous energy; of preventing the traffic arteries from seizing up under the impact of the torrent of motor cars which pours into them on every working day; of planning the sprawling metropolis in a way which will have some regard to order, beauty, convenience, health and amenity; of providing new or reconditioned housing at a rate which is not always lagging behind the growth of slums and sub-standard accommodation; of trying to remedy or restrain the mounting figures of crime, drug addiction, suicide, homelessness, juvenile delinquency, gangsterism, illegitimacy, broken homes, prostitution and other evils which flourish to a disproportionate extent in the greatest cities. Often there is the paradox that the municipal governments of the wealthiest metropolitan cities are in the most serious financial straits. And everywhere the integration of the teeming millions of the city into a genuine community presents one of the most difficult political problems of the present age.

It is no wonder, then, that the problems of metropolitan areas have become one of the leading pre-occupations of governments, international organizations, social scientists, planners and officials the world over. Here is a subject of common interest which transcends differences of politico-economic régime, language, race or culture.

Here is a subject on which the United Nations can organize seminars and conferences in the confident knowledge that the participants will discuss their common problems rationally and seriously without rhetorical assertions or wild accusations. Here is a subject on which forty great cities from as many countries thought it worthwhile to attend an international conference organized by the Bureau of Municipal Research in Toronto in 1967. Here is a subject on which a cascade of books, pamphlets and articles comes pouring out of the printing presses and publishing houses in an endless stream.

Yet although there is much analysis and discussion in the world of thought, surprisingly little has been attempted in the world of action to relieve the pressing problems of the giant city. We may note that it is now becoming clear that the solution to some of those problems lies outside the sphere of the Metropolitan Government. This indeed is the significance of the urban policies which some national governments have adopted; and still more of the regional planning and development which is now familiar in Britain, France, Poland, the Soviet Union, and several other countries. But whatever may be the implications of the city region, nothing can detract from the overriding need to reform the obsolete and obsolescent system of local government which prevails in most of the world's giant cities.

In this context the reform of local government in Greater London which took effect on 1st April 1965 is of the highest importance. It was, and has remained, the most outstanding example of an attempt to create a system of Metropolitan Government for one of the world's greatest cities which would enable it to respond to the needs of the modern age.

It is a far more drastic reform than that which took place in Metropolitan Toronto; and unlike the highly centralized reforms recently introduced in the District of the Region of Paris, it remains true to the traditions of genuine local government.

In addition to its significance in the wider context, the reform of London government was an event of considerable interest in the history of local government in this country. Not since the structure of local government was devised in the latter part of the nineteenth century had there been any fundamental reorganization to meet the vastly changed social and economic circumstances of Britain in the twentieth century. There have been many enquiries and reports and a limited amount of adjustment within the system; but at no point did these changes result in reform of the structure. Thirty years ago in *The Government and Misgovernment of London* I showed how antiquated and obsolete was the structure of London Government and how clear the need for reform. It was not until the passage of the London Government Act of 1963 that a new structure was devised for an area containing one-seventh of the population of the United Kingdom. Whatever changes may result from the report of the Redcliffe-Maud Commission, there can be little doubt that the London reforms gave a powerful impetus to the idea of a more searching enquiry into local government in the rest of the country than was provided by the ill-fated Local Government Commission.

For these reasons the Greater London Group decided to make the London government reforms the subject of a major research project. The object is twofold. First, to examine the origin and course of the reforms and to show how and why they came about; secondly, to describe and assess the working of the new system in practice. I have already indicated that this undertaking is important in itself. I believe that it is also particularly fitting that the Greater London Group should be the body to carry out this research.

The Group was formed under my chairmanship in 1958 in response to an appeal addressed to the Vice Chancellor of London University by Sir Edwin Herbert (now Lord Tangley) the chairman of the Royal Commission on Local Government in Greater London. He urged that a group of scholars should do research and prepare evidence on matters within the Commission's field of enquiry. The evidence submitted by the Greater London Group to the Commission in 1959 was extensive and detailed. It had a considerable influence on the Commission's thinking and recommendations. These in turn were a major factor in the events which resulted in the Conservative Government's commitment to a scheme of reform. Furthermore, the Group's proposals in regard to the number and size of the London Boroughs were closer to those adopted by the Government than were the recommendations of the Herbert Commission. Thus the Group can claim to have played some part in the reform of London government.

During the course of preparing the evidence and in subsequent years the Group assembled a unique collection of documentary material on these events and established close contacts with many leading participants. We have retained a continuing interest in the problems and processes of London government, and have carried out investigations into some aspects of them which have already been published*.

Accordingly the Group initiated a large-scale research study of the reforms in 1965. The present volume represents the first phase of this project. It describes and analyses the events which culminated in the introduction of the new system on 1st April 1965, concentrating in particular on the period from 1957 when the decision was taken to set up a Royal Commission. The study gives an account of the various stages through which the reforms passed and recognises the importance of both political and administrative factors in influencing the decisions which were taken.

The present volume does not evaluate the merits of the reforms. In a further study, which is now in the course of preparation, the main features of the new system of local government in Greater London will be examined more critically. The extent to which it has fulfilled the hopes and fears which were expressed about it will be looked at and its merits and demerits assessed.

Mr Gerald Rhodes was appointed Senior Research Officer in charge of the project. The detailed research was carried out by him or under his supervision. All the chapters of this volume were drafted by Mr Rhodes and discussed in detail by members of the Group. Each chapter has been subsequently revised.

On behalf of the Greater London Group I wish to express our warm thanks to Mr Rhodes for his prolonged and excellent work on this project.

WILLIAM A. ROBSON
Chairman, Greater London Group

*London School of Economics
and Political Science*

* See S. K. Ruck *London Government and the Welfare Services* (Routledge & Kegan Paul, 1963); S. K. Ruck *Municipal Entertainment and the Arts in Greater London* (Allen & Unwin, 1965), and the series of Greater London Papers of which 13 have so far been published by the London School of Economics and Political Science.

Acknowledgements

My first and greatest debt is to the Greater London Group and especially to their Chairman, William Robson, for entrusting this study to me, and for exhorting, persuading and cajoling me to try to improve it once it was under way. Their comments and criticisms on successive drafts at many lively Group meetings helped to give the whole work a depth and coherence which it would otherwise have lacked. I have also learned a good deal from Group discussions about the pitfalls of doing research of this kind. Whether I have always avoided the pitfalls is another matter.

A study concerned with contemporary politics and administration must rely heavily on the readiness of those closely involved in the events described to provide information and comment. I was fortunate in securing a ready response from nearly all those whom I approached. I should particularly like to thank Lord Brooke of Cumnor, formerly Minister of Housing and Local Government; Mr A. E. Coventon, formerly Deputy Director of Establishments, GLC: Mr A. G. Dawtry, Town Clerk of Westminster LB and Hon Sec London Boroughs Association; Viscount Eccles, formerly Minister of Education; Sir Harold Emmerson, Chairman of the London Government Staff Commission; Lord Fiske, formerly Leader of the Greater London Council; Lord Hill of Luton, formerly Minister of Housing and Local Government; Mr George Hooper, Town Clerk of Hillingdon LB; Sir Keith Joseph, formerly Minister of Housing and Local Government; Professor W. J. M. Mackenzie, member of the Royal Commission on Local Government in Greater London; Alderman H. T. Parkin, Bromley LB; Mr C. J. Pearce, Ministry of Housing and Local Government; Sir Norman Prichard, formerly Chairman of the London Boroughs Association; Lady Sharp, formerly Permanent Secretary, Ministry of Housing and Local Government; Mr T. W. Sowerby, Treasurer, Bromley LB; Lord Tangley, Chairman of the Royal Commission on Local Government in Greater London; and Mr R. H. Williams, Town Clerk of Barnet LB. For the time and effort which they and many others devoted to helping me I am immensely grateful. It goes without saying that they bear no responsibility for the views expressed in this study.

Mr K. G. Young, one of the Group's research assistants at the time, worked with me on this project for a year. He performed prodigies in reducing the vast amount of information which we assembled to usable material, particularly in the preparation of Chapter 11. His indefatigable quest for relevant facts was invaluable to me. I am very grateful to him for all his work. I should also like to acknowledge the help given by other members of the Group's research staff at various times.

Finally, I should like to thank Miss Pauline Billingham of the LSE Geography Department for drawing the maps, and the Group's secretaries who worked hard to produce readable texts of the study, particularly Miss Doreen Mann, Mrs Elaine Steinhart, and, latterly, Mrs Eileen Bedford.

G. R.

London School of Economics
and Political Science
May, 1969

The Greater London Group

The Group was formed in 1958 under the Chairmanship of Professor W. A. Robson from among members of the teaching staff of the London School of Economics and Political Science. It carries out research into problems of Government and Administration in Greater London and the South East Region and for this purpose employs a small full-time Research Staff. Its current list of members is as follows:

Professor W. A. Robson, Professor Emeritus of Public Administration (Chairman)

Mr A. J. L. Barnes, Lecturer in Political Science.

Mr B. P. Davies, Lecturer in Social Administration.

Professor A. C. L. Day, Professor of Economics.

Mr D. R. Diamond, Reader in Geography.

Mr J. B. Goddard, Assistant Lecturer in Geography.

Professor J. A. G. Griffith, Professor of English Law.

Professor Emrys Jones, Professor of Geography.

Dr G. W. Jones, Lecturer in Political Science.

Dr P. H. Levin, Senior Research Officer, Dept. of Social Science & Administration.

Miss A. A. Nevitt, Lecturer in Social Administration.

Dr R. A. Parker, Lecturer in Social Administration.

Mr W. J. L. Plowden, Lecturer in Government.

Mr G. J. Ponsonby, formerly Sir Ernest Cassel Reader in Commerce.

Mr D. E. Regan, Lecturer in Public Administration.

Professor P. J. O. Self, Professor of Public Administration.

Mrs E. P. Tate, Lecturer in Social Administration.

Mr J. M. Thomson, Rees Jeffreys Research Fellow in the Economics and Administration of Transport.

Professor M. J. Wise, Professor of Geography.

1
Local Government in London

Nineteenth-century developments

To devise an effective system of local government for London has for a long time presented special difficulties. The latest system, brought into being by the London Government Act of 1963, has created, as did all previous attempts to change London's government, a pattern of local authorites and functions different from that of the rest of the country. To make intelligible the purpose and effects of the 1963 reforms therefore requires some understanding of the historical context within which the unique position of London's government has developed.

By the early years of the nineteenth century the built-up area of London extended well beyond the boundaries of the ancient City, and included practically the whole of what later became the Metropolitan Boroughs of Holborn, Finsbury and Southwark together with large parts of Westminster, Stepney and other areas.[1] Whereas the population of the City at the first census in 1801 was nearly 130,000, that of Westminster was over 150,000, of Southwark nearly 70,000 and of the remaining part of the continuously built-up area over 500,000.[2]

Two elements in this situation were of great significance for future developments. First, the jurisdiction of the City of London, which alone at that date had any system of effective local government in the area, extended only to a relatively small part of the population of the metropolis. Secondly, there was the sheer size of London, both absolutely and in relation to the rest of the country; one-tenth of all the inhabitants of England and Wales lived in London.

The first point became important when municipal reform was undertaken in the 1830s. The Royal Commission on Municipal Corporations in its second report of 1837 suggested that there should be a single form of Government covering the whole metropolis and not just the City. London, in their view, should be treated no differently from the rest of the country to which the recently passed Municipal Corporations Act applied.

This might have been done by the extension of the City's boundaries and administration of the extended area by a reformed municipal corporation on the lines of those established in the provinces. But the City Corporation used its considerable power and influence to ensure that its unique position was not changed. The result is that the City of London remains to this day a local authority in its own right besides retaining its ancient ceremonial dignities and privileges and also its own distinct sources of revenue for certain purposes. The profound effect which the success of the City's policy has had on the later development of London's government has been well put by the son of a former Lord Mayor of London, himself a former councillor and alderman of the City:

> 'There were occasions during the last century when, had the City been more outward-looking and more venturesome, the whole history of the local government of the Metropolis might have been very different. Last century, government after government begged the City to take responsibility for the growing mass of the Metropolis, but, time after time, the City turned its back on what would have been a very heavy duty and a very heavy responsibility but which might have solved a lot of our problems today.'[3]

But if the solution used for other municipal corporations could not be applied to London, it was equally certain that action had to be taken to deal with the problems of the great and growing metropolis. In 1829 the Government, largely at the insistence of Sir Robert Peel, had found an answer to the alarming problem of maintaining law and order by creating a metropolitan police force for an area extending roughly 6–7 miles from Charing Cross.[4] This force was under the charge at first of two salaried Justices of the Peace and later of a single Commissioner responsible to the Home Secretary. Its area was far larger than any which was regarded as feasible for local government purposes until the Greater London Council assumed its powers in 1965, and it included large tracts of open country. But the important precedent which it established was for a piecemeal and, particularly, a functional approach to London's problems. Sanitation, for example, was a problem which could not continue to be ignored but the solution which was devised for it was the creation in 1855 of the Metropolitan Board of Works, an indirectly elected body to be responsible mainly for drainage and sewerage,[5] although it later acquired a good many other functions. The area of the Metropolitan Board of Works was very much smaller than that of the Metropolitan Police District; it was, however, larger than the built-up area of London in 1855. Although the Metropolitan Board of Works became the most important body performing local government functions in London it was not the last of the *ad hoc* bodies to be set up to deal with specific problems as they arose. The Metropolitan Asylums Board, for example, was set up in 1867 and the Metropolitan Water Board in 1902.

In 1888 local government in the counties was reorganized. There was at that date no directly elected local government body for London as a whole. The Local Government Act of 1888 created a County of London, corresponding to the area of the Metropolitan Board of Works, for which there was to be an elected county council. Thus, unlike the other county councils established under the Act, the area of jurisdiction of the LCC was an artificial creation with no historical basis; it consisted of large areas of Middlesex and Surrey together with a smaller part of Kent. In addition, it was almost entirely urbanized and resembled in this way no other county in the country. The London County Council thus came into being as a by-product of the reorganization of the administration of the predominantly rural counties. It seems doubtful, however, whether this particular pattern of government would have been evolved for London if it had not been for the fact that a series of financial scandals affecting members of the Metropolitan Board of Works compelled some action to be taken about that body.[6]

The area of the London County Council did not correspond to the built-up area of London in 1888 since this already extended further (eg in West Ham and Willesden) in some directions; on the other hand, within the county there was a good deal of land (eg in Wandsworth and Lewisham) which was not yet built on. Its functions differed in important ways from those undertaken by other counties, mainly because the LCC inherited the powers of the Metropolitan Board of Works.

In 1899, under the London Government Act of that year, twenty-eight Metropolitan Boroughs were set up in place of the large number of local vestries and boards which had remained unaffected by the 1888 Act, largely to provide counterweights to the power and prestige of the LCC., But the powers of the Metropolitan Boroughs remained comparatively small. Although some of them eventually attained the size of large County Boroughs in other parts of the country,[8] in many ways their powers were less than those of medium-sized Municipal Boroughs; for example, they never had education functions.

The Ullswater Commission, 1921–23

The Act of 1899 completed the pattern of local government in the area which came to be known as Greater London.[9] That pattern lasted until 1965. Its main feature was a three-fold system for the performance of functions; first, the City of London containing an increasingly smaller proportion of the built-up area and residential population of London but retaining its own special structure; secondly, the County of London with its unique division of functions between the LCC and the Metropolitan Boroughs; thirdly, the normal County Borough, county and county district structure applying to the other metropolitan counties – Middlesex, Essex, Kent, Surrey and Hertfordshire. Throughout this period the London County Council exercised most of the major functions of local government in an area which had never been designed specifically for local government purposes. In 1888, as in 1855, it was used because it happened to have been used already.[10] Two major functions which the LCC never exercised were police and water supply, the latter being undertaken from 1902 by the Metropolitan Water Board, another functional and indirectly elected body exercising authority over an area a good deal larger than that of the LCC.

The growth of London beyond the boundaries of the LCC in the twentieth century brought increasing problems for London's government. By 1914 places like Walthamstow and Leyton to the northeast and Acton and Willesden to the west and north, had grown to be indissolubly part of London's built-up area, and had demonstrated the artificial nature of the boundaries between London and Middlesex or Essex. This development brought pressures for action to be taken, at least in certain spheres, over a wider area than that of any existing local authorities. Between 1905 and 1920, for example, four official committees investigated various aspects of London's traffic problems and all concluded that there ought to be a single authority responsible for traffic and indeed transport services generally over an area at least as large as Greater London.[11]

This point was taken up by the LCC which in 1920 sent a deputation to the Prime Minister to urge that an inquiry should be held into the whole question of London government particularly from the point of view that certain services ought to be administered over a much larger area than that of the LCC. This request seems to have been the main factor influencing the Government in their decision to set up a Royal Commission in 1921.[12] Its chairman was Lord Ullswater and one of its main tasks was to see 'what if any alterations are needed in the local government of the administrative county of London and the surrounding districts, with a view to securing greater efficiency and economy in the administration of local government services'.

These terms of reference seemed to be drawn sufficiently wide to permit a comprehensive enquiry into the needs of London government such as had not been made since the report of the Royal Commission on Municipal Corporations in 1837. The majority of the Royal Commission did not, however, see their task in this light. Although they recognized that their job was not simply to arbitrate between the LCC and the other authorities in the area on the former's proposals, they nevertheless felt that they were mainly there to hear the evidence presented, to weigh it up and come to a conclusion. The LCC, however, put forward their proposals for a more widely based authority rather as a general proposition than as a fully argued case, and clearly expected or at least hoped that the Royal Commission would themselves investigate them further. Most of the other local authorities in the area were content to argue that nobody had shown that they were not capable of doing their job. The majority of the Commission[13] drew the conclusion that no major changes were required. They were reinforced in this view by the thought that 'from a practical point of view' there was little point in recommending something which because it would arouse the opposition of so many local authorities would be unlikely to be put into effect.

But besides the majority report there were two minority reports which indicated the fundamental disagreements among the members of the Commission about how their enquiry was to be conducted. The first minority report[14] favoured the division of London into a number of County Boroughs with a central authority for certain matters such as main drainage; but the report remarked that because the proceedings of the Commission had taken very much the form of 'a litigious enquiry' they did not have sufficient information to decide whether there should be reform or not. The other minority report was more detailed and more sharply critical of the other members of the Commission.[15] It stressed the view that the Commission should itself have taken the initiative in presenting a constructive scheme of reform if it had believed that this would result in greater efficiency and economy. The signatories themselves advocated the creation of a directly elected Greater London authority to be responsible for major services such as traffic, town planning, education and water supply.

In accordance with the majority view of the Commission, no changes were made in the areas, status or functions of the authorities in the Greater London area. But the majority in this case consisted of only half the members, and the others felt in varying degrees a need either for further examination of the problems or for positive changes. Certain themes and arguments which figured in the proceedings of the Ullswater Commission are important because they foreshadowed much later debate about London government.

The arguments about London government

First, there is the argument for reform. The brief history of London's government given earlier shows how little the system which had grown up had been devised with the particular problems and difficulties of governing London in mind. It was a fundamental part of the Donald/Walsh minority report to argue that Greater London was a unity[16] and that a system should be devised which would best provide for the administration of services of Greater London significance.

Secondly, there is usually opposed to this argument the practical argument for leaving things essentially as they are. The argument takes various forms but basically it holds that whatever the theoretical justification for fundamental change it is important to preserve an established system provided that it works; and where change can be shown as necessary it should be based on as little disturbance of that system as possible. This is characteristically the attitude adopted by most existing local authorities. As the majority report of the Ullswater Commission put it, the other local authorities were almost unanimous in opposing the LCC's proposals, partly because

> 'great importance should be attached to preserving the continuity of the history and the sentiment which was based upon the existence of the county areas'

and partly because the County Councils

> 'had for over thirty years been building up a system of administration which was based upon the assumption that . . . their area would remain as it was.'

But

> 'neither the London County Council nor other witnesses had proved or even suggested that the administration of the existing Local Authorities was inefficient or uneconomical.'

Most suggestions from local authorities for meeting major difficulties were therefore confined to the setting-up of joint committees, advisory bodies etc. which would not fundamentally disturb the existing system.[17]

Clearly, both these arguments depend for their effectiveness on the question 'are there deficiencies in the present arrangements sufficient to make it necessary for action to be taken?' This critical third theme was abundantly displayed in the proceedings of the Ullswater Commission, and it revolved round the two interrelated functions of town planning and traffic and transport, whose problems most directly derive from the growth of London. Reference has already been made to the various official committees which from 1902 onwards had studied London's traffic and transport problems. The latest of these in 1920 had reported that 'immediate and effective action is imperatively needed' and would require a 'complete remodelling, co-ordination and increase of existing powers of control' which were 'quite inadequate, either effectively to alleviate existing conditions, or to offer any hope of permanent improvement in the future.'[18] And it was in relation to this kind of problem that the LCC had put forward its tentative proposals.

It was on the question of what action should be taken to deal with the problems which affected Greater London as a whole that the differences between the majority of the Ullswater Commission and the minority report of Messrs Donald and Walsh appeared most clearly. The majority recommended that a committee should be set up to advise the Minister primarily in relation to transport and town planning but also in some related housing and main drainage matters. An advisory committee was rejected by Messrs Donald and Walsh because 'it passes the problem by. At best it is only a palliative.'[19]

The Government's attitude

Important as these arguments were, in the last resort the problem of London government was a problem for the central government. From the time of the Ullswater Commission until that of the Herbert Commission, two linked viewpoints seem to have mainly characterized successive Governments' attitudes. The first was that very strong arguments were required to justify changing the existing system; the second was that any changes must be with the agreement of at least a majority of existing local authorities.

It has already been pointed out that the main reason for the setting-up of the Ullswater Commission was the pressure exercised by the LCC. When Lloyd George saw the LCC deputation on 9 December 1920 he told them:

'What you really want is agreement. A Report that would get 128 Local Authorities up in arms against you is not a Report that any Government could face with equanimity; . . . but I think a Royal Commission might achieve something in the nature of agreement.'[20]

There was some disagreement among members of the Ullswater Commission whether this was a considered view or only a 'casual reference'.[21] Yet it seemed to sum up accurately the views of the central government. Take, for example, the question of the creation of County Boroughs. Within Greater London there were by 1920 three County Boroughs, Croydon, East Ham and West Ham, all adjoining the boundaries of the County of London. As other similar areas grew in population to a size which elsewhere in the country would justify their applying for County Borough status, there seemed to be a need for a clear statement of what the government's policy was on this issue.

The Ullswater Commission did not deal with the question on the grounds that it was part of the task of the Royal Commission on Local Government (the 'Onslow Commission') set up by the Government in 1922 to examine, among other things, the procedure for creating and extending County Boroughs in the country generally. The Ministry of Health, in evidence to the Onslow Commission, pointed out that the Government had not been in favour of creating further County Boroughs in Greater London because they did not want to prejudice any general solution to the problems of local government in Greater London.

But a general solution would have required general agreement and, as the Ullswater Commission's report showed there was no general agreement on a solution either among the members of the Commission or among local authorities. There was, however, agreement among the latter on the preservation of the existing system. Quite consistently, therefore, with their general attitude the Government did not adopt any general solution but tried to deal with the problems within the existing system. So far as the County Borough issue was concerned, this meant that all applications for County Borough status within Greater London were opposed from the time of the Ullswater Commission onward.

From the Ullswater Commission to 1939

Among the problems identified by the Commission as requiring action London's traffic was among the most prominent. Under the Government's London Traffic Act of 1924, a London and Home Counties Traffic Advisory Committee was set up. As its name implies, it covered a much wider area than Greater London, including such places as Harpenden and Sevenoaks within its boundaries and its purpose was to advise the Minister of Transport. The boundaries of its area were chosen almost accidentally. The majority of the Ullswater Commission had said that 'the country within a radius of about 25 miles appears to us to be a suitable area' but for no stronger reason than the fact that a similar area had recently been used for the London and Home Counties Electricity District.[22] The Committee remained in existence until it was abolished by the London Government Act, 1963, but its powers were never as great as those suggested by the majority of the Ullswater Commission. In particular, it never acquired any town planning functions.

Town planning, however, provided further problems. In particular, the continued growth of London brought the need to concert plans over a wide area. As with traffic, a means of dealing with this problem was sought within the existing local government structure. In 1927, a Greater London Regional Planning Committee was set up at the instigation of the Minister of Health with representatives of local authorities in the London Traffic Area. But the Committee argued in its first report that an advisory body for regional planning was unsatisfactory because there was no obligation on the part of individual local authorities to carry out their agreed part.[23]

Nevertheless, it and successor bodies under various names continued in being until the 1939–45 War, although they met rarely and could achieve little.

In 1939 Professor W. A. Robson published *The Government and Misgovernment of London*, a vivid presentation of the argument for reform backed by a wealth of detailed analysis of the shortcomings in the performance of individual functions; this analysis was accompanied by positive proposals, most notably for an authority for Greater London as a whole. Robson thought that the best hope of achieving this was 'the inexorable pressure of facts' and the impossibility of existing tendencies continuing 'without the chaos and confusion reaching a stage at which the alternatives to reform will be seen to be infinitely more dangerous to established expectations than a bold measure of adaptation'.[24]

But there was no sign in 1939 that the Government viewed the position as seriously as this. Nevertheless, changes were taking place which were bound to affect the London government situation. One was the continued growth of London particularly in the outer area of Middlesex and in parts of Essex, Kent and Surrey. By 1939 Middlesex was a wholly urban county consisting of fifteen Municipal Boroughs and eleven Urban Districts. Several of the boroughs, such as Ealing, were large and populous and felt that they could perfectly well perform the functions of County Boroughs; they, therefore, pressed to attain this status but their claims were resisted by the county council and could make no headway in the face of the Government's general attitude.

The White Paper of 1945 and the Reading Committee

In January 1945 the Coalition Government issued a White Paper on 'Local Government in England and Wales during the Period of Reconstruction' whose main thesis was that 'there is no general desire to disrupt the existing structure of local government'.[25] By this was meant chiefly that there was no general desire among local authorities for change. The White Paper also needs to be seen in its context. The system of regional commissioners established by the Government during the war had aroused the apprehension of local authorities that there might be some move towards regional government after the war. The White Paper statement was designed to reassure local authorities on this point.

It is significant that apart from the views of local authorities the White Paper put forward as a further reason for not making far-reaching changes in the local government structure the fact that a full-scale enquiry would be needed and this could only lead to delays in important local government services such as housing and education. These two factors, the desire to carry local authority opinion with them and the belief that no major changes could be introduced without a lengthy enquiry were important elements in the thinking of post-war Governments on the question of local government reform.

There was, however, one important local government problem about which local authorities themselves were anxious that something should be done. This was the policy and procedure to be followed in the creation or extension of County Boroughs. The 1945 White Paper proposed the establishment of a Local Government Boundary Commission to revise local government areas outside the County of London. The Government, however, recognized the special position of Middlesex: 'if a process of creating County Boroughs were initiated, there would be no stopping short of removing the whole area from the administrative county and destroying the county government.'[26] Their solution was quite simply that the Commission should not be permitted to consider applications for county borough status in Middlesex.

But even more troublesome than Middlesex was the problem of London. The White Paper pointed out that there were two issues (i) whether the boundaries of the county of London should be extended (ii) whether changes should be made in the areas of the Metropolitan Boroughs and in the division of functions between them and the LCC. It did not come to any firm conclusion about the first issue. On the one hand, it said, 'there is much to be said' for having a much larger area as a single administrative unit for London government; on the other the county of London 'already contains a population nearly double that of any other local government area'. In any case the problem was too big to give to the Commission, it would require special legislation and 'the Government are not satisfied that the present time is opportune' because of all the big new tasks (e.g. in education) which local authorities were taking on; but 'it is recognized that experience of the working of the new services may disclose the need of more radical alterations'.[27]

To consider the second issue, the White Paper proposed that an authoritative body should be set up as a matter of urgency. On 12 April 1945 the Minister of Health (Mr Willink) duly announced the appointment of a committee of five members under the chairmanship of Lord Reading to examine the number, size and boundaries of the Metropolitan Boroughs, and the distribution of functions between them and the LCC. The Local Government Boundary Commission was also set up[28] but was excluded from considering the County of London or the establishment of County Boroughs in Middlesex. The election of the Labour Government in July 1945 did not at first appear to affect the situation. In December 1945 the Minister of Health (Mr Bevan) informed the House of Commons that the Reading Committee had met seven times up to that date.[29] But a few months later the Committee was wound up before it could make a report. Two grounds were given by Mr Bevan for this action, first, that the local authorities took the view that they 'could submit little more than factual evidence' to a committee which was dealing with only one facet of London's problems and, secondly, that an investigation was needed into the wider problem of Greater London but this would have to come after it had been settled what functions local authorities were to perform.[30]

Failure of Labour Government to investigate Greater London's problems

No attempt was however made by the Government in succeeding years to initiate this wider investigation. Apart from the reasons already given for the reluctance of governments to become involved in the wider problems of London government, there were additional reasons why the Attlee Government gave a low priority to the consideration of local government areas and functions. This may be illustrated from the fate of the Local Government Boundary Commission which was wound up in 1949. The Commissioners found themselves hampered in their work by the fact that they had no jurisdiction over the functions of local authorities; nor could they recommend new types of local authorities. They reached the conclusion that 'neither we nor our successors can everywhere create effective and convenient units of local government without some amendment of local government legislation.'[31] The Minister of Health (Mr Bevan) said that the Government accepted that it was difficult for the Commission to carry out the task allotted to them. But the solution they proposed was to abolish the Commission and restore the pre-1945 position 'until such time as the Government have had an opportunity of reviewing the structure and functions of local government.' At the same time, 'it is very doubtful indeed whether we would be able to come to an early decision on what the views of the Government are about the reorganization of local government.'[32]

The truth is probably that the Government's preoccupation with major legislation such as the nationalization of the railways, gas and electricity, meant that local government was neglected. In Aneurin Bevan's case the creation of the National Health Service took priority over the rejuvenation of local government. The piecemeal way in which local government lost functions under the Attlee Government's legislation is indicative of that government's order of priorities. Nevertheless the problems which the 1945 White Paper had referred to did not diminish but rather became aggravated with the passage of time. The denial of the opportunity of seeking County Borough status to the larger authorities in Middlesex is an example. Simply to leave the situation as it was in Middlesex, as proposed in the 1945 White Paper, could only further increase the tension between the county council and the district councils, which, as will be seen later, centred on a number of specific issues such as the arrangements for delegation in education.

But although in local government terms the Middlesex issue was prominent since it involved in an acute form the mutual antagonisms of county and borough which were inherent in the system established by the 1888 Act, it is even more important to consider the position of London's local government in functional terms. Mutual antagonism between authorities, however undesirable, does not necessarily imply that functions and services are not carried out satisfactorily.

The problem of planning administration

As might be expected, the services whose provision under the existing local government structure raised problems were precisely those in which social and economic pressures had produced changes which paid no attention to local government boundaries. Town and country planning, which became a function of major importance in the postwar years, is an outstanding example. Although both the City and the County of London had plans prepared during the war to assist in post-war reconstruction and development, the Government recognized that London's influence stretched far beyond the LCC boundaries. In 1942 it commissioned Professor Abercrombie to prepare a Greater London plan to cover an area of nearly 2,600 square miles stretching northwards and westwards from the LCC boundaries into Bedfordshire and Buckinghamshire as well as including the whole of Surrey and Hertfordshire. The boundaries of this area were thus much further out than either the Metropolitan Police District or even the London Traffic Area.[33]

Professor Abercrombie himself was in no doubt that 'there has been a lamentable failure to realize a need for co-ordination in planning all round London'[34], and he proposed the establishment of a regional planning board. The Minister of Town and Country Planning (Mr, now Lord, Silkin) in announcing the Government's views on Abercrombie's plan in March 1946 said that it was proposed to set up an advisory committee to examine the plan and for this purpose the 143 authorities in the area were grouped into 23 joint planning committees each to be represented on the advisory committee. But he also announced the appointment of a London Planning Administration Committee under the chairmanship of Mr Clement Davies[35] to consider 'the appropriate machinery for securing concerted action' on a regional plan for London.

This latter committee was immediately faced with the dilemma which had confronted all committees of inquiry which had had to consider the functional requirements of London government in piecemeal fashion. Either 'concerted action' required structural changes in local government, in which case the problem could not be adequately considered within the terms of reference of a committee looking at a particular function or group of functions; or some means for securing co-operation and co-ordination of action among local authorities would have to be used, with the risk of ineffectiveness which had earlier troubled the Greater London Regional Planning Committee.[36]

The Clement Davies Committee reporting in 1949 recommended that the larger question of the reform of London government should be investigated by a local government commission, but it could not reach agreement on what action should be taken meanwhile within the existing local government structure.[37] The majority of the members of the committee favoured the setting-up of a joint advisory committee of the planning authorities with limited powers, but the minority advocated a joint planning board on the grounds that an advisory committee would not be effective in securing action. No action was taken by the government on the first and major proposal; and in the face of the indifference of local authorities to an advisory committee and their opposition to a joint board, no special machinery of co-ordination was set up. Until the London Government Act of 1963 the Abercrombie plan provided the general frame-work within which the Counties and County Boroughs in Greater London prepared their development plans; and co-ordination of these plans was in the hands of the Minister who had to approve them.

This account of the difficulties in planning administration gives point to the view of the Herbert Commission that

'No independent inquirer has been satisfied with the machinery for planning in the Review Area whether before the Act of 1947 or since.'[38]

The White Papers of 1956 and 1957

The Conservative Government which took office in 1951 did not appear likely at first to carry out the investigation into the wider problems of London government to which Mr Bevan had referred in 1946. The first Minister of Housing and Local Government (Mr Harold Macmillan) was chiefly concerned with the first part of his title and the Government's pledge to build 300,000 houses a year. His successor (Mr Duncan Sandys) in 1954 approached the general question of local government reorganization from the point of view of finding how much common ground there was among the local authority associations. In the words of the White Paper published two years later:

'He told them [the local authority associations] that, in his opinion, it would not be fruitful to embark on any extensive reform unless there existed some broad measure of agreement among the local authorities themselves. Moreover, he made it clear that he did not consider that the existing system of local administration had broken down, and that he would not be prepared to contemplate eliminating either the two-tier system in the counties or the one-tier system in the big towns.'[39]

There was, however, agreement that there were special difficulties in the conurbations where either the retention of the existing pattern or the creation of a series of County Boroughs raised problems of co-ordination. As a result of these discussions between the Government and the associations it was proposed that a local government commission should be set up. Among other tasks it was to work out a formula for local government organization in the conurbations.

As in 1945, Greater London was seen to require separate treatment. The White Paper argued that in Middlesex either there must be no County Boroughs or nothing but County Boroughs. 'In all the circumstances, the Government consider that the two-tier structure should be retained throughout Middlesex.' Since the County of London had a different form of local government any changes in its organization 'would have to be specially considered.' But in recognition of the fact that there might nevertheless be a need for action on questions affecting Greater London as a whole the Government proposed that after consultation with all the authorities concerned, 'the Commission (i.e. the proposed Local Government Commission) should be entitled to make such recommendations as they may think desirable.'[40]

Implicit in these proposals was the belief that London government needed at most some rearrangement of areas and functions within Middlesex and some devolution of powers from the LCC to the Metropolitan Boroughs with possibly a joint board for functions affecting Greater London as a whole. In a further White Paper published in May 1957[41] the Government gave no indication that much thought had been given to the special consideration of the organization of local government within the County of London but merely pointed out that until this had been done nothing could be done about redistributing functions between the LCC and the Metropolitan Boroughs. And on Middlesex they proposed to have further discussions with the local authority associations about the distribution of functions.

The appointment of the Royal Commission

On 29 July 1957 the House of Commons was invited to take note of the White Papers which had been produced as a result of the discussions initiated by Mr Duncan Sandys. So far as Greater London was concerned, they seemed to promise little that was new. When, therefore, the Minister of Housing and Local Government, Mr Henry Brooke,[42] announced that the Government had decided to appoint a Royal Commission to look into the problems of Greater London, his announcement came as a surprise. It is of some interest to try to assess the reasons for this decision.

To begin with, there are the reasons put forward by Mr Brooke himself. The Government, he claimed, had come to the conclusion that the proposals put forward in the White Papers in relation to Greater London had two unsatisfactory features; first, it did not make sense to give the Local Government Commission power to look at London but exclude the County of London; secondly, there was 'no definite proof' that the refusal to create any County Boroughs at all in Middlesex was in fact the right course. 'It may be impossible to determine what is the right structure for Middlesex, except in the context of the Greater London area. The plain fact is that Greater London needs to be looked at as a whole.'[43]

The 'plain fact' had not, however, led the Government to this conclusion in 1956. One significant change in the situation was that in January 1957 Mr Brooke had succeeded Mr Sandys as Minister of Housing and Local Government. The most obviously interesting point about Mr Brooke in this context is that he was experienced and well known in London local government. In particular he had been a member of the LCC from 1945 to 1955 and leader of the Conservative opposition for the greater part of that period.[44] This fact was later to be used against him when the Labour Party accused the Conservative Government of gerrymandering and of being motivated primarily by the desire to destroy Labour's control of the LCC.[45] Nothing was heard of these charges in 1957. Nevertheless his knowledge of London government and his awareness of the political realities were reasons why he took a closer look at London than his predecessor had done. His character may also help to explain what happened in 1957. Henry Brooke's political career was marked by an essentially practical, down-to-earth approach to problems. There was something of the manner of the higher civil servant in the way in which he looked at problems as difficulties to be unravelled.[46] It was a pragmatic, limited approach with no hint of any desire to make sweeping, radical changes.

What one must look for, therefore, is some immediate practical issue which could be the occasion for looking again at the White Paper proposals. Undoubtedly the Middlesex issue was a major factor here. To begin with there was the general problem of boroughs which were eager to acquire County Borough status. After the failure of the post-war Boundary Commission in 1949 a number of

B

boroughs, among them Ilford and Ealing, promoted private Bills to acquire CB status in 1949, 1951 and 1952. The main Government argument in opposing these Bills was always that it was wrong to deal with each in isolation and that nothing should be done until after a general review. This was an argument which as the years passed was bound to wear thin unless the Government at least appeared to be tackling the general problem. At first the Government view was that no attempt could be made to deal with the general problem until the local authority associations had had time to discuss and formulate proposals. By 1954 when Ilford again and Luton for the fourth time promoted bills the Government, under a certain amount of pressure, acknowledged with a good deal of hedging and imprecision that something must be done soon.[47] Although this problem was not confined to Greater London it was there that it was particularly acute. In Middlesex alone apart from Ealing there were eight boroughs which, but for the peculiar circumstances of that county, would have had strong claims to become County Boroughs.[48] The proposal in the 1956 White Paper to preserve the existing two-tier structure in Middlesex without any kind of independent enquiry as had been agreed for other conurbations, left the problem unresolved.

But within local government as it existed at that time there was no alternative to a ban on County Boroughs in Middlesex. It is true that the 1956 White Paper had said that the alternatives were either to have all County Boroughs or to have no County Boroughs, but the abolition of a county and the substitution of a series of contiguous County Boroughs as part of a continuous urban area would have been a far more radical departure from the system established by the Acts of 1888 and 1894 than anything which had hitherto been attempted.[49]

It was quite clear, therefore, that if there was to be any solution of the Middlesex problem it would involve some departure from the established pattern of local government in the area. And acceptance of this was only a stage away from acceptance of the need for a major enquiry to cover at least London and Middlesex counties which indeed could hardly fall short of looking at the whole of Greater London.

This view probably reflected not only Mr Brooke's outlook but also that of his departmental advisers at the Ministry of Housing and Local Government headed by the Permanent Secretary, Dame Evelyn (now Lady) Sharp. Later, in evidence to the Royal Commission, she stressed that it was the different pattern of local government in London which had been a major factor in the decision to appoint a Royal Commission.[50] But it must be remembered that, as with the Ullswater Commission of 1921, the Government's decision to appoint a Royal Commission meant no more than that a case had been made for an enquiry. If the presentation of that case was Mr Brooke's responsibility and if he stressed the immediate difficulties which the 1956 White Paper had not removed, this did not mean that either he or the Government were committed to a reform of London government. It is often believed that the appointment of a Royal Commission can be a convenient means of shelving an awkward problem. The choice of members of the Commission, discussed below, suggests that this was not Mr Brooke's intention. But it may have been in the minds of some of his Cabinet colleagues that the setting up of the Commission would enable the Government to show that they recognized that there were problems in Greater London, without implying any commitment to making changes. The Prime Minister (Mr Harold Macmillan) was after all the man who, three years earlier, had promised to do something about the County Borough issue. He would have appreciated that the 1956 White Paper did nothing to settle that issue so far as it related to one important area, Middlesex.

Membership and terms of reference of the Royal Commission

There was an almost total absence of public comment on the announcement to set up a Royal Commission and on the later announcement (in November 1957) of the membership of the Commission. This in itself is not surprising, but it is worth making this point in view of the criticisms which were made at a later stage, particularly of the membership. The Chairman of the Commission was Sir Edwin Herbert (now Lord Tangley), one of that body of public-spirited men and women whose names appear constantly in the lists of members of official committees of inquiry. His name was probably best known for his chairmanship of the committee of inquiry into the Electricity Supply Industry in 1954. By training a solicitor, his experience had largely been in the commercial life of the City of London, apart from a war-time spell in the civil service;[51] and he was in no way connected with local government either in London or elsewhere.

It was the choice of the remaining six members of the Commission that raised some interesting points.[52] On the face of it they represented the usual mixture of different interests and professional viewpoints – an accountant, a retired civil servant, a businessman and so on. But the important point was that they were all free of any known fixed attitude towards questions of local government reorganization, either generally or in relation to London. Nothing illustrates better how far Mr Brooke had moved away from the Sandys position of trying to act only with the basic agreement of the local authority associations. There was no agreement on what should be done about London, or indeed on whether anything needed to be done at all. An enquiry on which local authority interests were represented was therefore unlikely to carry the argument much further than Mr Sandys' discussions had done. An independent enquiry might do so. On this point it seems clear that the Chairman and the Minister were in agreement about what kind of enquiry was needed. Nevertheless, although the members of the Commission were not identified with particular local government interests, they were not without knowledge and experience of local government. Apart from Sir John Wrigley, who had served most of his civil service career in the Local Government Board and its successors, two members had served as councillors[53] and one had at least an academic interest in local government.[54]

One other fact of major importance about the Commission also needs to be emphasized, although it is implicit in what has been said earlier. By setting up the Commission the Government adopted a different approach to local government reorganization in London from that for the rest of the country. The proposals in the White Papers of 1956 and 1957 which were put into effect by the Local Government Act of 1958 provided for reviews by the Local Government Commission for England, mainly of county and county borough boundaries; only in the 'special review' areas (i.e. the major conurbations outside London) was the Commission given powers to suggest a reorganization of areas and functions analogous to those of the Herbert Commission.[55] But the Commission was restricted by statute in the procedures which it had to follow. Every proposal was subject to lengthy consultation with the local authorities affected by it and to the normal procedure of public enquiry, the effect of which was inevitably to narrow the scope for change.[56] A Royal Commission by its very nature operates differently and is free to make what enquiries and recommendations it chooses within the limits of its terms of reference.

In contrast to the decision to set up the Royal Commission, its proposed terms of reference were, as is usual, discussed with the local authorities affected before they were publicly announced by the Prime Minister on 19th November 1957. Two crucial points which need to be considered in more detail about the terms of reference are first the area and secondly the functions to be considered by the commission.

Area. The area chosen did not coincide with any area already in use for any purpose. It was rather larger than the Greater London conurbation as used for statistical purposes by the Registrar General, and the Metropolitan Police District (a very similar area). It was much smaller than the London Traffic Area established under the 1924 Act following the report of the Ullswater Commission, and therefore very much smaller than the area covered together by the County of London and the Greater London Plans. The main object seems to have been to include all the local authority areas which were or could conceivably have been regarded as forming part of the continuous built-up area.[57]

An obvious starting-point in trying to delimit an area in this way would have been to take the inner edge of the Green Belt as the boundary but for two reasons this could have been unsatisfactory. First, some local authority areas contained sizeable areas both of continuous urban development and of Green Belt land; an example was Orpington. Secondly, some tongues of development protruded right into and in some cases almost right through the Green Belt. To draw a line round such areas was therefore bound to be to some extent arbitrary. Thus Walton and Weybridge was included in the area but not Chertsey; Staines but not Egham. To some extent the decision to include or exclude must have been governed by the desire not to get involved in too much argument with the local authorities concerned. The case for inclusion became more difficult the further one moved outwards, given the general principles on which the determination of the area was based; the case for including Twickenham was stronger than that for Walton and Weybridge, and for the latter stronger than that for Chertsey. As it was, eight of the 111 authorities who were consulted on the proposed terms of reference thought that they should not be included at all, and although they were in fact included the terms of reference were reworded to make it clear that it was not essential for the Commission to recommend changes in the existing system.[58]

In the case of the inclusion of Watford and adjacent areas rather different considerations seem to have applied. Certainly Watford could be said to be joined to London by continuous development but even more relevant perhaps was the fact that it was a large and ambitious town in the Green Belt which had plans of achieving County Borough status. There were advantages in having this case debated before the Royal Commission rather than leaving it to be settled by the more cumbersome procedure of the Boundary Commission.

Thus in the end the Commission's review area included, apart from the City of London, two complete counties (London and Middlesex), three County Boroughs (Croydon, East Ham and West Ham) and parts of four other counties (Essex, Hertfordshire, Kent and Surrey). Only in one case did the boundary of the review area correspond to a major local government boundary, that is, the western boundary of Middlesex from Sunbury-on-Thames to Uxbridge.

Functions. The most notable point about the functions which the Commission was given to review is the fact that police and water supply were specifically excluded. The reason was basically that the task of the Commission was viewed as being a review of the functions which were actually being performed by local authorities in the area, and water and police[59] were not among these.

There seems, however, to have been some confusion even at this stage over the question of water supply and not all the local authorities were happy about the exclusion of the police; some too wanted to take in other functions which in some parts of the country were either wholly or partly a responsibility of local government, notably public transport.[60]

It will be seen that the terms of reference are consistent with the general approach of the Government outlined above. They did not see this enquiry as an attempt to examine the whole question of what constituted London in the mid-twentieth century and what form of local government structure might be appropriate for such an area. Instead, they set the Commission the more limited objective of trying to rearrange the pattern of local government administration within an area which possessed what unity and cohesion it had from the fact that it had grown physically to be part of a single urban mass spreading originally from one centre, the City of London. There were practical considerations too for limiting the terms of reference; the job which the Commission was given to do proved to be a tough enough assignment and, as the Prime Minister claimed, to have given them further tasks such as looking at public transport would have been a very big undertaking.[61]

Appendix

Royal Commission on Local Government in Greater London 1957-60
Terms of Reference and Membership

To examine the present system and working of local government in the Greater London area; to recommend whether any, and if so what, changes in the local government structure and the distribution of local authority functions in the area, or in any part of it, would better secure effective and convenient local government; and to regard, for these purposes, local government as not including the administration of police, or of water, and the Greater London area as comprising the Metropolitan Police District together with the City of London, the Boroughs of Dartford, Romford, and Watford, the Urban Districts of Caterham and Warlingham, Chorleywood, Hornchurch, Rickmansworth, and Walton and Weybridge, and the Parish of Watford Rural in the Watford Rural District.

Sir Edwin Herbert (Chairman). b. 1899, created Life Peer, Lord Tangley, 1963. A solicitor by profession, Member of the Council of the Law Society from 1935. Chairman, Industrial and General Trust Ltd, and director of several other concerns.

Mr P. S. Cadbury. b. 1895. Life-long connections with the family firm of Cadbury Bros Ltd, of which he was Chairman from 1959 to 1965. Author of *Birmingham–Fifty Years On* (1952).

Miss A. C. Johnston. b. 1902. After graduating at Lady Margaret Hall, Oxford, her life work had been mainly in the social services eg member of the National Assistance Board from 1948–1964 and Deputy Chairman 1961–1964; Social Services Administrator, WVS from 1954 onwards.

Mr W. H. Lawson. b. 1899, knighted 1962. A chartered accountant by profession, Member of the Council of the Institute of Chartered Accountants from 1946 to 1966 and President in 1957–58.

Professor W. J. M. Mackenzie. b. 1909. Fellow of Magdalen College, Oxford, from 1933 to 1948; Professor of Government, Manchester University from 1949 to 1966; Professor of Government, Glasgow University from 1966. His publications include *Free Elections* (1958).

Sir Charles Morris. b. 1898, created Life Peer, Lord Morris of Grasmere, 1967. Fellow and Tutor in Philosophy, Balliol College, Oxford, from 1921 to 1943; Vice-Chancellor of Leeds University, from 1948 to 1963. His publications include *Locke, Berkeley, Hume* (1931).

Sir John Wrigley. b. 1888. After graduating at Corpus Christi College, Cambridge, his career was in the civil service. Local Government Board, 1912–1919; Ministry of Health 1919–1951; Ministry of Local Government and Planning/Housing and Local Government, 1951–1952. He was Deputy Secretary from 1943 to his retirement in 1952.

2
The Herbert Commission (1)

Evidence of Local Authorities
and
Local Authority Associations

General

Superficially there is a great similarity between the tasks which the Ullswater and Herbert Commissions were asked to undertake. But in practice there were fundamental differences in the approach which each made to the problems of London government. In contrast to the atmosphere of 'litigious enquiry' of the Ullswater Commission[1], the Herbert Commission believed that 'it was our duty to inform ourselves of the problems of the government of London by all means available to us'.[2] Where the Ullswater Commission had relied almost exclusively on the evidence of local authorities, their associations and government departments, the Herbert Commission in addition wrote to and invited evidence from over 200 bodies and organizations which might conceivably have views on London's government, from the Federation of British Industries to the Fabian Society and from the London Labour Party to the London Master Builders' Association; they also wrote to every British University to see if any research work was being undertaken which could throw light on the problems of London government. The Ullswater Commission did not see it as part of their duty to carry out extensive visits to local authorities in the area, whereas the Herbert Commission laid stress on the value they found in informal visits to local authorities which they carried out before beginning their public hearings and on which they in fact spent more time than on public hearings. In addition they carried out their own enquiries into questions such as the delineation of the boundaries of Greater London.

No doubt part of this difference in approach can be attributed to general changes in attitudes in the thirty-six years between the appointment of the Ullswater and Herbert Commissions. But there can be little doubt that the Chairman and members of the later Commission were determined to avoid as far as possible the kind of situation which had arisen on the Ullswater Commission. To this end the method of procedure which they proposed was first of all to find out if there were any defects in the existing arrangements for the performance of local government functions in the Commission's area; and then to consider whether any defects so disclosed were the result of defects in the administrative machinery.

Inevitably, the great bulk of the evidence, both written and oral, which was presented to the Commission came from the local authorities in Greater London of whom there were 117 in the Commission's review area. In attempting to assess this evidence two separate questions need to be borne in mind; first, what the Commission were looking for, secondly, the major points of view which local authorities wished to convey.

On the first point it has been claimed[3] that the Commission in inviting evidence were too restrictive and gave the impression that they were mainly interested in the working of a few major functions. But although the letter which was sent to authorities in February 1958 concentrated attention on six major functions it left scope for any authority which wished to do so to make radical suggestions for reform.[4] Some indeed did suggest to the Commission that a new approach was needed to local government in London, but the great majority argued only for what they thought best for their own areas. By and large, this meant that they saw no need for change in the existing system. The Commission stigmatized this attitude in strong terms,

'notwithstanding the many virtues of local government today the parochial outlook that has been one of the great obstacles to any serious reform of London government is still very much alive.'[5]

But they recognized the reasons why most local authorities adopted this attitude; there were, first, tactical reasons in some cases where, for example, authorities had the immediate and principal aim of trying to secure county borough status; secondly, councillors and officers tend to be immersed in the affairs of their own area, to the exclusion of a wider view of local government. Part of the Commission's criticism may also have been inspired by the need to make clear their own position. They had reached the conclusion that something more was needed than tinkering with the existing structure of local government in London, but past history as well as their own enquiries, made it clear that few local authorities held this view. They were therefore anxious to make plain why they felt that a very large part of the evidence which was presented to them was inadequate to meet the situation as they saw it.

Nor did the Commission find the evidence of the local authority associations helpful on this point. Mainly because of the dual nature of the local government structure based on the Counties and the County Boroughs, the two major associations, the Association of Municipal Corporations and the County Councils Association, have developed as champions of particular and opposed views about the best organization of local government and this has directed their energies away from taking a wide and concerted view of the problems of local government as a whole.[6]

Thus the Commission spent a great deal of their time reading and listening to evidence which was largely directed to one of two ends: either the preservation basically of the existing system with the least modification necessary to meet any problems which might have arisen; or pleas by particular authorities for higher status, particularly by Municipal Boroughs wishing to become County Boroughs. Although this failed to meet the Commission's needs, this is not to say that the evidence of local authorities was of no value. It provided a vast amount of factual information about local authorities as they existed in the London area in 1957–58; it provided revealing illustrations of how local authorities regarded their functions; above all it threw light on the working of existing administrative arrangements and on the strains to which these gave rise in certain cases.

As one would imagine, the factual information provided by local authorities was in general detailed and thorough and provided the essential background to the Commission's activities. It also provided incidental illustration of that pride in achievement which is so characteristic of English local authorities. Perhaps the prize here should go to the Borough of Uxbridge whose 62-page volume of written evidence included information about geology, population, staff and their salaries, departmental organization and much more besides.[7] But most authorities submitted fairly weighty memoranda and it is not surprising that these fill four large volumes of nearly 2,500 pages in all in the printed version.

These volumes also throw light on the attitudes of local authorities particularly to their own place in the system. It is very revealing, for example, to find Chelsea, a Metropolitan Borough with a generally hostile outlook to the LCC, arguing that the creation of the LCC in 1889 'in no way altered the feeling of the people as belonging to their own parish community' and that effect was given to this popular feeling in 1900 by the creation of Metropolitan Boroughs.[8] Whatever the merits of this argument, there is no doubt that it indicates how tenaciously the borough council clung to the preservation of Chelsea's identity. This standpoint was to be found among all sizes and types of authority and, as will be seen, it later played an important part in the reactions which the various local authorities made to the Herbert Commission's proposals.

It is of interest to see how the local authorities' views and the Commission's approach to them were exemplified in a number of specific instances.

The London County Council

The written evidence of the LCC consisted of twenty pages, 19 of which were a sober and factual account of the existing system of local government in the LCC's area; on the final page they found that the only specific difficulty in these arrangements was in relation to the control of water-courses, and their general view was 'the Council is confident that, so far as its own area is concerned, no greater efficiency could be secured by any alteration in the methods of administration'.[9]

These twin pillars of their belief, that they could only speak for the LCC, and that there no fundamental change was required, came out very strongly in their oral evidence. When the Commission asked whether in view of their belief in the great virtues of the system operating in the administrative county of London, they would advocate its extension to other parts of Greater London, the Leader of the Council, Mr (now Sir Isaac) Hayward, replied:

'I think one of our great prides – although we do not always succeed – is that we have friendly relationships with all the counties around us. I rather think we should strain it very much if we expressed an opinion on that.'[10]

The Commission also pressed the LCC on what should be done

about problems which were too big for the LCC alone in that they affected the whole of Greater London. Again, Mr Hayward saw no difficulty about this:

> 'if you are going to keep these matters within local government the present system is the right system, because the co-ordinating centre both for planning and for transport is the Government departments; the Ministry of Housing and Local Government is responsible for the town plans of all the local authorities and is able to co-ordinate all the facilities – they have the expert staff, they have all the information by which they can co-ordinate town planning throughout the area, irrespective of the difference in the authorities who control it.'[11]

The commission were particularly critical of the LCC for refusing to budge in any way from this position.[12] But apart from the general reasons which have already been given why most local authorities saw no reason for change in the system, there is another complicating factor which was particularly important in the case of the LCC. The LCC had always been run on political party lines and since 1934 the Labour Party had been in continuous control. Any fundamental changes in local government areas and functions in Greater London could have put this control in jeopardy. This fact was clearly in the minds of Mr Hayward and his colleagues in framing their evidence. Equally, the Conservative opposition on the LCC made clear their belief that some changes were needed in the local government structure both by forcing a lengthy debate when the question of the evidence to be presented to the Commission came before the Council[13], and by taking the unusual step of themselves submitting a separate memorandum of evidence on which they also gave evidence orally.

To some extent the Labour Group on the LCC had been placed in a difficult position by the Government's action in setting-up a Royal Commission. On the one hand they could hope that either no fundamental changes would be recommended by the Commission or if they were the Government would shelve them; on the other hand, if there was to be change it was clearly important that they should try to influence the direction which it was to take. They seem to have had no hesitation in relying on the first alternative, an attitude which they maintained until the bitter end. In large part, this seems to have been because they found it inconceivable that any government would go so far as to abolish the LCC of whose record they were immensely proud.

Greater London problems

A major aim of the Commission, as shown by the questions put to local authority representatives, was to elicit their views on suggestions which had been put forward for dealing with problems which affected Greater London as a whole. An important question which the Chairman of the Commission put to all the major authorities in the area was the extent to which the existing local authority machinery was adequate for putting into effect and revising development plans to ensure co-ordination in Greater London. All but one of the major authorities agreed with the LCC that this was a matter for the central departments. Thus Middlesex 'does not see the need for the creation of any regional authority'; they were content with the Ministry of Housing and Local Government 'acting fully as a policy-making and co-ordinating body'.[14] Kent thought that 'the best method of co-ordinating the planning operation of various local authorities in Greater London is through the appropriate government departments'.[15] Croydon believed that when the Abercrombie plan needed revising 'it would be appropriate for the Minister to call in another Professor Abercrombie, if you like, to prepare a basic plan'.[16] Only Surrey did not join fully in this chorus, but reverted to a suggestion of the Clement Davies Committee on London Planning Administration for 'a joint advisory committee to deal with major planning in the whole of the London area' with the Minister having the final word 'as to whether he would accept or whether he would reject the recommendations' of the committee.[17]

These views are interesting in several ways; in the first place, all the authorities responsible for planning in Greater London, with the exception of Surrey, had clearly not considered the possibility or need for altering the arrangements for the production of a general framework of planning for the whole area. Secondly, none of the authorities, again with the exception of Surrey, saw any need for local authorities to take any initiative in revising the pre-conceptions of the Abercrombie plan, preferring to leave this to the Minister. Thirdly, the suggestion made by Surrey although it recognized that there might be some need for effective co-ordination, did not carry the idea very far; a joint committee had been suggested by the majority of members of the Clement Davies Committee as the best in the circumstances and within the limitations of their terms of reference. But they had not by any means regarded it as an ideal arrangement; and the minority of members had rejected it as inadequate in favour of a joint board.[18]

Here then was one important field where the local authorities most directly involved did not see any need for any major changes and yet, as was noted earlier, it had seemed to most independent observers to be a field where the existing administrative machinery had failed to achieve effective action. It is true that a number of authorities did put forward suggestions involving major changes in the structure and functions of local government in Greater London; in particular some advocated a new authority to be responsible for certain functions over the whole area. It is significant, however, that these suggestions came mainly from Metropolitan Boroughs (especially Chelsea, Hampstead, Kensington and Westminster) which were of a different political complexion from the LCC; and the main object of the proposals was to strengthen the boroughs and to give them major powers.[19] The proposal for a Greater London authority was, therefore, in part designed as a means of overthrowing what, in the eyes of these boroughs, was an unpopular and unwieldy authority, the LCC.

Second-tier authorities' support for the existing system

Few of the second-tier authorities advocated any fundamental change in the existing system of local government. Many of them wanted increased power and to the extent that boroughs aimed at County Borough status, the effect, although not perhaps the intention of their proposals, would have been to create a very different pattern of local government in Greater London.[20] It was the preservation of their own identity as individual local government units, however, which took precedence in the evidence of most second-tier authorities and to this they devoted many and indeed picturesque arguments. Stoke Newington, for example, one of the smallest of the Metropolitan Boroughs, after citing its mention in Domesday Book claimed 'we have still preserved the village atmosphere'.[21] Barnet, in its attempt to show how different it was from suburban London said 'it is really at the bottom of Barnet Hill that you almost get an Iron Curtain coming down'.[22] But probably the attitudes of those who wanted as little change as possible are most effectively summed up in the words of St Pancras:

'we are a very happy and contented borough. We do consider that the present set up of local government so far as London is concerned is the right one for London government'.[23]

At first sight, it seems surprising that St. Pancras and indeed the great majority of the Metropolitan Boroughs were not seeking increased powers and status. The Metropolitan Boroughs had fewer powers than second-tier authorities elsewhere in Greater London, despite the fact that the largest of them, such as Wandsworth, Islington and Lambeth were of a size to justify elsewhere County Borough status.[24] They certainly wanted increased powers, but not on the whole by claiming County Borough status. An essential part of the evidence of the Metropolitan Boroughs' Standing Joint Committee was concerned with arguing that the LCC covered a coherent area and should not be broken up.[25]

The explanation of this state of affairs is largely to be found in the political situation. Most of the Metropolitan Boroughs had Labour majorities and many of them could be described as permanently Labour. Through the medium in particular of the London Labour Party a fairly close relationship had developed between the various Labour groups on the Metropolitan Boroughs and the majority party group on the LCC, and the former preferred the known hazards of attempting to negotiate a greater share of powers with the LCC (and ultimately the Government) to the unknown risks which would follow a change in the system. Thus, with the solitary exception of Fulham,[26] only the Conservative-controlled boroughs put forward proposals which would disturb the existing basis of local government in the county of London.[27]

Delegation in Middlesex

But perhaps of more interest to the Royal Commission was the evidence of those authorities who were dissatisfied with their powers or status (or both) under the existing system. The Commission had to decide what were the reasons for this dissatisfaction and how important it was to an assessment of the working of the system. Delegation in the county of Middlesex provided a classic example.

Delegation is an important administrative device in local government; under it a county council retains control of policy, and especially financial policy, in a local government service, but delegates powers in the running of the service to district authorities. Usually, these arrangements are governed by specific statutory provisions under which district authorities have to satisfy certain conditions (eg of population size) before being able to exercise delegated powers.[28] District authorities generally regard delegation as a second-best; they would much prefer to have powers directly conferred on them.

These general points were exemplified in much evidence from second-tier authorities to the Royal Commission. Those authorities which sought increased powers, whether, like Ilford or Harrow, they aimed at County Borough status, or, like Carshalton, they had more limited aims such as responsibility for the personal health services, asked for direct conferment of powers and not an extension of delegation. In Middlesex, however, this request was accompanied by severe criticism of the way in which the county council had operated delegation arrangements in the education service.

One factor which played a part in this situation was the large number of second-tier authorities affected by delegation arrangements in Middlesex. Of the twenty-six county districts, 16 were excepted districts for education, that is, they were authorities which before the Education Act, 1944, had exercised elementary education powers, and were therefore automatically entitled to delegated powers under that Act. In addition, there were four divisional executives exercising delegated powers under the Middlesex County Council's scheme of delegation under the 1944 Act.[29] This situation was largely the consequence of the development of Middlesex into a wholly urbanized county.

The first question the Commission had to consider was whether criticism of delegation arrangements in Middlesex was exaggerated and whether it represented the target of authorities frustrated in their ambitions for County Borough status. This was the view put forward by the county council:

'It is to be expected that some difficulty and sense of frustration is likely to occur under any system of two-tier organization. Nevertheless, it is considered that the difficulties and frustrations have been of a comparatively minor order . . . and that the position can best be met by improvement in the operation of delegated powers'.[30] 'I think it is ambition, the frustration that arises from frustrated ambition is the major cause. I would say in the day to day running of the services it just does not happen.'[31]

Some of the written evidence of the second-tier authorities seemed to suggest that difficulties arose largely because Middlesex was an unsuitable area for delegation. The Borough of Tottenham, for example, claimed:

'The difficulties, frustrations and lack of progress . . . arise to a large extent inevitably in a system where the County Council has a legal obligation to control, over so large and varied an area as Middlesex, an essentially personal and local service like Education.'[32]

But what precisely were the authorities' complaints? Nine defects were listed by a group of ten medium sized authorities.[33] These included remoteness of financial and policy control; duplication of work; delays and extra costs in administration; friction between the county and local councils; interference in matters of detail; and confusion in the minds of members of the public. More specific examples were given by the Middlesex Excepted Districts Association to show that there was 'overlapping and frustration' leading to inordinate delay in reaching decisions and unnecessary administrative work. Their main criticism was the excessively detailed financial control exercised by the County Council. These defects were

'largely due to the inability or unwillingness of the County Council to grasp the significance of or to rise to the opportunities given by the Education Act 1944'.[34]

Alderman Jordan, the Chairman of the Association, and a member of Harrow Borough Council, summed it up by saying:

'I think the main point of the defect is the loss of authority, really, in the sense that we have not the real powers that are presumed to go with delegation'.[35]

In oral questioning of both the County Council and the second-tier authorities, the Royal Commission showed particular anxiety to find out whether delegation was itself a bad system or whether there were special reasons in Middlesex for the undoubted hostility of the second-tier authorities. What emerged most clearly, however, was the impossibility of reconciling the tensions within the county as long as there were so many boroughs with ambitions for County Borough status. Perhaps this was more important to the Commission's enquiry than the question whether the County Council had been too rigid or the boroughs too obstructive. There was little in the evidence to show that the service provided to the public had suffered from the internal strains of the system. Nevertheless the Commission were much concerned with the general question of delegation versus conferment of powers and returned to it in other evidence.[36]

The Local Authority Associations

The local authority associations' evidence was very much in accordance with their general standpoints.

The Association of Municipal Corporations, with their belief in the superiority of the one-tier system, advocated dividing up Greater London into a large number of contiguous county boroughs. This posed the problem of how to secure effective co-ordination of action in matters which affected the whole area. The AMC's written evidence was brief and brushed aside the difficulties. For dealing with such matters as sewage disposal, 'some aspects' of education and the preparation of development plans they proposed joint arrangements between authorities, preferably joint consultative committees.

Not unnaturally, this point received a great deal of attention from members of the Commission when the AMC representatives gave oral evidence. At each point the AMC stuck to their view that there would be no difficulty in getting their proposed county boroughs to act jointly whether over children having to cross borough boundaries to get to school, or over the preparation of a master development plan or over the provision of housing within Greater London. As the following exchanges over housing indicate, the proposition seemed less plausible to the Commission the more often it was advanced:

Mr Cadbury: The point I am putting is that under the existing machinery, there is a way of equalizing, at any rate to some extent – not entirely – the needs of the various parts of London. What I am putting to you is how do you secure that, if you can?

Mr Bentley (Town Clerk of Paddington): If some authority for getting together is necessary, it should be just as simple over this as over many of the other things on which local authorities get together.

Mr Cadbury: Yes, we have to do it as we go along. Your answer is that it is always simple to get together, but we will have to weigh up at the end of the day what are the size and importance of the subjects on which you have to get together, because supposing it was to cover a large variety of important subjects, it would begin to throw doubt on the efficacy of your main thesis . . .

Sir Harold Banwell (Secretary of the AMC): I thought it was clear that there was a problem in relation to London, whatever the form of local government within it; and because there is a problem in relation to London and housing, we do not think it ought to destroy the basic principle upon which you ought to build local government.[37]

The County Councils' Association, in contrast to the AMC, did not recognize that there were any problems in Greater London. Their view may be summed up as 'Existing arrangements work well' and although, unlike the AMC, they were prepared to consider possible alternative forms of local government, their conclusion was that there was an 'absence . . . of any really major problems necessitating radical changes'.[38] Their oral evidence really added very little to this statement of their point of view. Naturally, they did not agree with the suggestion that there should be a series of County Boroughs covering the whole area of Greater London because

'our experiences make us look to joint boards and joint committees, and the like, only in the last resort.'[39]

Their answer, therefore, to the boroughs, such as those in Middlesex, which were claiming County Borough status was that in every sphere a two-tier system could provide a superior service largely because the counties could take a wider view of problems. The difficulty was that this depended on a smoothly-working system of delegation. On this they affirmed their belief in the possibility of delegation working, given the right conditions.

Other Local Authority Associations

Apart from the Urban District Councils Association, who were predictably in favour of increased powers for county districts, the remaining local authority associations were concerned only with limited parts of the problem, either territorially as with the Hertfordshire Borough and District Councils' Association or functionally as with the National Association of Divisional Executives for Education. Of these, perhaps the most interesting evidence was given by the Middlesex Excepted Districts' Association, to which reference has already been made,[40] and the NADEE.

The latter's evidence was particularly illuminating on a point which very much pre-occupied the Commission, the necessity for reconciling the functional needs of a service like education with local control. The Association held strongly to the view that local intimacy and control were essential to the running of education, not least because 'the more people we can bring into the actual administration of education . . . the better'.[41]

But clearly they then faced the fundamental dilemma of whether the kind of size of authority in which this local control would apply would be capable of running the education services effectively. Here, the Association proposed an ingenious compromise between the two existing systems of local government. For distinct towns of population roughly in the range 100,000–250,000 they suggested a most-purpose status, with responsibility allocated to them for the whole of education except for some matters, such as advanced technical education, which required a wider area of administration and for which the counties would continue to have responsibility. For the remaining areas they suggested a system basically similar to the existing pattern of excepted districts and divisional executives, but with improvements in the system of delegation. On this latter point the Association's representatives were closely questioned by the Commission. One important point which emerged from these exchanges was how much the successful operation of schemes of delegation depended on the spirit in which those who had to work them interpreted them.[42] Nevertheless it was agreed that the form of financial control adopted by the county could play a large part in contributing to the success of schemes.[43]

3
The Herbert Commission (2)

Evidence of Government Departments, Political Parties, Professional Bodies and Universities

The government departments

With one exception, the Ministry of Transport and Civil Aviation (as it then was), the written evidence of the departments gave little indication of any real difficulties in the existing system of administration in Greater London or indeed of why it should ever have been thought necessary to set up a Royal Commission.

The Ministry of Education, in a remark which not surprisingly was quoted by a number of authorities during the course of the Commission's proceedings, said 'There is no part of the area in which the present system of education administration does not work at least tolerably well.'[1] This might almost be taken as the theme song of the written evidence of the departments. Thus the Ministry of Health concluded that 'the local services for which the Ministry are responsible in the Greater London area are not regarded as unsatisfactory or inefficient'.[2] The Home Office, when asked their general views on local government organization in the Greater London area for the children's service replied 'There seem to be no particular disadvantages in the organization of child care in large local government units such as the London County Council and the Middlesex County Council'.[3] The Ministry of Housing and Local Government which could be expected to take a wider and deeper interest in local government than other departments, did indeed see some disadvantages in the existing system, finding some authorities, such as Holborn, to be too small to be housing authorities; deploring the lack of co-ordination over the housing problem; and drawing attention to the difficulties of overspill housing – 'this means perhaps that overspill does not fit any local government set-up . . . Yet local government is and must be intimately concerned with overspill.'[4] On the all-important question of overall planning for the Greater London area the Ministry thought that within the framework of the Abercrombie plan 'the plans of the various authorities have been on the whole well co-ordinated' but 'it is a question whether some machinery is not required for continuous review of the whole region'; only traffic congestion appeared to the Ministry a major failure in planning and this 'does illustrate the difficulties which arise out of the existing local government organization when it comes to the really big problems of the region'.[5]

Two features are evident in the written evidence of these government departments. One is that although they did not find much wrong with the existing system, they certainly did not show any great enthusiasm for it; the cautious statements of the Ministry of Health and the Home Office aptly illustrate this point. Secondly, where faults were found in the system, eg by the Ministry of Housing and Local Government they were referred to in tentative terms with little hint of possible remedies. All the more remarkable then is the written evidence of the Ministry of Transport and Civil Aviation. They not only found much positively wrong with the existing system of local authorities in the area but were also quite ready to suggest remedies. They found that many authorities were too small to be efficient highway authorities and 'would like to see the number of highway authorities in the metropolitan area considerably reduced'. The arrangements for dealing with traffic problems they considered to be even more unsatisfactory; the 'multiplicity of authorities concerned and the fragmentation of responsibility for traffic control . . . makes it impossible to deal efficiently with present-day problems', so that 'even the simplest measure takes an inordinate time to put into effect'. And in one of those rare public expressions of frustration by a government department they declared, 'The purpose of any regulation which the Minister eventually decides should be made can easily be frustrated by any local authority which for its own parochial reasons decided to be dilatory about the erection of the necessary signs or any other works involved.'[6]

The Ministry's proposals to deal with this situation also fell into two parts; on highways they wanted authorities with not less than 200,000 population[7]; for traffic purposes they suggested that if the Commission recommended a top-tier Greater London authority for other functions this should have traffic powers too. Otherwise they favoured either a separate executive agency or traffic powers going to the reorganized highway authorities with some kind of overall co-ordinating authority.

Before considering why government departments should have adopted these particular attitudes, it should be pointed out that as described below, the written evidence was in some cases modified when the departments gave oral evidence. In part, this may be explained by the fact that the departments gave their oral evidence at the beginning of 1960 after the local authorities had given theirs; they therefore had by then had the benefit of local authority comment on the written evidence. But modification was also forced on departments by the evident desire of the Commission, and especially of the Chairman, to get departments to take a more positive line, particularly over questions such as the minimum size of authority.

The key to the attitudes of most of the departments, however, is that they were extremely reluctant to say anything which could be construed as being a criticism of any individual local authority. Perhaps the Home Office best exemplify this cautious attitude; in their written evidence on the care of children they had said[8] 'It is important that child care should be organized in units large enough to support a reasonable number of trained staff' without committing themselves to any specific figure. Sir Charles Cunningham, the Permanent Secretary, was pressed by Sir Edwin Herbert to give a specific figure and replied, 'Speaking quite personally, I would have guessed that a population of 200,000 to 250,000 was probably nearer the figure you would want to support, generally speaking, an efficient child-care service', but he hastened to add, 'I hope I have not said anything to suggest that the smaller County Boroughs are not operating an efficient child-care service.'[9]

Allied to this attitude was the fact that there was no overall view of local government by the central government. Each department tended to view the problems from its own specialized point of view. Thus on the important question of the size of authority necessary to perform particular functions, departments generalized from their experience of which authorities performed functions most efficiently under the existing system. The Ministry of Health, for example, suggested that the range of size for the adequate performance of personal health and welfare functions was between 100,000 and 1 million, and they seemed to be thinking mainly of the fact that many good authorities were in the 250,000 – 500,000 range, although, at least in arriving at the minimum figure, they had examined such detailed questions as the work-load for individual officers, the amount of supervision required, and the fact that there was a tendency for newer services (as in the mental health field) to require bigger case-loads.[10]

The Ministry of Housing and Local Government in their oral evidence did go rather further in pointing to what, in their view, was wrong with the existing organization of local government. The Permanent Secretary, Dame Evelyn Sharp, said that it had become obvious that especially in the conurbations,

> 'the areas of local authorities and the distribution of functions between them are no longer matched to the social pattern, nor so arranged that local authorities have a clear and manageable job to do.'[11]

But on the whole what emerges most clearly from the Ministry's evidence is their identification of the functions where difficulties in performance had arisen, with few indications of what they thought the implications were for the future organization of local government. For example, on overspill housing they recognized that the problems

> 'must need some organization or organizations larger than a borough organization.'[12]

but this did not go very far towards a specific solution. Again on the difficulties of overall planning for Greater London, a subject which, as has been seen, was given a good deal of attention by the Commission in the oral evidence of the major local authorities, the Ministry pointed to the advantage of a single authority responsible for the plan 'looked at simply from the point of view of achieving the best broad planning for the whole of Greater London', but then immediately qualified this by asking whether

> 'you can achieve that result without paying too big a price in your whole local government organization or in destroying existing and well-established local authorities.'[13]

In other words, the basic problems were left fairly and squarely with the Commission with only hints here and there of what the Ministry really thought should be done about them.[14]

Even the Ministry of Transport and Civil Aviation which, in its written evidence, had boldly advocated fundamental changes was not quite so decisive when it came to giving oral evidence. As the spokesman for the Ministry Mr (now Sir James) Dunnett, freely admitted, they were much influenced by the criticisms which had been made of their original proposals. In particular they withdrew their suggestion for an *ad hoc* executive agency with over-all powers in traffic matters. Local authorities in general had condemned these proposals, some in very forthright terms. Thus Middlesex said:

'How such an arrangement could be an improvement on the present organization is difficult indeed to conceive',[15]

and the South-West Essex Authorities:

'We find the Ministry's views unacceptable generally'.[16]

To the Metropolitan Boroughs Standing Joint Committee they were,

'a root and branch attack on local democratic government'.[17]

The Commission in their report commented that it was the one occasion in the whole course of their inquiry when local authorities were unanimous.[18]

The reasons which led the Ministry of Transport and Civil Aviation to put forward their views and the reasons for the hostility of the local authorities are revealing for the light which they throw on the strength and the weakness of the evidence from the departments. The Commission criticized the Ministry's original proposals as indicating that 'its general knowledge about the working of local government is rather slight'.[19] But they were perhaps nearer the mark in their general remark that, with the exception of the Ministry of Housing and Local Government, government departments are mainly concerned with seeing that particular services and functions are run and maintained to an average standard rather than with whether the local government system is working well as a whole.[20] On the whole they have tended to take the system as they found it and have been reluctant to condemn publicly and, particularly to condemn individual authorities.[21]

It is significant, for example, that the Ministry of Education in discussing the performance of each local education authority in the area, adopted a judiciously balanced attitude; indeed some of the written evidence reads rather like a headmaster's report. Most of the authorities were given a 'satisfactory but could do better' mark, and only West Ham became really indignant at being told that it 'has not a very high reputation as a local education authority . . . but there are signs of some improvement.'[22] Nothing better illustrates the tone of the Ministry's evidence than their remarks in the written evidence on delegation in Middlesex. After acknowledging that the system was obviously not working well there – with faults on both sides – they came to the optimistic conclusion that there was no reason why it should not work but 'every effort needs to be made by all concerned to improve its working in Middlesex.'[23]

This substitution of exhortation for positive proposals and the unwillingness to disturb existing arrangements, or at least to admit openly that they should be disturbed, are characteristic to a greater or lesser degree of all the departments' evidence except that of the Ministry of Transport and Civil Aviation. But the difference is not perhaps as great as it appears. The Ministry of Transport and Civil Aviation had responsibility for an area of administration where, it was generally agreed, existing arrangements in London were not proving satisfactory. Undoubtedly there was a good deal of truth in the Ministry's analysis of this situation, although the local authorities might justifiably complain that the blame for the delays was not entirely to be attributed to their parochial attitude. It was in the circumstances impossible for Transport to argue, as did Health and Education for example, that the existing system could be kept working tolerably well. The traffic situation in London alone demanded that some measures should be taken. The dilemma of the Ministry was that they could only suggest solutions which in their view might meet the traffic and highway problems without knowing how this would fit in with solutions to other problems.

The same problems would undoubtedly have arisen with some of the other departments if they had taken the logic of their arguments further. The Ministry of Health, for example, placed a good deal of emphasis in their written evidence on the need to achieve co-ordination of the different branches of the health service, and Dame Enid Russell-Smith drew attention to this point quite specifically in her opening remarks when the Ministry gave oral evidence,

'It is the great object of policy to get exactly the same degree of co-ordination and planning in the home care of the patient as exists in hospital'.[24]

But they were far less clear about how precisely such a policy could be achieved in practice, and whether it would involve any fundamental change in the pattern of local authorities in Greater London. Their attitude was summed up as being

> 'we believe that the services at the moment are efficiently run, but we are not saying they could not be better run, and we are certainly not taking up any line on the question of change'.[25]

They were therefore content to state what was needed and the criteria by which they would judge whether an authority had sufficient resources to perform adequately the personal health and welfare functions without drawing any conclusions about the application of such criteria to existing authorities in the Greater London area.

Thus the Ministry of Health, unlike the Ministry of Transport and Civil Aviation, were able to avoid having to commit themselves to a specific form and pattern of local government simply because they were not prepared to say that deficiencies in the existing arrangements were sufficiently serious to make changes necessary.

What is at first sight surprising is to find much the same kind of attitude as the Ministry of Health's being taken by the Ministry of Housing and Local Government. There is a curious kind of ambiguity about some of the latter's evidence. On the one hand they analysed with great force and clarity many of the basic problems and were prepared to be critical of at least some authorities. The view that

> 'In the exercise of some functions local authorities sometimes seem to allow their anxiety about the possible effect of what they do on their areas and status to influence them as much as the needs of the service in question'[26]

might well serve as an apt commentary on a good deal of the evidence put to the Commission by local authorities. On the other hand, they were unwilling to suggest any particular solution to these problems, as opposed to stating in general terms the conditions which would have to be met by any solution. As Dame Evelyn Sharp put it:

> 'Almost every service requires a different organization for its ideal consideration, and it is the extreme difficulty of reconciling these different ideals created by the different services and somehow fusing them into a strong well-based healthy local government system – well, it is so much too difficult for us that we thought it needed a Royal Commission!'[27]

For the Commission, the Departments' evidence provided much

useful analysis and information; in particular, it gave some indication of where the existing system was proving unsatisfactory. But it gave them little guidance on what should be done about improving the system.

The political parties

For the most part, the evidence of the political parties was submitted by bodies which did not cover the whole of the Commission's area. The London Municipal Society which said that it 'supports the Conservative Party, but is not a part of the Conservative Party Organization' stressed that its activities were confined to the County of London. The London Labour Party was concerned only with London and Middlesex counties although it had had consultations with Labour parties in Kent, Essex and Surrey before submitting evidence. Even so its evidence related largely to the LCC area only. As might be expected, it followed closely the LCC's evidence particularly in stressing the necessity of retaining goodwill 'by respecting the integrity of long established local government units',[28] and in its emphasis on the view that 'the Government of London works'.[29] The party's representatives were subjected to some close questioning by the Commission at the oral hearing, particularly on the implications which could be drawn from its evidence that different systems of local government should continue to apply in London and Middlesex. On this the London Labour Party could advance little beyond 'historical considerations'.[30]

That the Party's defence of the existing system derived from a genuine belief that local government was well run in the County of London was evident. The Party's treasurer, Mr (as he then was) Herbert Morrison had missed few opportunities in the twenty-five years during which Labour had controlled the LCC to put forward this view. At the same time it was obvious that politically the Labour Party in London, though not necessarily in Middlesex, had most to lose from any reorganization of local government. There is a certain irony in the fact that this same Herbert Morrison had, on behalf of the London Labour Party, advocated a Greater London Council in evidence to the Ullswater Commission over thirty years earlier.

The Conservatives, in the form of the London Municipal Society, at least had some definitive views on what was wrong with local government in the County of London. The LCC was too big, and therefore too much influenced by its officers. They drew the conclusion that the LCC's administration was becoming 'increasingly out of touch with the ordinary citizen' and that 'what enthusiasms or loyalties there may be for local government in London is now focused almost entirely upon the metropolitan boroughs'.[31] This view was quite consistent with the avowed purpose of the Society which had been founded in 1894 among other things,

> 'to extend and complete the policy successfully presented by the Unionist Ministry of 1886–92 for the reform of London government. . . . . . by the establishment of district councils or corporations.'

Their evidence went further in asserting that there was 'extravagance and duplication of effort' in the existing arrangements and in pointing to alleged defects in specific functions performed by the LCC. In housing there was inflexibility and lack of co-ordination with other departments leading to mistakes such as 'the placing of housing applicants suffering from heart trouble on the top floor of five-storey flats without lifts'. In education they claimed that electors who raised problems with their divisional executives 'rarely receive the attention which elected members would give'.[32]

In view of this analysis the Society at first came to a surprisingly indefinite conclusion about how local government should be re-organized. They thought there should be a top-tier authority for such things as traffic co-ordination, and that the second-tier should be strengthened by having such functions as education conferred on them, but they left open the precise form which these authorities should take. It was not until after they had seen further evidence presented to the Commission that they put forward a second memorandum in far more definite terms advocating a Greater London authority for a limited range of functions and most-purpose boroughs of around 250,000 population for the remaining functions.

When they came to give oral evidence the Society's representatives were not able to add very much on precisely how their proposals would work in practice. When challenged specifically on the case for splitting up the LCC education service among fourteen or fifteen boroughs they fell back on the view that 'the very fact that a system has continued for one hundred years is in itself ground for revising it', a remark which provoked Sir Edwin Herbert into saying 'I realize that life is topsy-turvy in London. The Conservatives are the revolutionaries now.'[33] The evidence of the minority party on the LCC followed similar lines. The London Municipal Society disclaimed any political motive in their evidence. But they could not have been unaware that the abolition of the LCC and the creation of a Greater London authority with, as they proposed, members indirectly elected by the boroughs would have given the Conservatives a greater chance of political control in London than they had on the LCC.

The evidence of the London District Committee of the Communist Party was the most uninhibited of all the political parties. As they pointed out

> 'we here are in the fortunate position in that we have no vested interest in the present structure of London Government, apart from our interest as citizens. We are not in the immediate running for wearing the mayoral robes.'[34]

Apart from wanting to show that the organization of local government was part of the class struggle, they advocated a Council of London to be responsible over a wide area (eg the London Transport area) not only for major planning and similar functions but for hospitals, gas, water and electricity, police and local passenger transport. District councils of around 200,000 would be responsible for other services.

In oral evidence they were able to let themselves go:

> 'we are not as a matter of fact' they said 'being terribly revolutionary about this. . . . . We find it difficult to understand the attitude of so many witnesses before this Commission, who seem blithely to ignore, or to wish to ignore, the fact that the London of to-day is not the London of 1855 or 1888.'[35]

And for good measure they quoted with relish earlier Labour views that fundamental changes were needed in London government. But their strongest criticisms were reserved for those witnesses (mainly local authorities) who had argued 'please do not touch our boundaries' or 'please make us all-purpose authorities and damn the rest'. Apart from the merits of what they suggested, the Communist Party added some liveliness to the somewhat staid oral hearings of the Commission. After sixty days the Commission must have been grateful for that.

Professional and other bodies and associations

The evidence of these bodies was chiefly notable for what it added in the way of outside views about the limitations and difficulties in the existing system and about what seemed from a specialized viewpoint to be required for the proper functioning of particular services. Thus both the main professional bodies in the planning field, the Town Planning Institute and the Town and County Planning Association, took the view that over-all planning needed to be carried out over a far wider area than that of any existing local authority, or indeed of the Royal Commission's area. What they were not so clear about, and this was perhaps only natural in the circumstances, was what kind of authority was needed or implied by such a view. The Town Planning Institute, in particular, was quite clear that the Abercrombie Plan was in urgent need of revision especially because of the traffic problems of London, a view which was in striking contrast to that of the major authorities in Greater London.[36] With the views of these two authorities one may also link that of the Royal Institute of British Architects who advocated an *ad hoc* body for 'strategic issues' affecting Greater London, because, as they claimed, there was no local government body which could do this.[37] The Royal Institution of Chartered Surveyors also did not believe that the Abercrombie plan was the last word, particularly on road planning, but definitely came down in favour of a regional elected authority, rather than a joint committee of local authorities. Their argument against the latter was almost a classic statement of the case:

> 'Local authority representatives can never regard themselves as representatives viewing the problem as a whole. They always think of themselves as delegates and watchdogs. I know of no exception to that.'[38]

But for the most part the evidence of these bodies was much more limited in scope. The Royal Colleges of Midwives and of Nursing, for example, could add very little of substance to views which had already been expressed. The Institute of Public Cleansing came out firmly in favour of planning refuse disposal on a regional or Greater London basis and setting up some kind of research organization, but appeared to favour an ad hoc body.[39] The Institution of Municipal Engineers favoured most-purpose authorities of 100,000 – 250,000 population, but were not prepared to commit themselves on how this was to be applied to Greater London.[40] The London Teachers' Association strongly supported the LCC's arguments for preserving the existing system on the grounds that having got something that worked it would be disastrous to break it up.

Of more interest was the evidence of a body which called itself the District Medical Officers of Health (Greater London) Committee. This body came into being specifically to try to put forward the views of the Medical Officers of Health of the 'second-tier' authorities, and it thus differed from practically all the other societies and associations which were of course established bodies. This enterprise however met only a limited success since only fifty-five of the eighty Medical Officers positively supported the memorandum put in by the Committee. Its main contention was that the existing system was unsatisfactory for the personal health and welfare services leading to duplication of work and delay; and that a reorganization of authorities was needed to create second-tier authorities of a size which could effectively deal with these services and co-ordinate them with the environmental health services. The oral evidence was spirited particularly in relation to the cumbersomeness of the existing procedure. As the Medical Officer of Health for Ilford (Dr Gordon) put it:

'whenever I wish to send one of my doctors or a health visitor or domestic help organizer on a course of instruction, that has to be arranged through the county council . . . we are not supposed to correspond directly with certain bodies such as ministries, regional hospital boards, other county councils or county boroughs.'[41]

This of course is the essence of all complaints against the working of delegation arrangements but it was particularly interesting that the point was raised by a group of local government officers who did not constitute a formal organization.[42]

There were of course submissions by a great variety of other bodies and indeed of private individuals. The great majority of these were concerned with very specific and often very local issues, as with the Chelsham and Woldingham Association Limited who wished simply to be left out of London or the St Marylebone Chamber of Commerce who thought that Metropolitan Boroughs should collect rates only for the purposes of their own expenditure. Some submissions came from rather surprising quarters. The Manorial Society of Great Britain, for example, claimed that the Manor was a definite unit of local government, that therefore the Royal Commission was concerned with Lords of Manors 'and for the latter this Society is the premier (if not the only) representative and voice.'[43] And the Middlesex Touring Society wanted Middlesex 'restored to its former greatness' as it was before 1888.[44] The Director and General Manager of Sun Printers Limited claimed that 'Industry in Watford and District would view with grave dismay any change which brought them into the area controlled by London County Council'.[45]

More important however than these submissions from what without disrespect might be called marginal bodies in relation to the Commission's main task were the sometimes rather surprising omissions from bodies which were specifically invited to give evidence. Prominent among these were associations of local government officers. It is true that both NALGO and the LCC Staff Association (who for some reason were not invited to give evidence) did submit evidence, and that some of the professional bodies, such as the Institute of Public Cleansing, did likewise. But there was nothing from the Association of Chief Education Officers or the Association of Children's Officers, the County Planning Officers' Society or the Institute of Municipal Treasurers and Accountants. No doubt local government officers suffer from certain inhibitions in giving evidence particularly to a body which was concerned only with the problems of one part of the country but the result was that their views were under-represented.[46]

The contrast between the NALGO evidence on the one hand and the evidence of the LCC Staff Association and the District Medical Officers on the other illustrates the difficulties or reluctance of the national bodies. NALGO confined themselves in their brief evidence to one point, the difficulties of divided loyalties where one officer served two authorities. The LCC Staff Association gave in effect a spirited defence of the LCC based on the view that a large-scale organization was necessary for London – and for good measure they threw in the suggestion that any future major authority for London might take over the administration of the hospitals and water supply.

The universities

As was shown earlier, one of the innovations of the Herbert Commission was to invite evidence from the universities. This not unnaturally, brought no response from places like Belfast and Durham, but there was a rich reward from London particularly from two bodies, the Greater London Group of the London School of Economics and Political Science and the Centre for Urban Studies based on University College.

First, however, mention must be made of two items of evidence which were submitted by individual university teachers. Dr Peter Richards of the University of Southampton was already known as the author of a work on delegation in local government and his evidence concentrated on this topic. He advocated direct conferment of powers in preference to delegation and favoured a two-tier system in Greater London with functions divided between the two tiers.[47] He argued that there was a conflict between general agreement that delegation should be as unfettered as possible and the practice of some counties in insisting on 'detailed returns of administrative minutiae'. He criticized Middlesex in particular for emphasizing uniformity at the expense of local opinion, but admitted that where there was a sharp clash of interest such as existed there because of the ambitions of Municipal Boroughs for County Borough status,

'some conflict is inevitable: delegation merely provides a more complicated institutional framework in which negotiations can take place'.[48]

In giving oral evidence he elaborated on the disadvantages of delegation and particularly the fact that formal and fairly rigid agreements were necessary when it was a 'question of handing down executive powers'.[49] His evidence enabled the Commission to put the Middlesex situation in perspective and considerably influenced their own views on the advantages and disadvantages of delegation in general.

Professor John Griffith fell into a rather different category. As Professor of English Law at the London School of Economics he had originally been a member of the Greater London Group, but broke away on a fundamental point of disagreement. He believed that the problems of local government in London should be approached primarily in terms of administrative efficiency and not in terms of local democracy. The point of view he put was novel, in that it did not even pay lip-service to conventional views about the values of local democracy. It is true that he acknowledged that there were advantages in elected bodies but 'there is no inherent virtue in elected bodies over those not elected'. In a candid statement he claimed that 'the principal reason for apathy at local elections is that it does not much matter who is elected'.[50] Whether he was cynic or realist it at least could not be argued that he spoke only from his scholar's ivory tower; he had spent ten years as a councillor first on Marlow Urban District and then on Buckinghamshire County Council.

The conclusions which Professor Griffith drew from this viewpoint were not, however, startling. Only highways and planning were not efficiently administered under the existing system and he therefore proposed that these functions should be taken out of local government and entrusted to a nominated board. All else was to remain exactly as it was.

Whatever the merits of his conclusion, it is a pity that the arguments for and against local democracy were not more fully debated before the Commission. They were quite fundamental to much of the evidence and, as will be seen, to the Commission's recommendations. Professor Griffith's challenge to accepted assumptions deserved fuller debate.

The Greater London Group

By far the weightiest and most comprehensive piece of evidence submitted to the Herbert Commission was that of the LSE's Greater London Group. The origin of this evidence throws some interesting light on the status of academic studies of local government. In March 1958 Sir Edwin Herbert wrote to each of the universities in the United Kingdom asking whether any members of the academic staff wished to give evidence. At London University this request naturally found its way among other places to the London School of Economics where William Robson who, as was seen earlier, had long advocated the reform of London government, held the Chair of Public Administration. The Commission's ostensible reason for writing to the Universities was that 'we believed (rightly as it turned out) that research work might be going on which would be of value'.[51] The statement is, however, somewhat disarming; academic study of local government was at that time limited and mainly confined to rather formal discussions of such things as the constitution, powers and duties of local authorities. Studies of how local government worked in practice in particular authorities, of the problems it faced, its achievements and shortcomings were rare. What the Commission really sought was to stimulate such study and with the LSE they succeeded.

It is true however that the idea of giving evidence to the Commission had already occurred to some members of the academic staff, aided by informal contacts with Professor Mackenzie, a member of the Commission, and Professor Robson had agreed to act as chairman of a group of interested members. There were obvious difficulties especially of time and money in organizing the necessary research for such a project, but by June 1958 the Greater London Group was actively in being for the specific purpose of carrying out research and giving evidence to the Royal Commission.

It consisted, apart from Professor Griffith, of thirteen members, all teachers at the London School of Economics and Political Science in subjects as diverse as economics, geography, law and social administration as well as public administration. The Group's evidence was completed at the end of July 1959, by which time the Commission were well advanced in their oral hearings.

Underlying all the proposals made by the Group was a certain view of what local government was about which was presented as an article of faith.

'We wish, therefore, to affirm our belief in the value of a strong and healthy system of local government as a fundamental part of democracy.'[52]

Among the disadvantages which they saw in the existing patchwork of local authorities were

'disadvantages which limit the political consciousness and inhibit the civic sense of the people of Greater London. There is at present no democratic or representative organ which can both express and develop the latent consciousness among Londoners, which lies beneath the surface, of belonging to a great metropolitan community.'[53]

And they saw such imponderable factors as being those which might ultimately 'tell in favour of bold and imaginative reform'.

The importance of this viewpoint is in its bold assertion of the need for a directly elected Greater London Authority. Defenders of the existing system asserted that an elected body for eight million people would not be local government. The Greater London Group were prepared to take as a main plank of their platform the idea of

Greater London as a community and to brush aside the objection of mere size to a representative body for such a large area.[54]

The idea was subjected to some criticism in the oral hearings because the difficulty of assertions of this kind is that, as was freely admitted, they must largely depend on personal experience. The following exchanges illustrate the point:

'Professor Robson: We think there is this growing consciousness of Greater London as a metropolis, but as I say, we cannot produce any kind of market research evidence.

Sir Edwin Herbert: There is a great psychological danger always of projecting into other people's minds something which you are conscious of yourself . . . I doubt whether there is as much as you think in this sense of oneness with London.'[55]

Important as this approach was in shaping the Group's views it formed only one limb of their evidence; the other was devoted to showing that the existing structure of local government, in addition to its limiting effect on London's civic consciousness, also affected adversely the performance of functions. In strong and characteristically forthright terms the Group argued the case for a Greater London Authority to be responsible for such functions as overall planning, main drainage, overspill housing, refuse disposal, major highways and technical education. Thus, on planning, after rehearsing the history of the Greater London plan and the Clement Davies committees[56] they concluded:

'the results of this failure by successive governments to set up any comprehensive machinery to take responsibility for the over-all planning of Greater London have been disastrous. There is no systematic co-operation or co-ordination between the twelve[57] local planning authorities and very little exchange of information. Questions of the utmost importance . . . are considered and determined in relation to the relatively small fragment of the area which happens to fall within the jurisdiction of the individual county, or even county borough, council concerned. Moreover there is no organ which is charged with the duty of keeping the needs of the metropolis under review . . . . . The need for a Greater London Council to be the planning authority for the Metropolis is unquestionable.'[58]

On technical education the Group criticized severely the lack of a single comprehensive plan for Greater London and pointed to the ineffectiveness of the London and Home Counties Regional Advisory Council for Higher Technological Education, set up in 1947, 'because of its inability to take positive and independent action' leading to 'misplaced colleges and resources misdirected in terms of priority of need'.[59]

It will be obvious that many of the points raised by the Group were not new. What was new was the vigour with which the points were made and the comprehensiveness of the case which was made in functional terms for a single authority for Greater London. Even so, the Herbert Commission and indeed its predecessors in looking at London's problems or parts of them, had had views in plenty and often well argued views. Why then should the Commission be expected to pay any particular attention to the Group's views beyond the respect due to the standing of its members? The answer lies partly in the fact that the members of the Group, like the members of the Commission, had no vested interest in any particular form of London government. A case, however well-argued, presented by a body such as the London Municipal Society or the Association of Municipal Corporations was bound to be treated with some reserve because of their direct interest in the form which local government took, and this was obviously still more true of evidence presented by individual local authorities.

But quite apart from this it was a feature of the Group's evidence that the general statement and argument was supported by a series of detailed papers dealing mainly with major functions such as education, town planning and housing, but also with more general questions such as population and employment in Greater London and the political structure of local government in the area. Some idea of the scale of these research papers may be gained from the fact that of the 200 pages which the Group's evidence occupied in the printed record of evidence these papers account for 120. It was these detailed research papers which gave substance and backing to the Group's general arguments. Those arguments were not, however, only concerned with the need for an elected Greater London authority. The Group also argued that the existing second-tier authorities did not constitute a satisfactory pattern for the performance of local government functions. What was needed in addition to the Greater London authority was a series of larger two-tier authorities. Ideally, these should be balanced and combine both richer and poorer areas.[60]

The Group were divided in their view of what was the ideal size of these local authorities which were to carry out all local government functions, except those assigned to the Greater London Council. Supporters of Scheme A advocated authorities of the size of large County Boroughs (250,000–500,000 population); those of Scheme B, authorities of the size of large counties (1,000,000–1,500,000). But it was not just a disagreement about population size; the significance of the split lay in drawing attention to a fundamental question which still remains unresolved – namely, what size of authority is necessary to provide an adequate standard of specified services and at the same time remain an acceptable unit of representative local democracy. So far as London is concerned, Scheme A provided one answer, Scheme B another. Later the Herbert Commission was to provide a third and finally, the Government yet a fourth.

The difference between Scheme A and Scheme B was a matter of emphasis, and this was clearly brought out in the supporting arguments which were used. Scheme A was strongly based on analogies. The size of the boroughs – Greater London Boroughs as they proposed to call them – was similar to that of provincial County Boroughs such as Leicester and Bristol and similar too, to that of the administrative divisions adopted by the LCC for education and health services; indeed they admitted that the LCC's educational divisions 'have carried great weight in determining the size of our proposed second-tier units'.[61] At the same time they wanted these units to be 'based on local centres of communal loyalty and sentiment'.[62]

Scheme B by contrast put much more emphasis on functional efficiency and the increasing need for large units of administration in, for example, education, health and welfare services to provide a good standard of services and to employ the highly qualified staff which the services demanded. Correspondingly they placed less emphasis on the community basis of their proposals:

'We consider that the London counties provide as good a focus for local democracy as it is possible to devise in the special circumstances of Greater London . . . The most definite local communities which can be distinguished in the London area tend to be fairly small units, which are too small in any case to serve as a basis for local government organization.'[63]

The strength of their arguments therefore turns on the importance of functional requirements. Here the great weight of influence of the personal and social services is evident in shaping their view of what size of second-tier authority was needed. A separate memorandum on the children's, personal health and welfare services was largely devoted to showing that authorities ought to be similar in size and strength to existing county councils; it explicitly rejected the Scheme A solution since

> 'sooner or later a system based on some twenty-five boroughs would inevitably result in a transfer of powers from the lower to the higher tier'.[64]

which would be 'unthinkable'. It is significant that both the members of the Group from the Social Administration Department were Scheme B supporters including D. V. Donnison, who later criticized the Herbert Commission's proposals for health and welfare functions.[65]

The Commission took the unusual step of devoting two whole days to oral questioning of the Group, a recognition of the fact that, as the Chairman put it, 'there is no doubt whatever that the work you have done will be of the utmost help to us'.[66] In addition to detailed discussion and elucidation of many of the Group's proposals, a number of major themes tended to recur, particularly the necessity, as opposed to the desirability, of instituting a Greater London Council. Members of the group were eloquent on the need in functional terms for an authority or body which could look at the problems of London as a whole. But that this must be a single local government authority rather than, for example, an ad hoc or joint consultative board of existing local authorities was not something which in the last resort could be demonstrated. As Professor Robson put it,

> 'It is not a necessity in the sense that bread, water, heating are necessities; but we think that things will be better done by a Greater London authority than they have been done in the past . . . and that some things will be done which are beneficial . . . (and) which will not be done if some sort of provision of this kind is not made.'[67]

These words sum up the fundamental philosophy of the Greater London Group and the reasons which ultimately led them to suggest a complete recasting of the structure of London government.

One of the difficulties of such a viewpoint was that it left uncertain the principles on which second-tier authorities should be created. As the Commission pointed out, the Government had accepted for the rest of the country the view that a town of 100,000 population was prima facie capable of running the full range of services of a County Borough and yet the group were proposing a minimum population of 200,000 or, in the case of Scheme B, of 1,000,000. Again, the Group were eloquent on the kind of considerations which had led them to take this view, particularly functional considerations and problems and costs of staffing, but again it was emphasized that in the last resort it must be a matter of judgment.[68]

Ultimately perhaps what counted in giving importance to the Group's evidence was not only whether they had contributed original research – the intractable nature of the problems and the shortage of time in any case limited what could be done – but the fact that over a period of several months a group of uncommitted, independent observers had tried to thrash out the whole problem as dispassionately as possible using as much available information as they could get and drawing on their experience of local government and of particular aspects and functions of it. Paradoxically the split between supporters of Scheme A and Scheme B may have helped and not hindered their case. The Chairman of the Commission hinted as much at the oral hearings and a similar point is made in the Commission's Report.[69] Certainly the questions over which the two schemes split were quite fundamental and it is not surprising that there was no unanimity. Professor Robson, on behalf of Scheme A, claimed, 'I do not think that the so-called London counties of Scheme B are local authorities', to which Mr (now Professor) Self, on behalf of Scheme B, replied, 'We think it is anomalous and retrograde – perhaps even a little absurd – to think in terms of large numbers of separate Londons.'[70] It was a difference of view which the Commission too had to resolve.

The Centre for Urban Studies

There could hardly be a greater contrast than that between the two main academic pieces of evidence. Although the Centre for Urban Studies was, like the Greater London Group, an inter-disciplinary body and included historians, geographers and statisticians, its evidence to the Herbert Commission and in particular the detailed research appendix on 'The Growth and Structure of Greater London' was primarily sociological in character. But even more important was the deliberate limitation of the scope of the evidence, to exclude the examination of the performance of different functions by local authorities. So far from thinking, as the Greater London Group had done, that a Greater London Authority was necessary, the Centre quoted with approval the Government's 1956 White Paper on 'Areas and Status of Local Authorities in England and Wales' that

'there is . . . no convincing case for radically reshaping the existing form of local government in England and Wales.'[71]

Specifically, they wanted to retain the 'status, functions and boundaries' of the London County Council.

To some extent the Centre's evidence is a reply to that of the Greater London Group. It was not presented until December 1959, over four months after the Group had submitted its evidence, and some of the points it makes seem to be directed specifically against the Group,[72] but it would be wrong to see it simply in these terms, as Smallwood does.[73] Much of the most interesting part of the evidence is the analysis of census and other material to show the different socio-economic zones of Greater London, and this is complementary to the much more limited analysis made by the Group. One conclusion drawn from the data by the Centre is that the boundaries of the administrative County of London correspond to an area of 'distinct social identity' and this is one of their supporting arguments for the maintenance of the LCC. However, in detail the correspondence does not appear to be quite so close, especially on the south side, where there is an intermediate area stretching from Wandsworth to Croydon.[74] But one of the main values of this research appendix is its detailed presentation of some of the hard facts about Greater London which were conspicuously absent from so much of the evidence to the Herbert Commission.

In the main body of their evidence the Centre rejected the view that there was a need for a Greater London Authority. They recognized 'the need for the integration of development and services in Greater London and beyond' but they did not see this as specifically requiring a local government solution. It could be met, indeed, in their view, could only be met, by a strengthening of central government regional organization.[75] There were also other arguments against a Greater London authority – the boundaries of Greater London were indefinite, it would not work, it would be an alien innovation. Their conclusion was that existing authorities, and especially the LCC, should be preserved.

The Centre devoted some space to examining certain aspects of local democracy, particularly what they regarded as 'misconceptions'. Much of this was an interesting commentary on voting figures and the social class composition of councils in which they rightly drew attention to the fact that the voting figures in Greater London compared favourably with those of England and Wales as a whole. Their main purpose seems to have been to defend the LCC from the charge of remoteness and to suggest that reorganization of local government might not in fact strengthen local democracy. But they also argued, against the Greater London Group, that there was not necessarily any advantage in the idea of *political* balance, that is, a deliberate attempt to create socially heterogeneous areas for this purpose.[76]

In oral evidence, the Centre's representatives were pressed particularly hard to say how the strengthened central government regional organization would work in practice. They saw it as a body which in planning

'would have the job of initiating requests for information, getting the information and formulating general policies'.[77]

but leaving the existing planning authorities with their powers of preparation of detailed plans and reviews. The real difficulty, however, which the Centre had to contend with was in defining the precise status of this regional committee particularly in relation to the parent departments. On the one hand they wanted it to be an advisory body, on the other they wanted it to have 'teeth', by which they intended in the first place an independent Chairman and in the second some kind of delegation of powers from the central departments themselves. This provoked an unusually frank exchange of views between Sir Edwin Herbert and representatives of the Centre:

'*Chairman:* Not another form of delegation?

Mrs Glass: I do not know why the term 'delegation' is so despised in this context. We had in mind the delegation of certain functions to the central government regional organization: those relating to the approval of development plans, for example, and also possibly to the allocation of certain grants. Alternatively, as Sir William Holford envisaged, there might be so close a partnership between government departments and the new regional organization, that the former would be practically bound by the recommendations of the latter, unless there were very strong reasons to the contrary.

Professor Sir William Holford: We hope, sir, the Commission would agree that delegation in Government Departments was a little easier than delegation in local authorities.
Chairman: I should have thought it was impossible frankly.'[78]

These exchanges illustrate clearly the Centre's dilemma. They were being pressed to be specific about something on which they did not claim to be expert. On the other hand, the question whether the initiation of any revision of the pre-conceptions of the Abercrombie Plan should or should not come from within local government had assumed a considerable importance in the course of the Commission's proceedings.[79] By the time the Centre came to give oral evidence it is probable that most members of the Commission had already made up their minds on this question.[80] It would probably have required, therefore, a much more precise plan than the Centre had been able to prepare to have any hope of persuading the Commission that 'Greater London needs integration, but not recasting, of its local government structure'.[81] But although the Commission rejected the main thesis of the Centre's evidence, they did draw on the considerable body of factual data presented by them; in the end this proved to be the most valuable part of their evidence.

Such were the main strands of evidence put before the Commission. An account of this kind cannot do justice to the range of the Commission's proceedings. This is particularly true of the oral hearings. In nearly 16,000 questions and answers members of the Commission probed hard to find out how the existing system worked and where any deficiencies lay. Often they found themselves drawn into great detail as when they sought to elucidate how refuse disposal was carried out or how the responsibility for highways operated in the County of London. All this took a great deal of time. This is a point which tends to be forgotten when one is trying simply to high-light the main points. Whatever view may be taken of the conclusions which the Commission reached it cannot be disputed that in their seventy days of taking oral evidence they covered the ground as thoroughly as it is possible to do so by this method. No person or body with an argument to put on London government lacked the opportunity to do so. As always with Royal Commissions, the main difficulty for the Herbert Commission was to sift this massive amount of material and decide what its implications were for the future of London government.

4
The Report of the Herbert Commission

The Commission's analysis of the problem

In October 1960 the Herbert Commission published their Report. It advocated a new series of authorities, of between 100,000 and 250,000 population, to be called Greater London Boroughs and to be responsible for the great majority of local government functions, and a new directly elected authority, the Council for Greater London, to perform those functions 'which can only be or can be better performed over a wider area'.[1] The main purpose of this chapter is to examine the reasons which led the Commission to these general conclusions, and to their detailed recommendations. In considering this account, it is important to remember that the Commission did not rely only on the evidence presented to them in reaching their conclusions. As they themselves noted, among the 'other means' which they had used to inform themselves were 'certain special enquiries' which they themselves commissioned and 'numbers of public documents' some of which were not mentioned in evidence.[2] This was in addition to their visits to local authorities in the review area. The special enquiries resulted in two important papers by Mr W. I. Carruthers, a research officer in the Ministry of Housing and Local Government,[3] but these appear to have been the only pieces of original research[4] initiated directly by the Commission. They considered but rejected a sample survey among members of the public because of the variety and complexity of the questions which they wanted to ask.[5]

It is important to note that in several places in their report the Commission stressed that they were not anxious to make changes. Their general approach was cautious and modest, and they claimed

'where a system is working or being made to work our predilection has been in favour of leaving it alone . . . We have only made recommendations for change where we have felt driven to do so in order to provide the machinery necessary, in our judgement, for the solution of London's problems'.

At the same time,

'we do not delude ourselves into thinking that one can solve problems by projecting changes of machinery'.[6]

Since they did advocate fundamental changes the logic of their case required them to show that there were great defects in the existing system. It will be necessary, therefore, to examine in detail the stages by which they reached their conclusions. But first it is also important that the Report was unanimous, in great contrast to the Ullswater Report. The account given in the Herbert Report is worth quoting; after saying that they did not discuss their recommendations until after taking oral evidence the Report refers to a week-end of discussions at Cambridge on 13 and 14 February 1960 when:

'at the conclusion of these meetings we found that each of us individually had been driven to the same conclusions'.[7]

Even allowing for the strength of personality of the Chairman which must have been an important factor in determining the scope and content of the Commission's recommendations, it is nevertheless remarkable that there was this degree of unanimity among the seven members of the Commission.

Two basic principles lay behind the Commission's detailed recommendations. The first was that some local government functions could not be satisfactorily carried out or even carried out at all by existing local authorities in Greater London; secondly, these functions ought to be performed by local authorities. From this it followed that there must be a reorganization of local government in the area.

There were thus two very different strands of thinking in the Commission's conclusions. One was concerned with administrative efficiency in the performance of local government functions, the other with what they themselves referred to as 'the health of local government' in the review area. There can be no doubt from a reading of the Report of the very great value which they attached to this latter concept. It represents a fundamental philosophy which transcends the functional approach, as will be seen in the following analysis of the Commission's Report.

It is natural, in view of the background to the Commission's enquiry to look first at what they had to say about planning and traffic problems. The main burden of their argument on planning was that the pre-suppositions on which the Abercrombie plan for Greater London was based needed re-examining largely because of social and economic changes since the war and that this required a body with the statutory duty of looking at the area of Greater London as a whole. The first part of this argument was hardly in dispute and the Commission presented the case forcibly and well. It was the implications of the second part which were of immense importance for their recommendations. They rejected any solution which would make such a body part of central government partly because they did not see how the Minister could properly be responsible for initiating a review and at the same time maintain his quasi-judicial powers under the Town and Country Planning Acts; partly because they viewed such a solution as leading to increasing intervention by the central government in London affairs and, in effect, the abandonment of local self-government for London.

'Town and country planning is, and always has been, an essential function of local government. To surrender even the initiation of policy to the central government would, we believe, fatally weaken local government.'[8]

Their belief in the values of local government was therefore a major factor in leading them to conclude that a reorganization of local government was necessary for planning purposes, but it was defects in the performance of the function which compelled them first to look at the possibility of change.

With London's traffic problems the Commission dealt more briefly. Here they showed that the existing machinery, involving not only local authorities but also the Minister of Transport, the Metropolitan Police and other bodies, was too cumbersome to get things done with anything like reasonable speed or at all effectively. It was 'chaotic, inefficient and totally out of date'.[9] The demonstration of the irrationality of the existing arrangements was done with gusto, the account being interspersed with remarks like

'the present machinery is so confused that it is difficult even to put down on paper a description of what it is, let alone how it works.'[10]

But they were careful to point out that improving the administrative machinery was not the answer to all problems. Rather, it was simply that the problems could not be solved under the existing machinery. They proposed instead that there should be a single authority responsible both for traffic management and for the construction, maintenance etc. of main roads in Greater London. In contrast to the chapter on planning where the arguments for a single authority and a local government rather than a central government solution were carefully set out, their conclusions on traffic and highways were badly stated without argument.[11]

It is important to note that these two chapters contain much the greater part of the argument for a single Greater London authority in the Commission's Report. It is true that there are other pointers in the same direction (especially 'overspill' housing) but it is very doubtful whether without planning and traffic the Commission could plausibly have argued that their inclination was to leave things as they were. Both these functions provided examples of things which were not being done at all under the existing arrangements or were not being done effectively. They provided therefore the motive force for change.

By contrast, the Commission's treatment of most of the other functions which they examined[12] depended less on the necessity for changes for the efficient performance of those functions. Education is an outstanding example. After a historical and descriptive analysis of the existing situation, the Commission posed seven questions the answers to which they believed would show whether the objects of the 1944 Education Act were being attained in Greater London. On most of these questions (eg an adequate number and variety of schools) they could find little in the way of defects. Nor in spite of the notorious friction in Middlesex between county and county districts did they in general find that the quality of education suffered from any defects in the system.

They did, however, put forward two closely related arguments. One was that there ought to be more local contact in education. This was chiefly directed against the LCC; they conceded that the LCC had a high reputation but then criticized the administrative system as 'huge and monolithic' and suffering from 'a certain rigidity and apparent inhumanity'. They went on:

'This fault – and it is a fault in a personal service like education – has been amply brought out in our evidence. It seems to us that in regard to the daily conduct of the schools, parents and other people like to be able to go to the Town Hall, or to approach their local councillors; and we think it right that in a matter which so intimately concerns the life of the individual and of the family they should be able to do so'.[13]

Their other argument was that every encouragement should be given to the interest of councillors in education:

'any organ of local government which has significant duties in regard to schools and colleges will for that reason tend to be a healthier and livelier body',

and therefore

'we cannot think of anything which is more likely to ensure a persistence of lively health in the boroughs of Greater London than that they should be given some active say in the conduct of their schools'.[14]

What is important about the Commission's discussion of education is that it illustrates most clearly the shift in their argument from considerations of administrative efficiency to what was necessary for the health of local government. In education they found little to indicate that changes in machinery were necessary to remedy defects in performance. What they proposed were ways in which the machinery might be improved to achieve what was, in their view, a better and healthier system of local government. Whereas they were driven to suggest changes for planning and traffic, they could not honestly claim that there was the same necessity for change in the education field except in terms of improving the health of local government.

The health of local government

In view of what has been said above, it is clear that the views of the Commission on what was required to maintain or to improve the health of local government in Greater London are crucial to an understanding of their precise proposals in terms of both areas and functions. The language of the Report, and especially of the early pages dealing with the historical background, gives a clue to their thinking. A key word is 'vitality'. In the space of two pages the word (or its related adjective) occurs five times. 'Here is a community of unrivalled vitality,' the Commission suggested and 'throughout its history London has had this astonishing quality of vitality.'[15] And the word occurs repeatedly throughout the Report.[16]

Just as the Commission emphasized this living quality of London as a community, so too they laid stress on the organic nature of local government. In two places in the Report they leaned heavily on this concept, the first time in relation to the nature and purpose of local government generally, and the second time in relation specifically to the Commission's review area. But like the concept of London's vitality, the importance of the health of local government is a theme which runs right through the Report.

'Local government,' they claimed 'seems to us to be much more like a living thing, an organism, in which each part or function is not self-contained or connected externally with other parts. Each part is integrally concerned with each other part.'[17]

In particular,

'no amount of potential administrative efficiency could make up for the loss of active participation in the work by capable, public spirited people elected by, responsible to, and in touch with those who elect them.'[18]

This led them to list the six qualities required of the ideal councillor and they summed up the position in the following words:

'It would seem that a councillor has the best chance of being active in these six respects without becoming a nuisance to the officials, or a busybody among his neighbours, if he represents an area and a body of constituents that are neither too large nor too small for the purpose for which he represents them.'[19]

From this basic philosophical position they developed their argument in two directions; first, by showing that all was not well with the health of local government in the review area and, secondly, by drawing attention to what in their view was needed to improve matters. The first part drew on a number of themes which were not specific to Greater London but applied to local government generally. They mentioned, for example, the effect of the transfer of functions in post-war legislation both as between local government and other bodies, and within local government as between counties and county districts; the difficulties in attracting councillors to serve on district councils; and the fact that county councillors tended to be drawn from different strata of the community from county district councillors.[20]

But in addition they argued that the situation in Greater London was made worse by the uncertainties over promotions to County Borough status and by the fact that 'the extraordinary complication of local government in Greater London is confusing to the electors'.[21]

The first of these was, as has been suggested, particularly evident in Middlesex. The second, once again, illustrates their basic philosophy, this time expressed in criticism of the elector:

'It does not seem to occur to the average elector that if responsibilities were clearly defined and if some local government authority on which he is represented by a Councillor were responsible and had the necessary powers, it would be practicable for the elector to bring his influence to bear through the medium of the ballot box'.[22]

They therefore concluded not only that local government was not functioning as well as it might but that: 'the present structure of government in the Review Area is not conducive to the health of representative government'.[23]

It became a major aim of the Commission in suggesting a reform of the structure to try to overcome these faults by eliminating the sources of conflict in Middlesex and by simplifying the structure and giving a clearer and more precise definition of powers and responsibilities.

Nevertheless, their conclusions owed little to the formal evidence presented to them. This evidence did, indeed, point to confusion of responsibilities but not in relation to the voter and his attitudes about which very little was said at all.[24]

What we are here concerned with is the Commission's statement of faith and belief in certain values in local government. Their views on this were formed at least as much by their informal contacts with councillors and officers as by reading and listening to the evidence presented to them. Nor did they set out with blank minds. They would hardly have agreed to serve on a Royal Commission concerned with local government if they had not had at the outset a belief in the value of local self-government. It is interesting to see how, in reaching their conclusions, these beliefs as formulated and refined led them to favour a particular structure and division of functions.

In particular, one needs to set their attachment to the health of local government against their claim that their inclination was to leave things as they were. It is impossible to make sense of the Royal Commission's proposals without bringing into account the fact that in many instances the health of local government was at least as important a reason to them for suggesting changes in structure as functional considerations.

This comes out most clearly perhaps in their general conclusions. The logic of their functional analysis pointed above all to the need for a Greater London authority to be responsible for certain functions, yet their first conclusion was:

> 'The primary unit of local government in the Greater London Area should be the borough, and the borough should perform all local authority functions except those which can only be effectively performed over the wider area of Greater London or which could be better performed over that wider area.'[25]

The expression 'primary unit' is ambiguous but there can be little doubt that in the Commission's view it was through the boroughs that the health of local government would be assured and the importance of this opinion was one if not the major factor leading them to put this as their first conclusion.

The Commission's recommendations

Appendix 2 (page 247) sets out the Commission's proposals and how they compare with the statutory provisions in the London Government Act, 1963. In the following pages some important aspects of those proposals will be considered in more detail.

Council for Greater London. Of particular importance were the arguments used by the Commission for an elected council for Greater London as opposed to either an *ad hoc* body, joint arrangements between existing local authorities, or a central government solution. In forthright terms they expressed their conviction that:

> 'the choice before local government in Greater London is, in truth, to abdicate in favour of central government, or to reform so as to be equipped to deal with present-day problems. There are great and growing problems to be solved and the present machinery of local government is inadequate to solve them. Unless this machinery is made adequate, the problems are so great and obtrude themselves so obviously on public attention that they will be taken out of the hands of local government.'[26]

In rejecting the solution of making central government responsible for major planning, traffic, highway and housing functions, the Commission argued cogently that the effect would be to destroy the independence of local authorities in Greater London. Not only would there have to be set up what would become in fact if not in name a Ministry for London or of London,[27] but once it was acknowledged that central government intervention on this scale was necessary, there was likely to be further intervention not only in London but in other parts of the country too with consequent diminution in the power and influence of local authorities.

This case was argued persuasively. It depended on a basic faith in the capacity of local government to deal with problems which hitherto it had been unable to because of defects in the structure. The Commission also rejected the view that these major functions which required to be carried out for the whole of Greater London could be performed either by an *ad hoc* body or by some form of joint action by existing local authorities. In advocating a Greater London authority, their recommendations were similar to those made by a few of the witnesses who had given evidence, but especially by the Greater London Group of the London School of Economics who had made this a key feature of their evidence.

One interesting recommendation made by the Commission was that the Council for Greater London should have 'a first-class Intelligence Department'. The necessity for research and information as part of the responsibility of a planning authority for Greater London had been argued in 1949 by the minority of the Clement Davies Committee,[28] and a similar viewpoint was put to the Commission by Dame Evelyn Sharp (for the Ministry of Housing and Local Government) and by Professor Allen of the Centre for Urban Studies.[29] But the Commission saw greater importance and a broader scope for this new department.

Characteristically their argument for an intelligence department had two bases. There was first the need for efficient administration requiring continuous research into problems affecting Greater London as a whole, and the collection and processing of information on such subjects as housing and education to enable intelligent planning to take place. But, secondly, in a wider context, the Commission saw this new department as a general clearing-house for information serving not only the Council for Greater London but also the central government, the boroughs, and the general public. By the latter they

chiefly intended the relatively small number of people who constituted an informed public opinion without whom 'democratic local
government is impossible'. And they concluded:

> 'without such a service we do not believe that local government in
> its traditional sense can continue to exist in London. If local
> government in Greater London does not do this job for itself
> central government must step in and do the job for it.'[30]

This was a bold claim but it illustrates clearly how the Commission
were influenced both by general arguments about efficiency and by
views on what would conduce to healthy local government.

On the constitution of this new council, the Commission had little
to say. It was to be a directly elected body with triennial elections and
109 members, one for the area of each parliamentary constituency
in Greater London. But they did not make recommendations whether
there should be aldermen, whether there should be a different system
of voting (eg the single transferable vote) or whether there should be
a form of payment to members or at least to committee chairmen.
They argued that in these matters they could see no reason why London should be different from the rest of the country.[31] No doubt too
there were tactical reasons. Having proposed a distinctive type of
local authority for London, the Commission could legitimately
have argued for different constitutional arrangements. But they were
aware that all these questions were controversial, and may well have
preferred to avoid what were to them side-issues.

Greater London Boroughs. The idea of Greater London Boroughs
was also prominent in Scheme A of the Greater London Group's
evidence but there were some obvious differences in what the Commission proposed. Scheme A supporters had stressed the need for
large authorities (250,000–500,000 population) to carry out effectively a range of functions which in most ways was similar to that
suggested by the Commission. The latter recommended much smaller and less powerful units of approximately 100,000–250,000 population. The Commission stated their preference for authorities which
were as small as possible consistent with their being able to perform
their functions efficiently. In an important passage they declared
their faith in the future based primarily on their visits to local
authorities:

> 'One outstanding impression' they said 'is that there is still left a
> great deal of vitality in local government amongst the Metropoli-

tan Boroughs and County Districts and that with the encouragement and stimulus of enlarged power and responsibility that
vitality can be quickened and invigorated.'[32]

And again,

> 'we also believe that it is best to give as much power and responsi-
> bility as possible to those who are in the closest touch with the
> people for whose benefit local government services are provided.'[33]

It is not therefore surprising that the Commission rejected the
Scheme B proposals of the Greater London Group. What is perhaps
surprising is the attention which they devoted to them. 'It may very
well be' they said, 'that if one were starting afresh in London . . . one
might devise a scheme of government of this kind.'[34] And the arguments which they used against it were not very strong, and did not
include what one would have supposed to be the most important of
all, that such proposals would be unlikely to make the contribution
to the health of local government which they considered so vital.
There is a hint here, one of the few in the whole Report, that much
argument and debate must have gone on before the Commission
agreed their scheme unanimously. That Scheme B should have had
much support in spite of the avowed leanings of the Commission is an
interesting comment on the complexity of the issues involved.

Areas of Greater London and the Boroughs. Fundamental to the Commission's Report was the view that there was a Greater London with
a 'recognizable civic unity and shape' and that 'the boundaries given
us do in general define an area recognizable as a city'.[35] This view
seems to have derived partly from what they had seen in their own
travels but mainly from certain special studies which they had had
carried out for them by W. I. Carruthers. They concluded that 'there
is an entity which is so closely knit, so interdependent, so deeply influenced by the central area and so largely built up, that it truly
makes up the London of today'.[36]

The Carruthers' studies were particularly directed towards delimiting the boundaries of Greater London. Their relevance to the Commission's general conclusion depends very much therefore on the vali-
dity of the criteria used for including or excluding areas from Greater
London. Carruthers analysed factual data for local authority areas
lying on the fringe of the area under review by the Commission, including the extent of the built-up area, frequency of trains to Central

London and the extent to which the population were employed in London. By means of a system of rating for each of the various categories areas could be identified according to whether they were definitely in Greater London, definitely outside, or marginal. It was the first time such techniques had played any significant part in delimiting local government areas, although the Commission were careful to point out that they had not simply relied on these analyses in reaching their conclusions. In the event, the Commission recommended the exclusion of: most of South-West Hertfordshire centred on Watford; Potter's Bar; Waltham Holy Cross; and Dartford. In all 60,000 acres and 276,000 population were excluded from the original area, representing 11 % and 3 % respectively of the total.

The Commission proposed rather different principles for determining the areas of the Greater London Boroughs. As far as possible existing boundaries were to be kept so that new boroughs were to consist of amalgamations of existing authorities; at the same time lines of communication and the existence of service centres were to be taken into account.[37] The underlying principle was that boroughs should be in the population range 100,000–250,000 since boroughs of this size should be able to discharge effectively the functions proposed for them.[38]

The Commission were reluctant to make specific recommendations for borough groupings, on the grounds that they were not a boundary commission and had not taken evidence on these matters. On the other hand, they did not wish to leave such an important question completely undetermined. They therefore proposed a provisional grouping of authorities to form fifty-two new Greater London Boroughs with populations ranging, with one exception, from 81,000 (Barnes/Richmond) to 249,000 (Croydon). They added a suggestion that if their recommendations were generally accepted there should be a further enquiry 'by a simple and expeditious procedure' into regrouping, and that this inquiry should follow the general legislation laying down the new structure of London government.[39]

There were two notable features about the list of boroughs; first it included the City of London as one of the Greater London Boroughs, despite its resident population of less than 5,000. This illogicality was defended with vigour but with something less than the Commission's usual persuasiveness on the grounds that 'it is in the national interest' that the City should remain unchanged. The second point was that no less than twenty existing authorities (including the City) remained with boundaries unchanged in the Commission's provisional list, their populations being large enough to meet the criteria laid down without the need for amalgamations.

Finance. The question of the financial effects of their proposals was dealt with briefly by the Commission. Nothing was said about it in their general conclusions and the short chapter which they devoted to it appears almost at the end of their report. Thus finance was, if not an afterthought, certainly a subsidiary question so far as the commission were concerned. This marked a contrast with earlier enquiries and particularly the Ullswater Commission who had devoted much effort to considering whether local government services could be provided more economically.

The Commission might have argued, as did the Government later, that since in their view reorganization was essential both for the efficient performance of functions and for strengthening local government, the financial effects were bound to be subsidiary. This was the implication of the way they presented the financial situation, but they claimed rather more than this:

'Our recommendations would not involve any material change in the aggregate rate expenditure in the Greater London area.'[40]

Such an argument was only tenable on the view that essentially what the Commission were aiming at was a redistribution of existing functions. But on their own analysis they were proposing to enlarge the scope of some functions, notably planning and traffic management, which were to go to the new Council for Greater London. And even apart from this could they reasonably hold that re-distribution on the scale they proposed would make no 'material change' in total expenditure? There were, for example, to be fifty-two separate children's departments, in place of the existing nine. Yet the Commission assumed[41] that there would be no difference in cost under the two systems. They were on firmer ground in pointing to the many uncertainties and difficulties in making any reliable estimates of cost; for example, the future incidence of general grant was not easy to forecast; and there were no accurate figures for the cost of county services in the proposed new boroughs.[42]

Nor did the Commission make allowance for any additional costs which might arise in the period of change-over, or for any effect which their proposals might have in stimulating demand for services. Whether or not these would lead to increased costs, and whether if so there were any means of calculating such costs were separate questions but one would have expected the Commission at least to have considered them if they had been seriously concerned with the financial effects of their proposals.

Instead, they confined themselves mainly to attempting to assess how, within the limited calculations which they made the proposed boroughs were likely to fare as compared with existing county districts, and came to the conclusion that most of the boroughs outside the LCC area would probably be able to levy a lower rate than that levied by their existing constituent districts. Although this would not be so in the case of some of the existing Metropolitan Boroughs, the Commission proposed here a new selective rate equalization scheme which would help to overcome this difficulty.[43] They also proposed that there should be limited transitional payments by the boroughs which were to be formed out of Essex, Hertfordshire, Kent and Surrey to their former counties in view of the exceptionally large disturbance which most of these counties would suffer.

Division of functions between the Council for Greater London and the Greater London Boroughs

The Commission recommended that some functions should be performed exclusively by either the Council or the Boroughs. Among the former's was to be responsibility for traffic management and for the fire and ambulance services. But the bulk of these functions were to be shared with the boroughs; these included town and country planning; highway construction, maintenance and lighting; education; and a number of lesser functions such as sewerage and land drainage. The list of functions to be performed exclusively by the boroughs was larger and included personal health, welfare and children's services; libraries; weights and measures; Food and Drugs Acts duties; and Shops Acts legislation. Also a number of functions were to be the boroughs main responsibilities, but the Council would have a limited responsibility; eg, the boroughs were to be responsible for parks and open spaces, but the Council was to retain control of Hampstead Heath and, possibly, Crystal Palace.[44]

Here attention will be concentrated on proposals for sharing functions between the Council and the boroughs and especially education which proved a difficult problem not only for the Commission but later for the Government too Divided responsibility for functions under the existing system by means of delegation arrangements was found by the Commission to have severe practical disadvantages. They stated their main principle to be:

'to give to each [sc. authority] functions and powers which are separate and distinct.'[45]

Where sharing of functions was necessary, they claimed that their proposals would be an improvement on the existing system, not least in getting away from 'the conception of superior and inferior or upper tier and lower tier'. It is therefore of some importance to see how they proposed to achieve this.

Planning. The Council for Greater London was to be responsible for the over-all development plan for Greater London and the boroughs for deciding planning applications with a few important exceptions. One of these was that proposals involving a departure from the development plan should be decided by the Council, but the decision whether a particular application did involve a departure was to be left to the boroughs. The risk in this that a borough might approve development which the Council would have regarded as a departure from the plan was, in the Commission's view 'well worth taking in order to avoid the double scrutiny of planning applications'.[46] They also proposed that the Minister should have power to designate classes of application in the central area of London (of which they found themselves unable to offer a satisfactory definition) which were to be referred by the boroughs to the Council. They had in mind here such things as applications which would greatly increase the number of office jobs and applications to erect tall buildings.[47]

Highway construction, maintenance, and lighting. Here the Commission proposed quite simply to divide London's roads into two categories, main roads and others, the Council to be responsible for the former, the boroughs for the latter. By main roads they intended roads whose major purpose was the carriage of through traffic, but they did not attempt a precise definition and thought the Minister should be empowered to declare which roads were to be regarded as main roads. They also left it to the Minister to decide whether any main roads should be designated as trunk roads.[48]

Housing. The Commission proposed that this should be a borough function except that the Council, alone in Greater London, should have power under the Town Development Act, 1952, to build outside London for the purpose either of creating a new town or of expanding an existing town. It was also to have power to build within London for two important reasons – for large redevelopment schemes[49] and to assist boroughs which were unable to meet their own needs; this was to be done by building in other boroughs. Ownership of houses in Greater London should be in the hands of the boroughs; in the case of houses built by the Council and of houses which they were to inherit from the LCC transfer was to be made by agreement to the boroughs in which they were situated within a period of 20–25 years.[50] Finally, although the boroughs were to be responsible for the allocation of their own stocks of housing, the Council was to have the power to co-ordinate the fifty-two separate housing lists.[51]

Personal health, welfare and children's services. The Commission thought these should be borough services, not only as a help towards restoring the morale of local government, but because they thought that borough administration would be more likely to make realizable the ideal of a domiciliary team in these services, a point on which they laid a great deal of stress.[52]

Education. At first sight one would expect the Commission to have recommended that education should be a borough function in conformity with their general principles and with their earlier analysis of the situation. It will be recalled, for example, that they had referred to the 'rigidity' of LCC administration and of the significance of councillor interest in education. But their reasons for rejecting this solution in favour of a division of powers between the council and the boroughs illustrate the dilemma in trying to reconcile criteria of administrative efficiency with those of healthy local government.

Three points are important here; first, the Commission's desire to associate the boroughs with the administration of education; secondly, their view that nevertheless there were many advantages in having a single authority for the whole area; thirdly, their dislike of the device of delegation of powers from one authority to another. Exclusive borough control was incompatible with the second of these viewpoints, which was linked in the Commission's view to the fact that education in the County of London had been under the control of a single body for nearly a century and that LCC policies such as freedom of choice of schools were important and should be extended to the whole of Greater London. In other words they acknowledged that for certain purposes at least functional requirements pointed in the direction of a Greater London education authority, but their views on the health of local government required them to give something more than delegated powers to the boroughs. The solution they proposed was a division between the Council and the boroughs on the following lines:

> 'that the Council should be responsible for the provision of a statutory standard of education throughout the area and that the boroughs should be responsible for the discharge of the executive work, subject to the budgetary and other controls by the Council referred to hereafter.'[53]

The Commission went into some detail to show how this division would work out. The council was to be responsible for the development plan for schools and colleges, their type and location, for promoting parents' freedom in the choice of schools (and therefore for control over selective entry) and for such things as teacher training and awards of scholarships. The boroughs were to be responsible for the maintenance of schools (and area and local technical colleges), for the day-to-day running of the schools and colleges (including such things as determining the use of premises out of school hours), and for a number of lesser but nevertheless important parts of the education service such as school welfare and the youth service.[54]

The object of these proposals was to give definite and assigned powers to the boroughs, thus avoiding the difficulties of delegation, yet at the same time to retain overall responsibility by an authority concerned with Greater London as a whole. The Commission believed that the plan which they were putting forward would 'avoid friction' between the Council and the boroughs, but inherent in that plan was a system of control by the former over the latter. The Commission insisted that the Council should limit its financial responsibility to controlling the budgets of the boroughs, which should be framed under limited number (six to nine) of heads, that general standards should be maintained by the Council's use of inspectors who 'should act primarily as friendly advisers', and that there should be genuine consultation between the Council and the boroughs over the location and type of new schools.[55]

Although the Commission were anxious to avoid the friction which delegation is liable to produce their proposals depended a great deal on a large measure of goodwill and co-operation between the Council and the boroughs. At the three critical points of financial control, consultation and inspection there was room for a great deal of argument and dispute unless both sides really had the will to make the system work. What the Commission themselves had said of the situation in Middlesex, 'it demands too much of the human nature of both councillors and officials', might be thought to apply to their own proposals.[56] Admittedly, the Commission were removing perhaps the main source of friction in Middlesex, the county v. county borough conflict. But places like Harrow, Croydon and Ealing, all proposed as boroughs under the commission's plan, might well chafe at restrictions on their powers in the education field especially when in other important fields (eg personal health and welfare) they were being offered full powers.

Factors influencing the Commission

This discussion of the Commission's proposals, and particularly of their education proposals, raises two important general questions about their report. The first is how much it owed to the evidence presented to them; the second is what part political considerations played in shaping their proposals.

On the first question, the general lines of the report followed the suggestions made by a few local authorities such as Westminster and Chelsea, but in a much more detailed way the evidence of the Greater London Group – and particularly Scheme A – closely parallels the Commission's proposals at most points. This suggests that the Commission were mainly influenced by the Group's evidence in reaching their conclusions. The Commission themselves stated categorically:

'we have arrived at [our own solution] independently and not by the process of elimination. We did not think we were obliged to choose between the solutions which had been presented to us.'

Nevertheless, in a reference to the Greater London Group, they remarked:

'we think it noteworthy, however, that it is those who have done the greatest amount of work on the subject who have reached the conclusions nearest to our own.'[57]

The latter quotation perhaps represents the key to the situation. The Commission could have reached the conclusions they did without the Group's evidence. Indeed in important ways their approach differed from that of the Group, notably in their treatment of education and the size of the boroughs. It is therefore an exaggeration to say:

> 'The London School of Economics testimony offered the Royal Commission the very thing it so desperately needed if it was to advance any comprehensive reform proposals at all: namely, a solid base of support upon which it could plead its case.'[58]

At the same time it was undoubtedly an advantage to the Royal Commission to be able to draw on the Group's findings, supported by their detailed research studies. To that extent the Group's evidence was an important influence on the Commission. But it is in the ways in which the Commission diverged from the Group's evidence that the most difficult questions arise.

On the need for a Council for Greater London and for stronger second-tier authorities, and on the allocation of most functions to the various new authorities the Commission closely agreed with Scheme A of the Greater London Group. The most significant divergence was over the size of the boroughs and over the allocation of education functions. Two obvious elements here were the Commission's predilection for boroughs which were not too large and, as has been shown, the dilemma, which became acutely obvious in the case of education, of reconciling democratic and functional claims. To this must also be added a third question, the extent to which the Commission were guided by political considerations and, in particular, the need to gain the support of the second-tier authorities to their proposals.

If the health of local government required strong but not too large boroughs it is easy to see why the Commission should reject the Scheme A suggestion of boroughs of 250,000–500,000 population. It is less easy to see what led them to conclude that 100,000–250,000 was the right range. In discussing this, they first pointed out that the Local Government Act, 1958, basically assumed that a borough of 100,000 population was capable of being a County Borough. They did not, however, deal at all with the question whether such an assumption was appropriate to a continuous built-up area like Greater London as opposed to a town standing on its own like York or Norwich. Next they mentioned that in the evidence submitted to them 200,000 had been the figure most often quoted, but immediately qualified this by saying, quite correctly, that none of these statements could be regarded as at all scientific.[59] Their own conclusion was that:

'there is no particular figure at which we should be justified in aiming as a scientific figure, but that there is a reasonably wide range of population (100,000 to 250,000) within which the functions which we propose for the Greater London Boroughs can be effectively discharged.'[60]

It has already been pointed out[61] that an important factor in the Greater London Group's Scheme A proposals for large boroughs was the need for strong units for education purposes. Here the divergence between the Commission and the Group was strong. Not only did the Commission take the opposite viewpoint that education should, as far as possible, be a local service although organized over the whole area of Greater London,[62] but the needs of education clearly played little or no part in shaping the size of their boroughs. Indeed, even boroughs the size of those proposed in Scheme A would not have met the Commission's requirements since they could not secure the overall planning and control of the education service throughout London.[63]

The divergence of views between the Commission and the witnesses whose plan came nearest to theirs was therefore quite sharp. It has here been presented mainly as a divergence over principles – over the size of authority necessary to sustain democratic local government and over the functional requirements of a service like education. On these points one can say that the Commission drew heavily on some of their witnesses, notably the Greater London Group of the London School of Economics, but modified the proposals put to them because they took a different view of what was needed for functional efficiency and the health of local government. A more difficult question is whether and to what extent political considerations also caused them to modify those views.

The Commission's recommendations for a Council for Greater London were certain to meet opposition from the counties, and, probably, the County Boroughs. Did they therefore seek consciously to gain support for their borough proposals from the existing County districts? As an American observer has put it:

'Whereas the first-tier County Councils and County Boroughs were to be the big losers in the reorganization process, the larger second-tier authorities were designated as the big winners. By driving a deep wedge between the first- and the second-tier units, the commission virtually guaranteed that its recommendations would not be met with unanimous opposition.'[64]

Perhaps few schemes of reform would have met *unanimous* opposition; the real danger from the Commission's point of view was that the Government would hesitate to act if there was any strong opposition from local authorities, and particularly from the major county authorities. The Commission themselves were perhaps acknowledging this when they said that they had originally aimed at putting forward recommendations 'based on a measure of general acceptance'. Once they had seen the evidence they had had to abandon this aim, fully realizing 'that whatever possible solution we offer . . . is bound to arouse strong opposition in one quarter or another'.[65]

Nevertheless, the question remains valid. The Commission might have argued that with the expected opposition from the LCC and other counties it was essential for them to show that there was a body of support, and preferably a strong body of support for their proposals within local government. This might not be of much use if the Government were unwilling to act against the opposition of the counties but it might help if they were at all open to persuasion. If the Commission had argued in this way the influence of the argument should show either in the proposed division of functions between the council and the Greater London Boroughs or in the fifty-two proposed borough groupings.

The stress on the boroughs as the primary units of local government in Greater London perhaps owes something to this argument. On the other hand, the conclusion was itself a logical outcome of the Commission's basic approach in terms of functional needs and of the health of local government. The Commission were doubtless aware that one argument which would be made against the proposed Council for Greater London was that it would be too remote and not truly local. It was therefore natural that they should stress the role of the boroughs as units of *local* government.

The size of the proposed Greater London Boroughs does not seem to owe anything to the need to obtain support from existing boroughs and urban districts. It is true that larger boroughs, as suggested for example by the Greater London Group, would have left intact fewer of the existing authorities than those suggested by the Commission.

But it was fundamental to the Commission's view of the health of local government that the boroughs should be as small as possible.[66] They claimed that it was impossible to give precise reasons for choosing the particular size range (100,000–250,000 population) which they proposed. But it seems doubtful whether the need to gain support from existing authorities was at all an influencing factor.

In considering the proposed groupings put forward, however tentatively, by the Commission, it seems relevant to quote their argument against the proposal of Scheme B of the Greater London Group for London counties of 1–1½ million population each that: 'it would destroy all existing Counties, County Boroughs, County Districts and Metropolitan Boroughs, a process which we should not wish to see unless it were absolutely necessary.'[67] It might be inferred that a conscious attempt was made by the Commission to preserve as many existing authorities as possible.

This is a question of degree. Many large existing authorities were to be left intact under the Commission's proposals; but many more with populations greater than the minimum were to be linked with others of considerable size;[68] others would be in groupings which, in terms of size, they would dominate.[69] Twenty existing authorities (nineteen excluding the City of London) were to form Greater London Boroughs, but seventy-five were to be grouped with one or more other authorities. Moreover, some authorities might attach just as much importance to gaining increased functions, even at the price of amalgamation, as to preserving their identity. The Commission could not therefore assume that the latter was the only aim to which they should have regard.

The inference must be that although the Commission clearly looked to some support from the second-tier authorities, it was very difficult to predict how much support they were likely to secure and how strong it would be. It is unlikely, therefore, that the aim of getting such support played much part in determining their specific proposals, but probable that it acted as a limiting factor to the extent that they were conscious of the need not to depart completely from the existing pattern of authorities.

There was one other direction in which political considerations might have played a part in shaping the Commission's proposals. Conservatives might be expected to welcome a plan which would abolish the LCC and thus end Labour's long rule at County Hall. Furthermore, the inclusion of many predominantly Conservative areas in Surrey, Middlesex and other metropolitan counties within the boundaries of Greater London might well give the Conservatives a greater chance of securing control of the Council for Greater London than they had had in the previous thirty years of capturing the LCC. Were the Commission aware of this and did it influence their conclusions?

They themselves stated categorically:

'we do not conceive it to be any part of our duty to have regard to considerations of party politics.'[70]

They must nevertheless have been aware of the political implications of their proposals. In view, however, of their own categorical statement and of the arguments which they deployed for the setting-up of a council for Greater London, it is difficult to believe that they consciously set out with the aim of getting Conservative support, or even that it was a motive for their recommendation that the LCC should disappear. Apart from the difficulty of inferring this from anything said in their Report, they would surely have had to take into account not only the political implications of abolishing the Labour LCC but the effects of their proposals in political terms on Middlesex, Surrey and Kent, all of which were predominantly Conservative.

In summing up the report of the Herbert Commission, the point which stands out is how effectively, in general, the case which they presented is argued. The report is free, not only of the encumbrance of minority reports, but of those vague statements and generalizations which tend, in reports of committees and commissions, to paper over splits and disagreements. Unanimity and the force of the arguments were factors giving weight to the Commission's report. Opposition had to meet a stiffer challenge than is often the case with Royal Commission reports. Nevertheless, it remains remarkable that so much of the report was actually carried into effect. The purpose of the following chapters is to trace the course of these events.

5
From the Herbert Commission's Report to the Government's White Paper

The publication of the Herbert Commission's Report on October 19 1960 was important mainly for two reasons: first, it proposed a comprehensive plan specifically designed to meet the problems of local government in Greater London; secondly, it presented this plan on the basis of clear, well-reasoned arguments and above all as a unanimously agreed plan of all the members of the Commission.

Thus, for the Government, who now had to make up their minds whether to accept, to modify or to reject the proposals put forward by the Commission, the issues were sharply put, far more so than in the case of the Ullswater Commission. Nevertheless, for those who wished to see as little change as possible in the existing system, it must have seemed unlikely that the Government would accept the proposals and still less likely that they would act with any speed over a report which was certain to prove controversial, especially to the local authorities who were most immediately affected by it. The reasons which had caused Governments to hesitate in the past, the political unattractiveness of local government reform and the prospect of prolonged opposition from many local authorities, tended to support this view.

Moreover, there is a widely held belief that one of the main reasons for setting up Royal Commissions is to shelve awkward problems, and that consequently controversial recommendations are liable either to be ignored altogether or to be considerably modified before being accepted, often after long delay. Generalizations of this kind need to be treated with caution. The author of a recent survey of Royal Commissions has pointed out that 'no study has yet been made of the time gap between issuance of the recommendations of every Commission and their implementation' and he suggests that Harold Laski's pre-war assessment of nineteen years for a unanimous recommendation and thirty years if the Commission were divided is 'probably an exaggeration'.[1]

A number of recent reports of Royal Commissions had in fact been implemented quite quickly[2]; nevertheless, the odds were probably in favour of slow rather than swift reaction to the Commission's proposals. In the event, 13 months elapsed between the time of the Commission's report and the Government White Paper of November 1961. During this period interest centred chiefly on the reactions of the various interested parties to the Commission's report and their attempts to influence the Government's decision on it.

General characteristics of the Herbert Report

Two elements in the Herbert Commission's plan were particularly important at this stage. First, there was the proposal for a single authority for an urban area containing $8\frac{1}{2}$ million people. Because of the sheer size of London, this might appear to be a startling innovation. But it should be remembered that the LCC too when it was created was a giant among local authorities with a population of over 4 million, and yet it came not only to be accepted but, as has been shown, to evoke from some quarters a remarkably spirited defence. In one sense, the proposed Council for Greater London was simply the LCC projected onto a larger scale, although of course with a very different range of functions.

In the distribution of functions between the Council and the boroughs lay the main innovations proposed by the Commission. What they suggested was a unique division of powers which did not correspond to anything which had hitherto been attempted. Their plan involved the creation of 'most-purpose' boroughs whose status and powers lay somewhere between those of County Boroughs and of Municipal Boroughs as they existed elsewhere in England and Wales.[3] Collectively the most obvious impact of these proposals was on the pattern of existing authorities in the area. In particular the effect of the introduction of a uniform system for the whole of Greater London depending on the strengthening of the second-tier or borough authorities was that two counties and three county boroughs would disappear and three other counties would lose considerable parts of their areas and populations; and that many second-tier authorities would lose their identities in amalgamations with other authorities.

Press comment

Immediate reaction to the Commission's Report, in terms of newspaper comment, was generally favourable, although with some reservations particularly over the education proposals. Thus *The Times*, under a first leader headed 'Bold Reform' characteristically hesitated over whether 'the disruption of experienced administrative teams and of much of whatever civic cohesion the present pattern possesses is too high a price to pay for a new structure properly adapted to wrestle with the problems of the day', but finally seemed convinced by the Commission's argument over the health of local government:

> 'if action were to follow the principles there recommended, responsible local self-government would be rehabilitated in and far beyond the metropolis.'[4]

Both the *Guardian* and the *Daily Telegraph* welcomed the general principles on which the Commission had based their plan as relevant not only for London but for other areas too.

All these three newspapers gave extensive summaries of the Report with more or less adequate maps. Most of the remaining national dailies did not comment on the Report. Only the *Financial Times* seemed to have doubts about the proposals, giving prominence to views suggesting that the problems of roads and regional planning were perhaps too big for local government. *The Economist* called for the 'speediest possible implementation' of the Report, declaring that it was 'a bold and intelligent plan' although perhaps not bold enough.[5]

But if the Press was generally favourable, this certainly did not mean that there was to be no opposition to the proposals. 'Row Brews Over Plan to Scrap LCC' was one *Daily Mail* headline the day after the Report was published, quoting Sir Isaac Hayward's comment: 'There is a long way to go yet before anyone can speak convincingly of the end of the LCC'. And a week later the *New Statesman* was speculating whether any worth-while reforms would be carried out in view of 'the amount of prejudice, self-interest and special pleading which can so easily surround this subject.'[6]

Reactions of Local Authorities

But perhaps of more substance and concern to the Government, judging by past experience, were likely to be the reactions of those most directly affected by the proposals, particularly the local authorities.

Opposition to the proposals could obviously be expected from bodies such as the London and Middlesex County Councils which would disappear altogether under the Herbert plan.[7] But could it be assumed that all local authorities would react in accordance with the effect of the proposals on themselves and, if so, how would they assess the advantages and disadvantages? On 28th November 1960 the Ministry of Housing and Local Government sent a letter inviting comments from all authorities affected by the proposals. They were given three months to do so and they were specifically asked to look at six points:

   i the borough as the primary unit of local government;
  ii. the view that for certain proposals the whole of Greater London should be the unit of administration;
 iii. a directly elected council for Greater London;
 iv. the division of functions between the boroughs and the Council;
  v. the financial implications;
 vi. the view that most authorities had stronger ties with London than with any other centre.

In considering the replies which authorities made to this circular a four-fold classification has been used:

  a. authorities supporting the proposals and particularly the proposal for a Greater London authority, with no or only minor reservations;
  b. authorities supporting the proposals in principle but with reservations on at least one major point;
  c. authorities rejecting the proposals and particularly the proposal for a Greater London authority and putting forward alternatives;
  d. authorities rejecting the proposals in favour of the existing system.

Counties and County Boroughs. The County Councils, with the exception of Hertfordshire which was very little affected by the Herbert proposals, fell into category (c). Their tactics and the alternative proposals which they favoured are discussed below. East Ham and Croydon defended the existing system and only West Ham of the first-tier authorities accepted the Herbert proposals in principle.

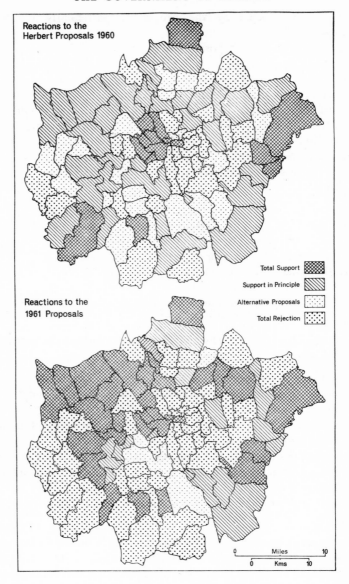

Figure 1. Reactions of County Boroughs and Second-Tier Authorities:
(a) to the Herbert Commission Proposals.
(b) to the Government Proposal of 1961.

Metropolitan Boroughs, Municipal Boroughs and Urban Districts.[8] The reactions of these second-tier authorities are best considered county by county.

London. The remarkable thing about the reactions of the Metropolitan Boroughs is how closely they followed political divisions. The eight boroughs (together with the City) which fell into category (a) ie general support for the proposals, were all Conservative – controlled and the only other Conservative Borough (Wandsworth) came in category (b). On the other hand all but two of the remaining Labour – controlled boroughs fell into either categories (c) or (d), the great majority being in favour of the existing system. Two Labour Boroughs (Fulham and Hackney) supported the proposals in principle.

Middlesex. (including also the two Hertfordshire authorities affected). Here there was much greater support in principle. A band of authorities from Uxbridge to Tottenham and from Harrow to Twickenham supported the Herbert proposals in principle; only four authorities (Staines, Sunbury-on-Thames, Acton and Barnet) wanted to preserve the existing system and another eight supported alternative proposals.

Essex. The ten Essex authorities were equally divided between those who supported and those who rejected the proposals. Of the five supporting, one (Hornchurch) fell into category (a) and of the five rejecting, four wanted to maintain the existing system, including two Conservative (Chingford and Chigwell) and two Labour authorities (Barking and Leyton).

Kent. The Kent authorities were even more in favour than those in Middlesex. Six of the eight supported the Commission's proposals, two of them (Crayford and Erith) enthusiastically. Only Bromley and Beckenham favoured alternative proposals.

Surrey. Like those in Essex, the Surrey authorities were very mixed in their responses. Of the seventeen affected, seven were in favour of the proposals, and ten opposed, most of the latter favouring an alternative plan.

It is clear from this brief summary of the replies made by local authorities that there was no simple pattern of response to the Herbert Report, except in the case of the counties. They alone, threatened either with extinction or considerable losses of territory, were unanimous in putting forward an alternative plan. Nor was this accidental. Surrey took the lead in formulating the plan and in consulting with the other County councils about it.[9] This Surrey Plan is discussed further below.[10] Meanwhile it is useful to consider the factors which influenced the reactions of the second-tier authorities, including the existence or possibility of alternative proposals.

Examination of the replies to the Ministry circular suggests that although most authorities[11] were chiefly concerned with how their own interests were affected by the Herbert Commission's proposals, this statement cannot meaningfully be interpreted unless at the same time it is made clear that a number of very different considerations could influence each council's view of where its interests lay. Status and powers, politics, relations with other authorities, social reasons – all these could, in varying degrees sway the view taken of the proposals.

A particularly difficult question for some boroughs was the extent to which the prospect of increased powers might have to be weighed against dislike of forming amalgamations with neighbouring authorities. There was no doubt that in a number of cases (eg Bromley, Beckenham) this dislike was at least a reinforcing factor for opposition views. At the same time, it must be remembered that as presented by the Commission, the proposals for borough groupings were intended to be tentative. It was not clear what view the Government took on this. Certainly the Ministry circular did not specifically ask for authorities' views on the proposed groupings and many must have felt that it was desirable to try to exert influence in case silence was taken for consent.

As was suggested above, political motives were probably predominant in the reactions of the Metropolitan Boroughs. The great majority of the Labour-controlled boroughs had supported the LCC in giving evidence in favour of the existing system. They continued to do so when the Herbert Commission proposals were published even though for a number of them, such as Islington and Lambeth, those proposals would have meant greatly increased powers and status with no disadvantages in terms of loss of identity. Some of the other boroughs (eg Bethnal Green, Poplar and Stepney) would have lost their identity but this factor seems to have been less important in determining their attitudes than the appeal of solidarity.[12] Fulham conspicuously failed to toe the London Labour Party line, just as they had done in giving evidence, and they were joined by Hackney; there were also one or two waverers (eg Greenwich, Shoreditch) who were prepared to concede that there was a case for a wider administration of certain functions without going so far as to support the Commission's proposals outright.

By contrast the Conservative boroughs such as Chelsea, Kensington and Westminster unhesitatingly supported the Commission's proposals. Here political motives, particularly dislike of a Labour-controlled LCC were allied to the hopes of functional gains as major reasons for their attitude. Even Holborn, with a prospect of a merger with the two larger Labour boroughs of Finsbury and Shoreditch, was generally in favour and merely urged that there should be a general consideration of boundaries by an independent commission. The City of London too supported the proposals no doubt because the Commission had accepted its pleas to retain its unique status.

The county districts in Surrey present a considerable contrast to the Metropolitan Boroughs. Perhaps the main point of contrast is that there seems not to have been a single predominant motive in the reactions of the Surrey authorities. Although there was a considerable degree of political and social homogeneity in the Surrey districts reactions varied from enthusiastic support to outright opposition. But there was an interesting parallel. In the LCC area the London Labour Party took the lead in trying to maintain a united front by Labour-controlled councils in defence of the existing system and, particularly, of the LCC. In Surrey, the County Council not only promoted an alternative plan to that of the Herbert Commission but sought, in meetings with the district authorities, to get their agreement in presenting a united front on this issue, with the preservation of the Surrey County Council and the districts as an essential element in the plan.[13] But in studying this parallel one sees the contrasting factors involved in the situation. The London Labour Party was concerned with two aspects; with the disappearance of the LCC (and to a lesser extent of the Metropolitan Boroughs) as individual entities; but even more with the likely effect on their political fortunes if the LCC disappeared and was replaced by a Greater London Council, which would include many predominantly Conservative suburban areas in Surrey, Middlesex, Essex and Kent. Surrey County Council were more concerned with the preservation of their identity and this factor outweighed purely party political considerations. Again, a significant element in the support of some of the Surrey county districts for the county's plan was the fact that for many of them it offered a chance to preserve their identity; reinforcing this were more intangible reasons concerned with social status. Some districts asserted that their area had less connection with London than with Surrey (eg Mitcham); alternatively or in addition it was argued that the area was mainly rural in character (eg Banstead). The fact that nearly all these areas could be shown (eg by commuting data) to have quite a strong connection with London was not regarded as relevant by these authorities. It was more a question of sentiment.

This view that although they were physically near to London they did not belong to London was increasingly put forward, particularly by district authorities, as a reason for opposing the Herbert Commission proposals and, later, the Government's proposals. For a number of authorities it became a principal aim of their policy to seek exclusion from the area which was to be reorganized. Staines and Sunbury-on-Thames in Middlesex, Barnet in Hertfordshire and Chigwell in Essex[14] were all authorities in addition to those in Surrey mentioned above which argued in this way in commenting on the Commission's proposals.

In Middlesex authorities seem to have been mainly influenced by the fact that the Herbert Commission's proposals gave most of the large districts a good part of what they wanted – greater power, greater status and freedom from the irksome control of Middlesex County Council.

What this analysis suggests is that for each council there was a need to balance a number of different factors. In so far as patterns emerged, as in the contrasts between London, Surrey and Middlesex, this was largely due to particular historical circumstances such as the long-continued antagonism between Middlesex CC and its districts which tended to make the Middlesex districts less inclined to favour the existing system or alternative plans than those in Surrey. But probably the most significant point about the district authorities generally at this stage was that the great majority of them did not react very strongly either for or against the Commission's proposals. Another way of putting this is to say that both supporters of the proposals and supporters of alternatives could claim that they had local authorities on their side. From the Government's point of view this left the way open for different possibilities, always remembering that the largest and most powerful authorities, the counties, had shown that they were utterly opposed to any scheme which involved giving power to a Council for Greater London.

The professional bodies

While local authorities were considering their replies to the Ministry's circular of November 1961, other bodies were pondering what the Herbert Report would mean for them. For the most part the professional bodies and associations whose members were likely to be most affected by the proposals were cautious and moderate in the way they reacted to them. Many of them had serious reservations about particular aspects of the proposals. The Town Planning Institute, for example, concentrated on the problems of regional planning and claimed that although the Commission had recognized these as fundamental, 'they appear to offer no solution consistent with their primary aims.'[15] They listed seven unsolved problems including a 'proper distribution and balance of work-places and homes throughout the region', regional planning of communications and the location of major projects such as airfields and power stations. They stressed again the view which they had put in evidence to the Commission that an executive planning authority was needed for an area at least as big as that of the Abercrombie plan.

These views were to some degree a criticism of the terms of reference given to the Commission rather than the Commission's proposals, but the Town Planning Institute also had detailed criticisms of the latter. They felt that the proposed division of planning functions between the Council for Greater London and the boroughs would not provide a practical planning organization; that the division of responsibility for major roads between the Council for Greater London and the Ministry of Transport was 'a fatal complication'. On the other hand, they endorsed the proposal to unify land-use and highway planning and to set up an Intelligence Department in the Council for Greater London. They argued that there should be fewer boroughs.

The Royal Institute of British Architects also argued, as they had done in giving evidence to the Commission, that the revised area was not big enough for dealing with the planning problems of the London region. But they thought that given the limitations of the Commission's terms of reference, their proposals 'open the way to far-reaching and long overdue reforms, particularly the planning of Greater London by a single authority'.[16] They wanted fewer and larger boroughs than those proposed by the Herbert Commission because they feared that there would otherwise be serious difficulties in recruiting staff of sufficient calibre; for the same reason they thought that boroughs should establish separate architects' departments and to this end they wanted the post of borough architect made a statutory appointment. They too did not think it right that the Ministry of Transport should retain responsibility for trunk roads, and they expressed alarm at the Commission's view that the boroughs would be capable of running parks and open spaces, arguing that it was not within their capacity to create major new open spaces.

The TPI and the RIBA were bodies which were broadly sympathetic to the Commission's Report. Other bodies. particularly those concerned with education, were more critical. The Association of Teachers in Technical Institutions, for example, complained that the Commission's education proposals 'are almost incidental to the report as a whole' and had not shown that the education service was not working successfully.[17] More mildly, the South-East Regional Association of Education Officers argued that the danger of the commission's proposals was that they would give the Greater London Council too much control of education rather than too little.[18]

The most outspoken criticism came from the London Teachers' Association. This body was the National Union of Teachers' Association for the County of London and claimed a membership of over 10,000. In November 1960, the Association's journal was expressing uneasiness at the education proposals and their president (Mr W. H. George) viewed 'with alarm and despondency' the handing over of day-to-day running of the schools to fifty-two boroughs.[19] The commitment of the LTA to the existing system of educational administration in the LCC area was emphasized in January 1961 when the Association petitioned the LCC asking them to oppose the education proposals of the Herbert Commission.

Basically, the LTA's position was that they were quite content with the present system, that it worked well and that there seemed little reason to change it, particularly as the alternative proposed by the Commission had in their view serious disadvantages. Smallwood has suggested[20] that underlying the teachers' concern was a fear that reorganization would in particular put in jeopardy the future of the comprehensive schools to which they had a strong commitment. This factor may well have weighed strongly with the executive of the LTA, but from a tactical point of view it was obvious that what they needed most of all was to publicize the general case against the Herbert proposals as much as possible and to get the widest support for it.

This they did with considerable skill. Opposition also came from other teachers' bodies such as the Surrey County Teachers' Association who wanted to maintain the existing system largely because they feared that they would be submerged in an 'impersonal' Greater London authority.

Defence of the London County Council

Other voices of opposition to the Commission's proposals were soon raised. A warning that any proposal to abolish the LCC was likely to be strongly resisted was given by Lord Morrison of Lambeth, who initiated a debate on the Herbert Report in the House of Lords on 21 December 1960. He urged the Government not to 'rush to conclusions' with the clear invitation that they should forget about the whole report.[21] Indeed his whole emphasis at this stage was on playing down the report. Tactically, this was no doubt sound. The history of proposals for local government reform clearly showed that the odds were against any far-reaching changes. By pointing out the obvious difficulties and dangers of such changes Lord Morrison might hope to encourage the idea that this was a report which was best forgotten.

However, at this stage, party political attitudes had not yet hardened; in the same debate in the House of Lords Lord Attlee said:

'reading this Report I am bound to say that there are extremely cogent reasons for having some services taken over by a larger authority.'[22]

He immediately qualified this, however, by saying that one should be cautious about destroying something which was working well.

Other defenders of the LCC added criticisms of the Commission's composition and approach to its task. A sociologist, for example, claimed that the lack of a social scientist among the Commission's members had led to a failure to accept a sociological approach to London's problems and particularly to assess 'the extent to which local services meet social needs.'[23]

The Surrey Plan

Major opposition to the Herbert Report came, as might be expected, from the counties who would be seriously affected by the proposal for a council for Greater London and, in particular, the counties of Surrey and London. Surrey, in replying to the Ministry's circular asking for comments on the Herbert proposals argued strongly that such a drastic change in the pattern of local government could only be justified by the presentation of 'an overwhelmingly strong case' and this the Herbert Commission had failed to do. They recognized, however, that some changes were desirable and proposed (i) that a joint planning board should be set up for certain purposes; (ii) that there should be some strengthening of the areas and powers of the county districts.

The first of these proposals represented an interesting development from the evidence which the County Council had given to the Commission in which they had proposed a joint advisory committee of the local planning authorities in the area of the Abercrombie plan. As the County Council themselves said, the lack of support for such a body

'calls for a proposal which goes further and the major Authorities in the London area must be prepared to sacrifice some degree of sovereignty in the broader interest.'[24]

The joint board, therefore, was to have 'executive and financial powers', and was not simply to be an advisory body as was the case with the previously proposed joint committee. It would have an independent chairman and co-opted members from industry, commerce, the trade unions, the police etc; this, in the County Council's view, would ensure that if there were any tendency, as the Herbert Commission had argued,[25] for local authority members to view problems too narrowly, it would be counter-balanced by the independent members. The joint board would have as its primary task the preparation of a master development plan for the Greater London region dealing not only with the broad pattern of land use, level of employment and the road network but also with such issues as the siting of airports. In addition, it would deal with overall traffic management, including making of regulations with the consent of the Minister of Transport and maintaining a traffic engineering unit; with the co-ordination of overspill and refuse disposal; and with any other regional problems referred to it by the authorities in the area. The development plans of the local planning authorities would be prepared 'to fit in with' the master plan.

The second part of the Surrey Plan was basically the application of the delegation provisions of the Local Government Act, 1958 to the whole of Greater London, with perhaps some modification to take account of 'the special position of the County of London'. The population criterion for delegation under the Act was a minimum population of 60,000. Surrey, therefore, proposed that, where necessary, district authorities in the area should be amalgamated to give a population of at least 60,000. In practice this would have involved comparatively few amalgamations. In addition to delegation in education, health and welfare as provided for under the 1958 Act and corresponding provisions under the Town and Country Planning Acts, it was proposed to apply delegation also to the children's service.[26]

This Surrey Plan was adopted by the five counties[27] as an alternative to the proposals put forward by the Herbert Commission. They were not entirely unanimous on the details (for example, the LCC did not want to go as far in delegating powers), but they all agreed on the broad terms of the plan. The significance of the plan was that it was the only alternative which was put forward to the Herbert Commission's proposals. It therefore became a rallying point of opposition to those proposals and, later, to the Government's proposals. It failed, however, as has been suggested, to win more than moderate support among the district authorities. For them, self-interest was a complicated issue in which allegiance to the county, whether, for political or other reasons, was only one element.[28]

An important question which the Surrey plan raised was whether Greater London as defined by the Commission was a unity for planning purposes. Professional bodies and others, both in evidence to the Commission and later, argued that planning for London required a much bigger area than that of the built-up area within the Green Belt.[29] The Commission themselves argued that although the problems of Greater London were inextricably concerned with those of South-east England as a whole, it did not follow that there was no value in treating the former as an entity for planning and other purposes.[30] More was heard of these arguments in the events leading up to the London Government Act, 1963.

Support for the Herbert Commission's proposals

No 'pro-Herbert' campaign emerged to match the anti-Herbert attitudes of the five counties. Even those who most welcomed the report tended to have serious reservations particularly about the education and planning proposals. Professor Robson, for example, at the London School of Economics suggested that the boroughs would

have comparatively little power in education, although it was difficult to tell from the 'somewhat confused and obscure' language of
the Report at this point. In the case of planning, he made the point
that some of the Commission's proposals, such as those dealing with
planning control, would tend to detract from the 'status, prestige
and effectiveness' of the Greater London Council as a planning
authority; moreover boroughs of the size proposed would be unlikely to attract outstanding planning officers. But he concluded opti-
mistically:

> 'I believe there would be much popular support for its [the Com-
> mission's] proposals if they were adequately explained to the 8½
> million citizens who dwell in Greater London.'[31]

It is worth adding that so strongly did Professor Robson and other
members of the Greater London Group feel about the limitations of
the Herbert proposals on planning that they addressed a memorandum to Mr Henry Brooke detailing their criticisms in August 1961.

There was little evidence, however, that the 8½ million citizens were
much concerned one way or the other about the proposals of the
Herbert Commission. In April 1961 the triennial county council
elections took place. Here, it might be thought, was a chance for the
electors to express their views on proposals which might vitally
affect the local government pattern of their area. This was particularly
so in London where the Herbert Report was a major issue of disagreement between the two main parties. But so far as the electors
were concerned 'all the indications are that it was a minor issue'.[32]
Of a sample of voters in Clapham, for example, nearly half did not
know which party was putting forward the policy of replacing the
LCC and Metropolitan Boroughs with the GLC and a small number
of boroughs.[33]

It was indeed one of the features of the public debates which took
place on the proposals of the Herbert Commission that it was carried
on either by interested parties, particularly local authorities, or by a
very small number of outsiders. Among the latter may be mentioned
the seven contributors to a series of lectures given at the London
School of Economics and Political Science in the Summer Term of
1961.[34] Each examined a particular aspect of the Herbert proposals in
detail. The attitudes expressed may be summed up as a cautious and
qualified welcome. Among the more pessimistic was Professor D. V.
Donnison who did not see how the structure proposed by the Com-

mission could last if there were to be any real improvements in the health and welfare services, since in his views this could only be achieved by larger authorities than the proposed boroughs.[35]

For the Government, who had to make up their minds what to do about the Herbert Commission's proposals, the various expressed attitudes and opinions served to show how little agreement there was on the subject of local government reform.

When finally in November 1961 a White Paper was published, it accepted what the chief opponents of the Commission's proposals most disliked, the need for a Council for Greater London. But it rejected the proposals for education and the size of the boroughs in favour of larger boroughs with full education powers except for a large area in the centre of London. Thus the Government committed themselves to a large-scale reform of local government in Greater London. Why they should have done so and how precisely their proposals differed from those of the Herbert Commission are questions which will be examined in the next chapter.

6
The White Paper on
London Government

What the Government proposed

The White Paper 'London Government: Government Proposals for Reorganization'[1] is an important document because in it for the first time since the existing system had been established in the late nineteenth century a government acknowledged that the system was no longer proving satisfactory for the effective performance of local government functions. Admittedly, the White Paper dealt only with London which in important ways differed from the rest of the country, but on London it stated quite categorically:

'The Government's main conclusion is that the Commission were justified in their criticism of the present structure of local government in Greater London, and that their broad design should be adopted as the basis for improving it. In particular the Government endorse the view that the boroughs ought to become the primary unit of local government; and that a new directly elected authority should be set up to administer functions which require to be dealt with over the whole of Greater London.'[2]

Furthermore, London 'has clearly outgrown' the system of government devised under very different physical and social conditions; moreover, Greater London has a recognizable civic unity and all its citizens are Londoners; to leave its problems to be settled by the central government would be disastrous; if the opportunity is not taken now to carry out effective reorganization 'local government will wither in the capital city where in the past it has been strongest'.[3]

All this is in close agreement with the spirit and recommendations of the Herbert Report. But the White Paper diverged from those recommendations on two important points, the size of the boroughs and the responsibility for education. This is the order in which the two points were stated and it is important to note that the White Paper made the case for larger boroughs independently of the needs of education, although, as will be argued later, the two are very closely connected. The White Paper claimed that although it was a presumption of the Local Government Act, 1958, that authorities of 100,000 population were capable of discharging the functions of a County Borough, larger units might be better (i) because they would in the personal services 'make specialization in staff and institutions more efficient and economical'; (ii) because they would be stronger in resources and therefore better able to maintain and develop services. Moreover, London 'has suffered in its local administration from too great a proliferation of not very strong authorities'. The White Paper concluded that boroughs of 200,000 population or more should be aimed at, without indicating on what basis this minimum figure was chosen.[4]

In all this it will be noticed that the emphasis is on efficient performance of local government functions. There was a brief reference to the fact that the services proposed for the boroughs would 'greatly enlarge the scope of the borough councillor' and that the plan was 'designed to attract into local government more men and women of real ability'.[5] But the White Paper did not argue, as did the Herbert Commission, that changes in London's local government were essential from the point of view of healthy local government.

Apart from education, the White Paper broadly agreed with the Herbert Commission's proposals for the division of functions. The education proposals, however, were criticized on the grounds that the division of functions between the Council for Greater London and the boroughs would be unlikely to work well, and that the division of the whole metropolitan area 'into fifty or so self-contained units would result in a too fragmented system'.[6] One would expect the conclusion from this to be that either the Council for Greater London or the proposed larger boroughs should be the education authorities. The first was dismissed summarily: 'the area is far too large to form a single education unit'.[7] The second was accepted but only for part of Greater London, since the Government:

'do not think . . . that this would be right in the centre of London, where the absence of administrative boundaries and the consequent complete freedom of choice for pupils and students, is of special value. Here they would wish to see one education authority for an area much larger than can be envisaged for the individual boroughs. It might well be that a central area with a population of the order of two million would be appropriate'.[8]

The area and the nature of this authority and the extent to which the boroughs were to be associated with it were all matters left for further discussion and decision.

On a number of other important matters the White Paper indicated that final decisions had not yet been taken; the planning powers of the boroughs, for example, and the question of the division of responsibilities for roads had not been settled. Nor did the Government commit themselves on the Commission's proposal that elections for the Greater London Council[9] should be based on parliamentary constituencies.

But in housing, health, welfare, children and the fire services, the Government plan closely resembled that of the Herbert Commission. The area of Greater London was also not finally settled. Although in general agreement with the Commission's principles for settling boundaries, the Government let it be known that when they consulted local authorities about the borough groupings, 'there will be opportunity for any peripheral authority to make known its views about its inclusion in or exclusion from the London area'.[10]

The White Paper also endorsed the Commission's proposal that the Greater London Council should set up an intelligence department. The financial effects of reorganization were barely touched on; nowhere in the White Paper is there a more remarkable indication of the change of approach to questions of local government reorganization that in the words:

'in the Government's view the financial arrangements should follow consequently on changes which are necessary for other reasons.'[11]

This was a far cry from the emphasis on economy as well as efficiency which earlier enquiries had followed.

External influences

As this last quotation makes clear, the White Paper indicated a Government commitment to reform which, in the light of the historical analysis given earlier in this volume, is remarkable. Two questions are of interest; first how did the Government come to accept this commitment? Secondly, why did they change the Herbert proposals relating to the size of the boroughs and to education.

The White Paper itself referred to the reactions of the local authorities and claimed:

'The Government have been impressed by the wide recognition among the local authorities concerned of the need for some change'

but then went on somewhat disarmingly:

'True, many would adopt a different and less radical solution than that proposed by the Commission.'[12]

In considering the influence of local authorities' views on the Government's decision, two things are important; first, the strongest pressures from local authorities were against fundamental change; secondly, as the White Paper itself showed, outright enthusiastic support for the Herbert Commission's proposals was rare.

If the Government had been mainly influenced by what the local authorities wanted, therefore, they would have been more likely to have followed the Surrey plan than to have proposed a plan based on the Herbert Commission's report. The Surrey plan, supported by the County Councils of London, Middlesex, Essex and Kent, offered an alternative which would not disturb the existing structure of local government. It was dismissed in scathing terms by the White Paper:

'The Government believe that a plan on these lines would not begin to meet the needs of the situation.'

It would ignore the view, fundamental to the Royal Commission's proposals, that the built-up areas outside the County of London were now part of London; it would confuse responsibilities and would be unlikely to lead to effective action in planning, traffic and road problems.[13] Thus the Government rejected what the most powerful authorities in the area proposed.

Again, though usually for different reasons, the pressures from professional bodies were strongest in the direction of modifying, if not rejecting altogether, the Commission's proposals. Bodies such as the Town Planning Institute and the Royal Institute of British Architects, although they might feel that these proposals would be an improvement on the existing situation, had reservations, and often quite serious reservations, on many points. They did not lead a campaign in favour of the implementation of the commission's report.

There were, on the other hand, campaigns against the Herbert Commission's proposals, or at any rate parts of them. The most prominent was the London Teachers' Association's attempt to secure the continuance of the LCC education service. Clearly the

LTA's views did not influence the Government in the direction of reforming London government. As in the case of the local authorities, if the government had paid attention to the loudest voices on the professional front, they would have been unlikely to have endorsed the main structure of the Commission's plan.

One may sum this up by saying that the strongest external pressure on the Government towards reform was the Commission's report itself, presenting a unanimous, unequivocal recommendation that the local government structure should be changed. Most of the other advice which the Government received from outside sources was, to say the least, urging caution at the prospect of change. We must therefore consider what internal pressures may have contributed to the Government's decision.

Political and administrative influences

As the Minister with direct responsibility for local government affairs it was for Mr Henry Brooke to take the initiative in proposing to accept, to modify or to reject the Commission's recommendations.[14] The 1961 White Paper falls into the second of these three categories, but the manner in which the Government's plan diverged from that of the Commission, particularly in relation to the proposed central area education authority suggests that as it finally emerged it was a compromise between conflicting views within the Government. It may be useful, therefore, to indicate the probable course of events before looking at the reasons behind them.

Mr Brooke was probably inclined towards accepting the Royal Commission's proposals. But if he was to get approval for this course he needed to get support above all from the Minister of Education, Sir David Eccles. This was mainly because of the importance of education as a local government service; but in part because neither the Minister of Health nor the Home Secretary could be expected to be enthusiastic about proposals which would give personal health, welfare and children's powers to boroughs, many of which were smaller than had been thought desirable by their departmental spokesmen in giving evidence to the Commission,[15] unless there were other compelling reasons (eg in terms of political advantage) for doing this. Perhaps only the Minister of Transport (Mr Marples) of the departmental ministers most closely involved was likely to be reasonably content with the Commission's proposals since they offered the kind of solution to the problems of traffic administration that the Ministry had been advocating.[16]

It is a clear inference from the White Paper's proposals that Sir David Eccles was not prepared to accept the education proposals in the Herbert Commission's report. He later indicated, particularly after he had ceased to be a member of the Government, that he favoured larger education authorities rather than smaller.[17] Perhaps he would have been prepared even to see the Greater London Council exercising exclusive education powers. At all events he was clear that the Commission's proposals were unworkable, and that at the least larger boroughs with exclusive education powers were necessary.

Mr Brooke may well have felt that the creation of larger and therefore fewer boroughs would not in itself damage the commission's proposed scheme,[18] and would have advantages in reconciling the Minister of Health and the Home Secretary to the proposals as well as meeting the views of some important professional bodies (eg the RIBA). But the hardest bargaining was over education in the County of London. It is not difficult to see that the White Paper's proposals for a central area education authority of undetermined size and character represents a hand-fought compromise between strongly-held views. The views in this case were those of Sir David Eccles on the one hand who regarded it as wrong to fragment the education service in the LCC area which had been a unity since the London School Board had been set up in 1870; and the views of Mr Henry Brooke on the other hand who saw the retention of this most important LCC service, as weakening the plan of reform and almost certainly leading to pressures for the retention of other services.

This probably represents the stages by which the White Paper proposals were arrived at. We now have to consider what were the reasons for the attitudes adopted by those chiefly concerned, and how the Cabinet were induced to endorse the proposals.

It seems likely that the Ministry of Housing and Local Government through its Permanent Secretary, Dame Evelyn Sharp, welcomed the Herbert Commission's proposals as offering a solution to those problems of overspill housing and planning to which she had referred in her oral evidence,[19] as well as dealing with the troublesome Middlesex issue. That Mr Brooke was in sympathy with departmental advice is probable, if the view taken of his outlook and attitude earlier is correct.[20]

The critical question is whether the logic of this situation sufficiently accounts for Mr Brooke's decision to try to implement the Commission's proposals. He knew that he would meet strong opposition from within local government, and that there was not likely, judging from past experience, to be much enthusiasm for a plan of local government reform considered purely on its merits from his own party.

It is natural, therefore, to look for a direct political motive as providing the immediate stimulus for Mr Brooke's action. Local government reform has generally been a politically unattractive subject precisely because it arouses intense opposition among local authorities but does not win many votes. Was the situation different in London?

Lord Morrison of Lambeth assiduously put forward the view that a major motive behind the Government's White Paper proposals was the aim of breaking Labour's control of the LCC. It was a view shared by others.[21] Mr Brooke's years as Leader of the Conservative Opposition on the LCC fitted neatly into this view. It suggests that he was anxious to see the Herbert Commission's proposals adopted primarily for the political advantage that he saw in them of putting an end to Labour's control of London.

There is no way of proving whether this was Mr Brooke's main motive. But if it was it implies that opposition to Labour's control of the LCC outweighed in his mind the other political consequences of the Commission's plan – the destruction or weakening of predominantly Conservative authorities such as Kent, Surrey and Croydon, as well as the merging of staunch Conservative areas like Wimbledon with other authorities with whom they might not see eye to eye.

It is possible to view Mr Brooke's actions in this way, but more plausible given the view of his character taken here, that in the first instance he was concerned with a solution to the problems of London government. Naturally he must have been aware of the consequences of the Commission's proposals for a Labour LCC. Perhaps psychologically they formed an unacknowledged stimulus. But it is unlikely that he saw what he was doing in these terms.

Whatever part the motive of party political advantage played in Mr Brooke's approach it can have played little part in Sir David Eccles' views. But again we must also consider not simply his views, but those of his departmental advisers as well and the influences on those views. One interesting fact about Sir David Eccles was that he had two separate spells as Minister of Education, and by the time of the Herbert Commission's Report he had had four years in all as Minister of Education.[22]

As has already been argued, Sir David had a strong commitment to large education authorities and, in particular, to the maintenance of the LCC. This accorded with the views of the department as expressed in evidence to the Herbert Commission. They had, for example, gone on record with high praise for the LCC.[23] It is reasonable to infer, therefore, that they would be opposed to the Herbert Commission's proposal to destroy the long history of centralized administration in the area, with its particular advantage of allowing freedom of movement over borough boundaries.

This does not mean that Sir David was simply a mouthpiece for Departmental views. There are several reasons for thinking that his defence of the LCC and of large education authorities represented his own convictions. The most important reason is that he fought so hard and tenaciously for this point of view in the arguments within the Government over the Commission's proposals. But, secondly, his own character and long association as a Minister with education make it unlikely that he would simply have been a mouthpiece. This is reinforced by the fact that the Permanent Secretary at the time had only recently arrived in the Department, and may well have been in a less strong position vis-à-vis the Minister than is usual with permanent secretaries.[24]

One may, however, well ask how the Department and the Minister had arrived at these views, and what, in particular, was the influence of the campaign of the London Teachers' Association against the Royal Commission's proposal to break up the LCC education service. These views, as the evidence to the Commission indicates, were long-standing. Not only were the Ministry reasonably satisfied with the existing system but they saw 'serious educational disadvantages' in the creation of a cluster of county boroughs in the metropolitan fringes of Essex, Kent, Surrey and Hertfordshire.[25] In other words their views on what constituted a good or a bad educational system were derived from their experience of the authorities and their performance under the existing system. Whatever facts or opinions these views were based on, they represented a commitment to the LCC and to large authorities which Sir David Eccles shared.

Immediate reaction to the Herbert Commission's proposals must have centred on the difficulty of working the proposed division of powers between the Council for Greater London and the boroughs.

No doubt the Ministry would have preferred to maintain the existing system; but if that was not possible some modification of the Commission's proposals was likely to be sought.

It is at this point that the campaign of the London Teachers' Association appears to become important. It has been claimed that their 'constant drumbeat of criticism' led to 'the first direct bullseye in the reorganization contest'.[26] It is true that the Government's White Paper proposals corresponded largely to what the LTA had asked for. But this is not the same as cause and effect. It seems doubtful, given the attitudes of the Ministry and the Minister, whether the LTA's campaign did more than reinforce views which were already held. To suggest that the Government's proposals were a direct result of that campaign is to give too little weight to other educational considerations which were prominent in the minds of the Minister and his advisers. This is not to question the fact that Sir David Eccles may have found it useful in arguing with Mr Brooke to use the LTA's opposition as an argument in favour of retaining the LCC education service.

If this view is correct – and as in the case of the Ministry of Housing and Local Government it necessarily depends on unprovable inferences about the relations between minister and department – the final question is how the agreement reached primarily between Mr Brooke and Sir David Eccles was accepted by the remainder of the Cabinet. Here one can only surmise that there were conflicting arguments about what was to be done. By its very nature the compromise plan did not give a clear lead either in terms of the functional effectiveness of local government or in terms of political considerations. Nor did the health of local government argument, to which the Herbert Commission had attached such importance, appear to point unequivocally in the direction of the scheme of reform now proposed by Mr Brooke with the support or at least the acquiescence of Sir David Eccles.[27]

It is very likely that the decision to go ahead and publish the White Paper was far from unanimous. The arguments of advocates like Mr Brooke pointing out the desirability of a functional reform of London government, or the political advantages of the disappearance of the LCC, could be countered by the argument that the reform would disrupt many local authorities performing services satisfactorily, and that there were many political disadvantages in antagonizing such authorities with support among Conservative back-benchers. And although it might be claimed that the proposed London Boroughs, like the Commission's Greater London Boroughs, would help to revitalize local government, it might equally be argued that the existing units more truly represented local democracy. Above all, the argument against the proposals must have been – is it really worth it?

Ultimately, therefore, the decision to go ahead, was the resultant of a number of delicately balanced forces. It is quite conceivable that the decision could have gone the other way. As subsequent events showed there was no consistent pattern of Government motivation whether in terms of strengthening local government or in terms of narrow political advantage. The White Paper's proposal that peripheral, and mainly Conservative areas, should have the opportunity of declaring that they wished to be excluded from Greater London, is an example of the ambiguity of the Government's aims. Again, people like Lord Morrison of Lambeth who believed that the Government were inspired largely by the desire to break Labour's control of the LCC found it puzzling that a Conservative Government should be 'so rough' on the largely Conservative counties of Surrey and Kent.[28] The White Paper and the Bill can only be meaningfully understood in the light of the very mixed motives and pressures which inspired the Government.

One paragraph in the White Paper does, however, show an awareness of political realities in a different sense. In November 1961 the Conservative Government had at most three years of life before the next election. And although the Parliamentary Labour Party had not proclaimed any view on the Commission's proposals it was very likely that they would oppose any radical reform proposals particularly if they involved the disappearance of the LCC. Given the great complexity, therefore, of any legislation to put into effect the proposals of the White Paper and the need to consult with the various affected bodies, the Government clearly had now to push forward vigorously if they wanted to ensure the success of the proposals. In particular, legislation would have to be brought in in the 1962–63 Session at the latest and the change-over from the old to the new system would have to be short to ensure that there was no possibility of 'unscrambling' if a Labour Government took office following the next election.

None of this was explicitly mentioned in the White Paper. What it did say was that the aim was that the new authorities should be elected in the autumn of 1964 and take over from existing authorities in

April 1965. Of the two reasons given for the need for speed, the first ('it is very difficult for the existing authorities to carry on once it is known that changes are impending') was a valid practical point; the second ('the Government believe that the changes proposed will provide . . . a more effective and a more firmly based system of local government, better fitted to meet the needs of the future'[29]) was a familiar peroration of a type found in White Papers but was hardly directed specifically to the need for speed.

The local authorities and the White Paper

The publication of the White Paper on London Government was the signal for intensified activity on the part of those who had opposed the Herbert proposals and, in particular, those who did not accept the idea that there was a need for a Greater London authority. It was also the occasion for many other bodies and individuals with special interests to plead for changes or modifications in the Government's plan. The period of one year between the publication of the White Paper and the London Government Bill saw the question of the reform of London Government become a major political issue, which culminated in the lengthy and tortuous proceedings on the bill itself. A major theme of the next chapter is to trace the stages by which this came about until, as *The Times* put it, 'The London Government Bill stakes out the main legislative battlefield for this session.'[30] But first the reaction of the local authorities to the White Paper will be described.

The publication of the White Paper in November 1961 was soon followed by a circular from the Ministry of Housing and Local Government addressed to 'local authorites in the London Area'.[31] The purpose of this circular was to put forward the Government's suggestions for the new London boroughs and to invite comments on them by the end of March 1962. Thirty-four boroughs were suggested in place of the fifty-two proposed by the Herbert Commission.[32] They had been drawn up, the circular claimed, having regard to 'present and past associations, to the location and areas of influence of service centres, to lines of communication and to the patterns of development.' But there was no indication of which of these factors had been treated as important in each grouping. It could be inferred, for example, that Borough 27[33] was mainly based on lines of communication; it was a funnel-shaped authority over ten miles long from the LCC Hammersmith/Chiswick boundary to the Thames at Staines with the A.30 as its spine. But it was less easy to see what had led to the grouping in Borough 28[34]; it was almost as long from north to south as Borough 27 but the main lines of communication ran across it; only a combination of the other three factors mentioned in the circular, applying in different degrees to each of the constituents could be held to justify this grouping.

The truth seems to be that although the Ministry had paid some regard to the factors they mentioned they were above all constrained by the need to amalgamate areas of sufficient size to give the minimum populations required. Particularly in the outer areas which were less densely populated this naturally tended to give large and awkwardly shaped areas.

With the publication of the circular, the local authorities affected by the Government's plan had one major question answered which the White Paper had left in doubt. Furthermore, the borough groupings were the only aspect of the Government proposals on which the local authorities were invited to make comments, although this did not inhibit opponents of the plan, such as the county councils of Surrey and London, from making their views known very actively. A particular feature of the Circular was that it specifically invited 'peripheral authorities'[35] to say whether they wished to be brought into or excluded from the London area, as had been promised in the White Paper. This provision indicated that the Government were open to pressures – largely from their own supporters – to reduce still further the area of Greater London from that originally considered by the Herbert Commission.

Inevitably, since they were so directly affected, the reactions of the local authorities were the most immediately prominent features of the situation in the first weeks after the publication of the White Paper and the circular. By March 1962 *The Times*, which emerged as one of the main supporters of reform (though not without criticism in detail of the Government's plan), was declaring 'The opponents of reform have in recent weeks been getting the better of the argument' and contrasting the report of the Royal Commission ('cogent, authoritative, and persuasively presented') with the fact that the Government 'have allowed the case for reform to look after itself'.[36] Whether this was so and if it was how it had come about is further discussed below.

E

The Counties and County Boroughs

So far as the Counties were concerned (and the two County Boroughs of Croydon and East Ham who had opposed the Herbert proposals) the Government plan confirmed their worst fears. It is hardly surprising, therefore, that the immediate reaction of the leading members of the London, Middlesex and Surrey County Councils was one of strong dislike of the White Paper; but significantly even at this stage the Kent reaction was couched in very moderate terms and Essex would make no comment at all.[37]

Nevertheless, all five authorities[38] sent representatives to a meeting (at London's County Hall) on 9 January 1962 convened by Mr Sydney Ripley, Chairman of Surrey County Council, to discuss possible joint action. A further meeting was held on 16 February but this time with only four counties' representatives since Kent had by this time withdrawn its opposition to the Government's plan. This second meeting issued a statement deploring, in predictable terms, the 'ill-considered experiment' and putting forward once again the Surrey plan as a less drastic alternative to the immense upheaval which the Government's plan would involve.[39]

But the possibilities of joint action were limited. Each county was faced with a very different situation, largely for reasons discussed earlier in relation to reactions to the Herbert Report. They were united only in their desire to see the least possible change in the existing system. Thus the tactics each adopted differed considerably.

The liveliest opposition came from Surrey. For this there were a number of reasons. Close and friendly relations with most of the county districts carefully built up over the years[40] which ensured a considerable measure of support among the districts for the county plan; the lack of sharp political divisions in different parts of the county such as marked off much of Essex within the Herbert Commission review area from the more rural parts to the north east; the fact that the proposed truncation of the county was likely to have severe practical effects because Surrey's greatest concentration of population was in the areas adjoining London; the fact that many of the County Council's most prominent members (eg Sir Cyril Black[41]) came from the metropolitan areas of Surrey. All these reasons contributed to Surrey's quick and decisive reaction. In January 1962 the County Council's General Purposes Committee issued a report condemning the Government's proposals. But realizing that this in itself was unlikely to sway the Government, they wished to 'request' Surrey members of parliament 'to consider opposing' the proposals. This carefully worded recommendation which was approved by the County Council on 23 January 1962 carried far-reaching implications. There were seventeen MPs for Surrey constituencies, all of them Conservative; they included a number of ministers and ex-ministers such as Sir Lionel Heald, Mr John Boyd Carpenter and Mr Harold (now Lord) Watkinson. They also included such redoubtable figures as Mr Charles Doughty, Mr (now Sir Peter) Rawlinson and, of course, Sir Cyril Black. Clearly any sustained opposition from Surrey MPs would be a troublesome matter for the Government.

The only question was whether, apart from committed fighters like Sir Cyril Black, these MPs could be induced to put any pressure on the Government.

In January 1962 the County Council began issuing leaflets stating their opposition to the Greater London plan and urging 'every Surrey man and woman who shared their concern' to write to their Member of Parliament. In spite of the entertaining cartoon (by courtesy of the *Surrey Comet*) included in the leaflet it made little impact on the Surrey man in the street, although it did provoke a sour comment from the *Daily Telegraph* which objected to its being 'sent gratuitously at the ratepayers' expense to those taking out car licences'.[42]

If the liveliest opposition came from Surrey, the bitterest came from the LCC. On the 12th March 1962 the LCC met to debate a lengthy report prepared by its General Purposes Committee much of this was taken up by an analysis intended to show for each service in turn that the Government's proposals were either unworkable, less satisfactory than the existing system or positively disastrous; the report went on to suggest that a number of important matters had either been left unsettled or not dealt with at all, and that in any case there would be a vast and unjustified upheaval. It ended with a peroration which must have come from the pen of the Leader of the Council:

'For seventy-three years the Council has spoken for the people of London, the capital of Britain, the heart of the Commonwealth: we do not believe that the people of London want that voice silenced. For that voice to be silenced without the people of London being allowed to express their view would in our judgment be an unforgiveable, destructive and irresponsible act and contrary to all principles of democracy.'

On the first part of this *The Times* bitingly remarked: 'Perhaps the LCC recognizes itself under that description: no one else will'[43], but it did concede that in some of the services, particularly the personal services, the LCC had made some valid points.

The debate at County Hall went on for eighteen hours and ended at 6 am, the second longest sitting in the history of the LCC. Nor is it difficult to see why the debate should have lasted so long. The Leader of the Council (Sir Isaac Hayward) set the tone of the debate: 'we have been asked to destroy ourselves,' he is reported as saying,[44] 'but we are not quite as simple as that. This is a political manœuvre, a determined move to destroy this Council.'

To which the Leader of the Opposition, Sir Percy Rugg, replied: 'I would not have supported the plan for a moment if I thought this was so.'[45] So far as the LCC was concerned discussion of the Government's plan had by now become a matter for bitter political debate and, as is discussed later, this debate was of more than local concern. The only immediate step to follow from the LCC debate, however, apart from acquainting the Government of their views, was a decision to send a deputation to the Prime Minister; this was duly done but did not give any satisfaction to the LCC.[46]

Middlesex County Council, although firm in its opposition to the Government's proposals, could not rely on much support from the Middlesex Boroughs and Urban Districts. In February, 1961 it had agreed proposals for 'devolution of functions' from the county to the districts including the conferment of personal health service powers. These had not met with any great enthusiasm from the districts then, and a proposal in March 1962 to call a conference of district councils to discuss them further had to be abandoned in the face of disagreement with the proposal from a majority of the districts.[47] Nevertheless, the County Council realized that 'every endeavour should be made in negotiation with the Government, to seek to obtain a final solution more nearly in accord with the Council's previously expressed views.' They also, however, went out of their way to state that they would co-operate fully in implementing whatever final solution was put forward.[48]

Essex, like Surrey, held a meeting with its district councils affected by the Government proposals, on 20 February 1962, and specifically decided to make a particular effort to help peripheral authorities who were pressing for exclusion from Greater London; if this policy failed, the County Council were to press for the new county boundary to be fixed at the inner edge of the Green Belt. The General Purposes' Committee of the Council, meeting on 13 February 1962, also pressed for a general policy of opposition to the proposals. But the meeting of the County Council to consider this did not take place until 6 March by which time, as is discussed below, the Government had made plain, in a debate on the 19 and 20 February that it intended to go ahead with the plan. Significantly, the County Council then decided to limit itself to the points listed above and to securing fair and equitable compensation for the remainder of the county.

Kent too, withdrew its opposition on the grounds that the Government proposals were both practicable and workable and that there seemed no likelihood that any alternative plan would be agreed. They concluded that the 'repetition of former arguments would be a waste of time and that so far as Kent is concerned there does not seem to be any sufficient reason for attacking the Government's scheme'.[49] This decision was not taken without criticism.[50]

It seems clear that two elements were strongest in determining how far the counties opposed the Government plan. One was the extent to which the proposals affected their existence and the other was the extent to which they had the support of the district authorities. In the case of London and Surrey both these elements were strong. In Middlesex the first element was strong but the second lacking. Of the other two counties, Kent stood to lose least, Essex rather more. Moreover neither of these counties had very strong support from their district authorities.

There were of course, other factors. Political opposition to the Government was, as has been suggested, a major factor in the position adopted by the LCC. And both Kent and Essex, with their county towns well outside the metropolitan area, would remain strong and important counties even with the loss of their metropolitan fringes, whereas Surrey was a county dominated by its urban and suburban function in relation to London.

The districts

Apart from the counties, most other local authorities in Greater

London were faced with the dilemma that, as compared with the Herbert proposals, those of the government offered increased powers, notably in education, but only at the cost of further amalgamations. Thus Croydon, East Ham, West Ham, Ilford, Twickenham and Hendon, among others, found that under the Government proposals they were to be joined with other areas to form the new London Boroughs instead of enjoying that status on their own as the Herbert Commission had proposed. Only three of the Government's proposed London Boroughs corresponded to the areas of existing authorities (Harrow, Lewisham and, inevitably, the City of London) as well as being identical with the boroughs proposed by the Commission.

A further six borough groupings were identical with those proposed by the Commission.[51] Thus, of the ninety-six authorities affected, eighty-two now found themselves either in a different set of groupings from that proposed by the Herbert Commission, or else in a grouping where formerly they had been in a position to preserve their separate identity.

Among the latter the proposed unions of East Ham and West Ham, of Wembley and Willesden and of Romford and Hornchurch all offered possibilities of discord between the partners for reasons of either political antagonism or civic pride. The question of the precise groupings of the new boroughs gave rise to a considerable amount of discussion as did, later, the question of what names to give to the new boroughs.

The most notable feature of the reactions of the County Boroughs and the districts to the White Paper was the intensification of attitudes adopted to the original Herbert Commission proposals. Those who had supported those proposals, but with reservations, now tended to accept the Government proposals; conversely those who had suggested modifications and alternatives to the Herbert Commission proposals, now tended to be completely opposed to the Government plan. The situation can be seen most clearly in Middlesex.[52] Here fifteen authorities had supported the Herbert proposals in principle but had particularly criticized the proposed distribution of education functions; all but Tottenham now came out in support of the White Paper. On the other hand Staines and Sunbury-on-Thames who had entirely rejected the Herbert proposals in favour of the existing system were joined by Feltham, Yiewsley and West Drayton, Hayes and Harlington and Southall as firm opponents of the White Paper proposals. Undoubtedly a major factor here was the 'escape route' provided by the White Paper, the possibility of being excluded from Greater London altogether. As will be seen later, both Staines and Sunbury-on-Thames achieved this exclusion; Feltham and Yiewsley and West Drayton tried but failed.

As in the case of the Herbert proposals, there were striking differences in the county patterns of reactions by the district authorities to the White Paper. No authority in Kent opposed the Government proposals whereas the great majority of the Surrey authorities were in total opposition. In Essex the reaction was mixed although support predominated. In general the same factors influenced authorities as in their reactions to the original Herbert proposals. In one or two cases, contrary to the general trend, there was a marked change of attitude. Romford, for example, which had supported the Herbert proposals in principle now opposed the Government proposals and aimed at exclusion from Greater London. Interestingly, the Borough listed possible changes in order of priority with County Borough status at the top of the list and amalgamation to form a Greater London Borough at the bottom, an indication of the conflicting pulls of self-interest for a medium-sized borough. In the case of the Metropolitan Boroughs the influence of party political attitudes was strikingly evident in cases where there was a change of political control as a result of the 1962 borough elections.

St Pancras, for example, went from Conservative to Labour control in May 1962; its attitude to the White Paper changed from one of support to opposition.

The White Paper of 1961, far more than the decision to set up the Royal Commission in 1957, was a critical point in the history of events leading to the London Government Act of 1963, because it seemed to indicate government determination to go ahead with a plan of reform in spite of all the familiar reasons against taking such a course, including notably the opposition of many powerful local authorities. But the decision to go ahead was not taken without misgivings; nor did the White Paper represent the final form of the Government's plan. The translation of the White Paper into legislative form, as will be seen, proved a considerable task.

7
Changes in the Government's Plan: the Labour Party's Opposition

So far as the Government were concerned, there were few surprises in the attitudes adopted by the local authorities. Certainly, the basic position had not changed since the Government had invited and received views on the Herbert Commission's proposals. As the Government had gone ahead with its White Paper in spite of the known opposition of powerful authorities such as the London and Surrey County Councils and in spite of the fact that many of the district authorities were either luke-warm in their support or positively opposed to reorganization, there seemed no doubt of their determination to push reorganization through. It seems all the more surprising, therefore, to find *The Times* criticizing the Government for its seeming lack of initiative in March 1962;[1] and for an academic observer writing after the event to comment that by May 1962, only six months after the White Paper 'the entire reorganization effort was now floundering in some very deep waters.'[2]

It is therefore tempting to suppose that other pressures on the Government, apart from those exercised by the counties, were causing them to hesitate or to give the appearance of hesitating in the early part of 1962. Three such sources of pressure may be identified (i) the activities of Conservative MPs, particularly in Surrey, aimed at trying to retain the existing system basically as it was or at least securing the exclusion of some of the peripheral areas; (ii) the activities of outside bodies such as the London Teachers' Association or of academic and other observers aimed at modifying the Government's proposals in particular directions; (iii) the activities of the Labour Party which came out in total opposition to the Government's proposals. The successes claimed for those who opposed the Government's plan in the first half of 1962 were two; first, the retention intact of the whole of the LCC education service, and, secondly, the exclusion, in whole or in part, of nine existing authorities from the proposed area of Greater London. Announcements on both these points were made by the Minister of Housing and Local Government, Dr Hill,[3] in the period between the end of April and the end of May, 1962.

Education: the central area plan

All three sources of pressure made some contribution to the Government's decision to make changes in the White Paper Plan. At the same time, as was pointed out earlier, that plan itself was an awkward compromise, particularly in relation to the proposals for education in Central London, which could hardly have stood unchanged. The proposal to preserve an area containing about two million people as a single education authority in the centre of London immediately raised the questions—what area and what kind of authority? These questions were posed in the White Paper, but left unanswered; they were still left unanswered when the House of Commons debated the White Paper three months later. The Minister of Education, Sir David Eccles, claimed that it was impossible to determine the area of this central London authority until the boundaries of the new boroughs were settled since it must consist of complete boroughs. At the same time, he gave as the reason for having an area less than that of the LCC the fact that the nearer to the centre one got, the greater the movement across borough boundaries, facilitated by good communications.[4] The argument was not altogether convincing. A glance at the map of 'London Boroughs: Possible Groupings' sent out with the Ministry Circular of December 1961 shows that it would have been impossible to devise from the proposed boroughs an area containing two million people which would consist only of the very centre of London.[5] The only way to have done so would have been to construct the borough groupings on a pattern of concentric rings round the centre of London but at no point was this attempted or even suggested.

If the view taken here of the steps leading up to the White Paper is correct, it is evident that Sir David Eccles himself did not accept the argument he was advancing. He wanted and in February 1962 was still seeking to change the awkward compromise decision which he had had to accept at the time of the White Paper. His view was that agreement to a single large education authority for Central London should be taken, the logical final step and the area extended to cover the whole of the LCC. No doubt the replacement of Mr Brooke by

Dr Hill gave him the chance to re-open this question. As late as 1st May 1962[6] the Minister of Education was publicly declaring that the precise area for the new education authority was not yet finally determined. Two days later Dr Charles Hill announced to the House of Commons that the education service of the LCC was to be preserved intact subject to a review within a period of five years.[7] Was it simply coincidence that this announcement followed only three days after Dr Hill's decision to regard three Surrey districts as falling outside Greater London? Or that a fortnight later he announced a further series of exclusions?[8]

There can be little doubt from the timing of these various announcements that they formed part of a single composite decision of the Government to deal with some of the most troublesome of the problems facing the reorganization proposals. The nature of the political struggle which preceded this decision was determined partly by the characters and personalities of those who were most closely involved and partly by the external factors and pressures to which reference has already been made.

To take the latter first. It will already be clear why even those who supported the idea of a comprehensive reorganization of London government had serious misgivings about parts of the Government's proposals for education. As the *Guardian* succinctly put it:

> 'The Government's plans for education in the new London seem to have no friends at all. . . . The Government has not made very clear why, if two million is a good size, the present $3\frac{1}{4}$ million population of the LCC education authority is impossibly unacceptable.'[9]

To those who were opposed to any fundamental change in the existing system the Government's proposal on this point was an obvious target. It was seized on by the LCC and by the London Teachers' Association.[10] It was also seized on by Lord Morrison of Lambeth who claimed that the break-up of the LCC education service was 'not far short of being criminally irresponsible'.[11] The LTA was, as in its opposition to the Herbert Report, active in publishing its campaign including calling parents' protest meetings, organizing petitions, and urging parents to write to their MPs. Among supporters of the plan, *The Times* consistently expressed doubts about this aspect of it.[12]

It is not surprising that the Government decision of May 1962 was seen as 'bowing to massive protests from thousands of parents and children',[13] but the reality is probably a good deal less dramatic than that. It is hardly likely that either Sir David Eccles or Dr Charles Hill seriously expected to satisfy anyone about the White Paper proposals on education in the central area of London unless they could produce more precise details of how the plan would work in practice. But this was what they failed to do, partly because Sir David did not believe it could work and wanted to retain the LCC education service intact and partly because Dr Hill was chiefly motivated by the desire to avoid conceding that the LCC service should be retained. Like his predecessor, he did not necessarily think that it would be a bad thing from an educational point of view but feared the pressures which might arise if this concession were made to the LCC's defenders, and the implications for the whole programme of reorganization. Undoubtedly, therefore, the fact that nobody had a good word to say for the White Paper's central area education plan strengthened the hand of the Minister of Education in seeking to change the White Paper's proposal. Dr Hill therefore struck a bargain with Sir David Eccles; the LCC education service was to be preserved intact, but not as a permanent arrangement. The provision for a review within five years would, as Dr Hill saw it, at least leave the door open for bringing the boroughs in inner London (the old LCC area) into the education picture. Sir David interpreted the review rather differently and more broadly as enabling a decision to be taken on what was the right future structure for education in Greater London. These ambiguities and differences of interpretation did not, however, emerge at the time. They first came into the open when the London Government Bill was in progress through Parliament and were a source of embarrassment to the Government.[14]

Nevertheless, important as the change from the White Paper was for the London Teachers' Association and other supporters of the LCC and however much it could be represented as a political setback for the Government, it must be remembered that it did not alter the crucially important fact about the Government's education proposals compared with those of the Royal Commission, namely, that education in Greater London should be a hybrid with differing arrangements for the centre and the outer parts. Politically, the disadvantage of making the whole LCC area a single education authority was that the Government might find themselves under pressure on two fronts, first to retain other LCC services intact and, secondly, to concede that the county pattern should be retained for education in other parts of Greater London such as Middlesex. There were, in fact, pressures on both these fronts but especially on the first.[15]

The boundaries of Greater London

In many ways a far more serious change in the Government's plan was the decision to exclude a further nine local authority areas wholly or partly from the area to be covered by Greater London. The grounds on which the Herbert Commission had excluded a number of areas, mostly in Hertfordshire, were reasonably consistent. It is not clear that the Government's exclusions were based on the same grounds. On 30 April 1962 Dr Hill announced that he had come to the conclusion that Banstead, Caterham and Warlingham and Walton and Weybridge should be regarded as falling outside Greater London, and that he was prepared to have discussions with the representatives of other authorities who had asked for exclusions to be made.[16] On 18 May he announced the results of these discussions: four authorities were to be wholly excluded,[17] two were to be partially excluded,[18] but six others had their claims rejected[19] as also were the county councils' requests for two other exclusions which were not however supported by the authorities themselves.[20] The effect of these exclusions was that from the original review area considered by the Royal Commission a further 80,000 acres (15%) containing 386,000 population (4½% of the whole) was taken from Greater London. Taking into account the exclusions made by the Commission themselves no less than 26% of the area and over 7% of the population of the original review area were now to be outside Greater London.[21]

It is true that for some of these areas – Cheshunt for example and Walton and Weybridge – it was open to dispute whether they did or did not satisfy the Herbert Commission's criterion of forming part of the continuously built-up area of London. The Government's changes, however, were not explicitly justified on these grounds nor was it made clear why in some cases local authority areas were split into two, something which the Herbert Commission had expressly tried to avoid.[22] On Epsom and Ewell, for example, the Minister merely said:

'The northern part of the borough . . . definitely forms, in my view, part of Greater London and must be included.'[23]

If, as is implied by this statement, the aim was to include all the continuously built-up area, then one might ask why Esher (which was totally excluded) or Romford (which was totally included) were not similarly split since they both included a built-up part adjoining Greater London and a green belt part. If on the other hand the factors considered by Mr W. I. Carruthers for the Royal Commission were to be taken into account, then both Chigwell and Esher had a higher dependence on London than Yiewsley and West Drayton.[24]

A major influence in these decisions was the Government's awareness from reactions to the Herbert Commission's Report of the strength of feeling of many of the peripheral authorities against being included in Greater London. This was particularly true in Surrey, an area in which support for the Conservative Party was very strong. It was therefore in the nature of a concession to their own supporters that the Government left the way open in the White Paper for some exclusions from the area of Greater London as put forward by the Herbert Commission.

The point was made clearly enough in the debate on the White Paper by Sir Lionel Heald, the Conservative member for a Surrey constitutency outside Greater London (Chertsey) and a former attorney-general:

'I am prepared to say at once, however—and I believe that this is the view of the great majority of my Hon. Friends who represent other parts of Surrey—that the area of Surrey at present proposed to be included in the scheme is far too big.'[25]

As if to emphasize the point, another Conservative lawyer, Mr Rawlinson made a vigorous speech in favour of taking Epsom out of Greater London.[26]

Dr Hill undoubtedly tried to find good reasons, for example in terms of the continuously built-up area concept, for excluding some areas and rejecting the claims of others for exclusion. There is no doubt too that he went to some trouble to find an acceptable solution for some difficult areas, in spite of which his solutions were not always readily accepted.[27] But his basic difficulty was that he did not have a great deal of room to manœuvre. The Government felt that some concessions had to be made but at the same time too many concessions would make it difficult to defend the idea of Greater London as a unity. It is hard to avoid the conclusion that on this issue Dr Hill fell between two stools. The concessions did not satisfy extremists like Sir Cyril Black who saw no reason for any change in the position of Surrey; and it may well be true that had the Government stood firm and not made these concessions they could in any case have carried their more moderate supporters in the House with them. Thus they probably gained very little in terms of increased support for their proposals as a whole.

On the other hand, the deletion of most of another nine areas from the area of Greater London represented a weakening of the main plan of the reforms. As *The Economist* put it:

'Dr Hill really must not let himself be browbeaten by suburban witenagemots. ... The Surrey Tories may dance in the streets because they still have sack and soke in Banstead ... (But) ... London's readjustment will not be advanced if Dr Hill's first action has to be to placate those of his political friends who make the loudest noise.'

And it concluded:

'The worst thing that could happen to London would be if ... it should find itself the prey of political deals and parochial primacy.'[28]

There was a further consequence of this decision to exclude a number of areas from Greater London. Because politically these areas were mainly Conservative, the Conservatives seemed to be weakening their chances of controlling the Greater London Council by making the exclusions. This reflects the conflicting considerations which the Government were trying to meet in order to make progress with their plans.

In all this the position of Dr Hill himself was an awkward one. He inherited the problems of education and the boundaries of Greater London from his predecessor. He had no particular commitment to London government reform as had his predecessor. It is hardly surprising that he did not give the impression of tremendous enthusiasm in the early months of 1962. Rather he was a man who had a job to get on with and one which he could not really get on with until these two stumbling-blocks in the White Paper had been removed.[29] How he did this will be described later but first the important question of the Labour Party's attitude to the Government plan needs to be examined.

The Labour Party opposes the plan

These two changes – in the central area for education and in the boundaries of Greater London – represented the final modifications to the general framework of the Government's plan. Other changes, some of considerable importance, were, as will be described later, being made up to the time of the introduction of the London Government Bill in November 1962 and later. But for the most part these further changes filled in details rather than affected the structure of the scheme.

The two changes described above were, however, made two months or more after *The Times* had claimed in March 1962 that the opposition to the proposals was having the better of the argument. Undoubtedly, one reason for *The Times* assertion derived from the two-day parliamentary debate on the White Paper held on 19 and 20 February 1962. This was the first occasion on which the Labour Party opposition in Parliament had challenged the idea of a reform of London government. Two points need to be examined here: first, the stages by which the Labour Party came to oppose the Government proposals and the reasons for their doing so; secondly, what influence this opposition had on the course of events.

Among the champions of the existing order of local government in London none was more prominent than Lord Morrison of Lambeth. During 1962 he was busy writing letters to the papers, and making speeches in the Lords and elsewhere in which he constantly returned to one single theme that the Government were primarily concerned with abolishing the LCC as a political manoeuvre to break Labour's control. Not everyone in the Labour Party, however, was so firmly convinced that it was all simply a Tory plot, but the fact that the result of the Government proposals would be the disappearance of the LCC was a major influence on the attitudes of the leaders of the party. Furthermore, they were very well aware of the strength of feeling on this issue not only of Lord Morrison of Lambeth, but of the majority group on the LCC and of the London Labour Party, both of whom exerted considerable pressure to get the parliamentary party to take a firm line of opposition to the Government proposals, particularly enlisting the support of Labour's London MPs such as Mr Michael Stewart (Fulham) and Mr Robert Mellish (Bermondsey), both of whom were active in the following months in putting the LCC case. The result was that the leaders of the party convinced themselves that there was nothing in the London situation which required the destruction of the LCC and their opposition to the Government plan was very largely a fighting defence of the LCC and the services it provided. There was scarcely any concern over the disappearance of Middlesex except from individual members of the party who were closely connected with that county.[30] Still less was there concern over the dismemberment of Essex, Kent and Surrey.

It is of course easy to see why the LCC meant so much to the Labour Party. At a time when the party had sustained three successive defeats in parliamentary elections, the fact that they had retained control over the largest municipal authority in the country was some consolation. And there was undoubtedly pride in what had been achieved since Labour had won control at County Hall in 1934. Nevertheless, the strength and determination with which the party fought the Government proposals in 1962 and 1963 remains puzzling. It was true that by 1962 there were signs that the Government's popularity was waning[31] and the Opposition were looking for a good opportunity to attack. But the reform of London government and the defence of the LCC were hardly issues to stir the country, and it would be surprising if the Labour Party's stand on this issue won them any votes. On the other hand their attitude laid them open to the charge of being reactionary and backward-looking, a charge which was used to effect by Sir Keith Joseph when he became Minister of Housing and Local Government. But certainly one factor in the party's adoption of an extreme position was that both the Labour Party and the LCC pressed the party very strongly in this direction, particularly through the person and influence of Lord Morrison of Lambeth.

The Labour Party's opposition to the White Paper proposals was publicly declared on the eve of the two-day parliamentary debate which opened on 19 February 1962. The Government had earlier proposed a one-day debate which was resisted by the opposition mainly on the grounds that there had been too little time to make an effective debate possible. When the Government announced that there was to be a two-day debate on a proposal to take note of the White Paper proposals, the Labour Party tabled an amendment which concentrated on two things, first that the proposals were inadequate to deal with the problems of planning and transport, and secondly, that they would 'wreck the humane and efficient performance' of certain functions particularly in central London. At the same time it was given out that they had so far refrained from coming out in outright opposition in the hope that the Government would respond to criticism and revise their policy.[32] Presumably, one thing which they had in mind was whether the opposition of some of the Conservative backbenchers would have any effect on the Government's determination. But it is more than likely that there was considerable internal debate within the Labour Party before they committed themselves to such an outright attack.

The debate on the White Paper

The Government themselves seem to have been a little apprehensive about this debate. It took place on a motion to 'take note' of the White Paper in spite of the fact that the Government were already committed to the main lines or reorganization.[33] The main government spokesmen were the Minister of Housing and Local Government (Dr Charles Hill) and the Minister of Education (Sir David Eccles). The former seemed to be in a very subdued mood; perhaps he hoped that a moderate approach would help to win over at least the dissidents on his own side of the House.[34]

He stated the case for reform largely in terms of the Commission's findings:

'This structure and this pattern – in the Government's view – flow logically and naturally from the two principles – indeed, the facts – established by the Commission'.[35]

He spent some time indicating what the Government saw as the weaknesses of the Surrey plan, particularly the proposal to set up a joint planning board:

'It would necessarily deal in generalities' and 'it adds another tier to an already complex structure, without giving it real power to solve the complex problems.'[36]

He also spent some time dealing with the changes from the Herbert Commission's plan which had been put forward in the White Paper. But he said little that was new on the reasons for accepting a plan of reform in detail. For example, he gave a list of functions to be performed by the Greater London Council and added:

'I do not need to go over the reasons for this choice of services; the House will know them. Indeed, the choice almost dictates itself.'[37]

On the following day, Sir David Eccles spoke about the Government's proposals for education. He claimed that where the Government had differed from the Commission it was

> 'because we think that the Commission did not give quite enough attention to the lessons of experience in local administration and particularly in the education service. Indeed, it is mainly out of regard for the education service that we are proposing a major change from the recommendations in the Commission's Report.'[38]

But he spent some time discussing the conflict between efficiency which implied larger authorities, and humanity which favoured smaller authorities.

He argued that the Commission's own arguments showed that a division of education powers between an upper-tier and a lower-tier authority should be rejected; this he described as 'a fundamental issue'.[39] He took it as generally agreed that the Greater London Council was too big to take over the whole of education for Greater London. But on the vital point of how the Central London Education Authority area was to be defined he could not add anything to the White Paper

> 'because we do not yet know the exact borough boundaries.'[40]

The main reason for not including the whole of the LCC area in this authority was however that

> 'as one gets towards the very centre of London so the pattern of schools and technical colleges is less and less related to borough boundaries, and, furthermore, the transport system is better and better'.[41]

He claimed that the Government had considered whether to make the boroughs in the central area of London education authorities but had rejected the idea as being impracticable largely because of the large movement of children across borough boundaries. On the constitution of the new Central London Education Authority he again could not bring forward any definite plans but said that the Government were anxious to obtain the advice of the House on this point.[42] Finally, he gave no new information on why the Government had decided on a 200,000 minimum population for the outer boroughs, beyond saying that it was 'extraordinarily difficult' to strike a balance between efficiency and freedom of choice of parents and children.

The opposition attacked the White Paper proposals strongly. In the first day's debate, Mr Michael Stewart presented the three-fold argument: (i) that for over-all planning and allied functions the GLC area was too small; (ii) that the proposals for the social services (especially children) were retrograde in that the boroughs would be too small; (iii) that the Greater London Council would not be electorally attractive. On the second day Mr Willey launched an attack on the Government's plan for education; if it was wrong to have the boroughs as education authorities in the central area why was it not wrong elsewhere; the central area plan was in any case half-baked; and the plan involved fragmentation of the existing administration of education in the Greater London area.[43] Sir David Eccles' reply to these charges was criticized by later speakers in terms such as 'vague and woolly' (Mr Chuter Ede) 'most ineffective' (Mr Clement Davies). It was left to Mr George Brown winding up for the Opposition to claim that the Minister of Education 'obviously adopted the brief from which he argued in Cabinet against the Royal Commission's proposals', and to refer to the Minister of Housing and Local Government's speech as 'one of the most unconvincing expositions of Government policy that the House has heard for a long time'.[44]

Undoubtedly, it was the debate in the House of Commons which mainly caused *The Times* to bemoan the fact that the opposition to the Government's proposals appeared to be having the better of the argument. The Government's apparent lack of vigour was largely due to the lack of enthusiasm of the Minister chiefly concerned and the uneasy compromise over education. Nevertheless preparations went ahead in readiness for the introduction of a Bill in the next session of parliament. To Dr Hill it may have been a job which had to be done; nevertheless, he did not shirk it. In this same debate in February he announced an ingenious formula for dealing with one troublesome question, that of the precise groupings of authorities to form the new London Boroughs. It was proposed that a small number of town clerks (later fixed at four) from outside the London area should be appointed to conduct discussions with the local authorities on this question. This interesting proposal will be discussed later.[45] Its merit was that it offered a relatively speedy way of settling an awkward question. It was therefore an indication that the Government were determined to push on with their plan.

Nevertheless while the Government were still wrestling with the problems first of the boundaries of Greater London and secondly of education, the opportunity for the voices of opposition to make themselves heard were numerous. Labour solidarity was emphasized when at the beginning of March 1962 the party's national executive committee met Labour representatives of affected local authorities and issued a statement that 'There was complete agreement . . . that the Government's scheme was not only impracticable and unfair' but would not meet the problems of Greater London.[46] On 13 March came the marathon LCC debate already referred to. And on the following day, the Lords met to debate a motion of Lord Morrison of Lambeth 'that the White Paper will not meet the needs of democratic local government'.

He attacked the Government in forthright terms. Their plan was simply a

'wicked attempt to destroy it (the LCC) for party political reasons. This is a plot, a rather contemptible plot – I almost said a corrupt plot – inspired by the London Municipal Society and the Conservative Central Office, not to destroy the London County Council because it is the London County Council, but because they challenge the right of the people of London to have anything but a Conservative majority at County Hall.'[47]

He went on:

'I say now, in the light of the White Paper, that the Government are madder than ever. It really is insane . . . Why do they want to land themselves into all this trouble? At the next general election, if this thing comes off, I will stump London and we will fight in London to denounce the Government for this piece of political jobbery . . . Hitler tried to destroy London and failed. Now the Conservative Party, for party political reasons are trying to destroy the municipality of the Capital City. It is my belief and hope that they will no more succeed than did Hitler.'[48]

Here was the authentic voice of Herbert Morrison who now, in his old age, could see nothing in the Government's plan beyond the fact that it would destroy the LCC, whose achievements under Labour and under his leadership were for him a matter of immense pride.

In replying for the Government, Viscount Hailsham repudiated the charges of Lord Morrison with vigour. Not only was it the view of the Government that the system of local government established by the 1888 Act was out-of-date and needed to be changed, but he suggested that Lord Morrison might himself be guilty of political bias:

> 'can it be that his passionate, almost religious attachment to the status quo of 1888 is partly influenced by the fact that he believes that if London were to be given more or less contemporary boundaries his built-in Labour majority which he has enjoyed for so long as a result of the 1888 status quo would disappear overnight?'[49]

Furthermore, there seemed to be some inconsistency between Lord Morrison's charge of gerrymandering and his view that the Government were mad to get themselves involved in something which would not win them any votes:

> 'He really ought to make up his mind ... whether in fact he is dealing with a devilishly clever Government trying to destroy the London County Council for political advantage ... or a particularly short-sighted and idiotic set of nincompoops who are offending their own supporters in the last Session of Parliament, destroying the financial basis of their subscriptions in the County of Surrey and rendering themselves liable to lose the next General Election.'[50]

The argument over the children's service

But the critical question for the Labour Party was whether their opposition could be made effective. If they could not get the Government to halt or modify their plan, there was always the possibility of delaying tactics, and ultimately perhaps a reversal of the plan if the Labour Party won the next General Election. Certainly Lord Morrison was in the early part of 1962 pressing the party to commit themselves to repeal of any legislation which the Conservative Government might pass.[51] There was a strong feeling, shared not only by Lord Morrison, and members of the London Labour Party but also by some members of the Parliamentary Party, that it would be a disaster if the services provided by the LCC were broken up. As Mr Michael Stewart had indicated in the Commons debate, this feeling was particularly marked in the case of the children's service, and an immediate aim of the Labour Party was to try to secure changes in the Government's proposals for this service. Mr Stewart advocated authorities of county size for this purpose on the grounds that the boroughs would be too small to make adequate specialized provision. This argument, it may be noted, was not applied to the personal health and welfare functions which it was conceded could be a borough function.[52] The implication was that existing counties should retain child-care functions, although this point was not made explicitly; and no doubt what he chiefly had in mind was that, as in education, there should be a single authority for the LCC area – or at least for the undefined central area of the White Paper proposals.[53]

Particularly after Dr Hill's announcement on 3 May of the decision on the education service, support for the Labour Party's stand came from professional bodies in the field. The association of Child Care Officers and the Residential Child Care Association, in a joint statement[54] urged that more research should be undertaken into the optimum size for children's departments before a final decision was made to transfer the service to the boroughs and that if the Government decided to go ahead with their plan, there should, as with the education service, be a review after five years.

Support for the retention of the LCC children's service also came from thirteen chairmen of Metropolitan Juvenile Courts who addressed a joint letter to *The Times* arguing that the courts could not do their job properly without the 'range of well integrated supporting services' provided by the LCC.[55] There followed a number of letters in support of this point of view not only from the chairman of the Association of LCC Child Welfare Officers and from the secretary of the Association of Child Care Officers but also from four members of the social administration department of the London School of Economics including Professors Titmuss and Donnison.[56] They were followed by two letters in support of the Government's proposals from the chairman of the General Purposes Committee of the Association of Municipal Corporations and from Professor W. A. Robson. The latter, apart from arguing that it was wrong to assume that the LCC was providing a better child care service than would the boroughs, attempted to bring the discussion back to the more general point that the object of the proposed reorganization was to establish a system of government in London with some relation to current needs: characteristically he ended his letter, in the spirit of *The Government and Misgovernment of London,* by saying 'It

is distressing to observe so many public-spirited persons apparently
defending the obsolete, ramshackle medley of authorities which at
present sprawls across Greater London.'[57] Finally, the chairman of the
LCC Children's Committee (Mrs, now Lady, Serota) accused Professor Robson of being misled by tidiness on the map 'in preference to
concern for the realities of human need'.[58]

Parallel with these events, the Labour opposition in Parliament was
maintaining its pressure. On 10 May the Minister of Housing and
Local Government was questioned about the decision to retain the
LCC education service, and pressed by the Opposition spokesman
(Mr Michael Stewart) to do the same for the children's service, but
replied that there were many advantages in making this a borough
service eg the need for close association with the health and welfare
services.[59]

On 31 May Mr George Brown returned to the point, this time in
questioning the Home Secretary (Mr R. A., now Lord, Butler). He
referred to the 'general disquiet' about the proposed fragmentation
of the county children's services and of how he was 'terribly fright-
ened' about what was going to happen. Would the Home Secretary
be prepared to see him and discuss the proposal further. Mr Butler in
replying was conciliatory but firm; he was ready to see Mr Brown and
his friends and agreed that there were some 'very difficult' problems
in the proposed transfer particularly in relation to residential
establishments. Nevertheless, the Government believed that this was
a 'proper function for the proposed London Boroughs'; again, he
stressed the need for close links with other services.[60]

As these exchanges illustrate, the children's service was not, like
the education service, a major influence on the structure of the
Government's plan. Perhaps the main question to be considered is
how and why the Government resisted pressures for the retention of
the existing arrangements for the children's service. In this the outlook
of the Home Secretary and his department are important, as also is
the general situation in which the Government found themselves by
May 1962.

As was indicated earlier[61] the Home Office in evidence to the
Herbert Commission had seemed rather reluctant either to comment
on the existing structure of local government for the performance of
child-care functions or to indicate the optimum size of local authority
for this purpose. Nevertheless, it seems likely, that if the existing
pattern were not to be retained the Home Office preferred the larger

authorities proposed in the Brooke/Eccles plan to the smaller authorities proposed by the Herbert Commission.

But there were two connected reasons why Mr Butler unlike Sir David Eccles, could not hold out for retention of the existing structure. First, the Home Office is responsible for many activities apart from the children's service; not only was the right organization of that service not vital to the department's interest as was that of education to the Ministry of Education, but the organization of the fire service[62] and civil defence, two of the Home Office's other interests, was, under the Commission's and the Government's plan, largely in accordance with what they thought desirable. Secondly, it must have been very clear to Mr Butler, as it was to the Home Office spokesmen subsequently on the London Government Bill,[63] that the main argument for abolishing the LCC and Middlesex and making fundamental changes in the structure was largely unconnected with the needs of the children's service. That service like education had to be fitted into the new structure but unlike education, it could not claim a leading place.

In favour of the Government's stand against the pressure to retain the LCC and possibly other existing children's services was, first, the argument used by Ministers. It made sense, as the Commission had argued, for the same authority to be responsible for the personal health, welfare and children's services; furthermore, there could be advantages in having links between the children's service and the housing and environmental health powers of the same authority as well as with education. But, secondly, there was the reality of the political situation. If it was conceded that both the education and the children's services of the LCC should be retained intact, it would be very difficult for the Government not to leave the LCC very largely as it was shorn perhaps of some of its powers in planning and highways. The argument about the need for links between the children's and other services would have made the case for retention of the LCC's personal health and welfare services stronger. Once that point had been reached, it would have been difficult to argue the need for the London Boroughs, since in the inner area of Greater London they would have been deprived of their major proposed functions.

Dr Hill and Mr Butler must both have been aware, therefore, that to have yielded to the pressures on the children's service could well have led to the collapse of the entire plan of reform. There is no indication either that Mr Butler pressed for this course or that

Dr Hill wished to yield. It was a critical point in the history of these events. If the Government had had second thoughts about the reform plan, this was the moment at which they could have chosen to retract. But they resisted the pressures: from then on there was no turning back.

For the Labour Party and their supporters at County Hall it was a critical point too. Fortified by genuine fears for the future of the service and with their hands strengthened by the views of the professional bodies and the metropolitan magistrates, they yet were unable to deflect the Government from the plan of reform first outlined in the 1961 White Paper. But if they could not stop the programme they might at least attempt to delay it. As early as March 1962 the *Guardian* was probably not far from the truth in arguing:

'even the bravest Labour spirits at County Hall recognize that only a general election and a change of Government could save them'.[64]

For the Labour Party, therefore, it made obvious sense to use every opportunity to hold up the Government's time-table in the hope that the general election might come before the plan had been finalized.[65] Equally for the Government it was essential for them now that the two awkward stumbling-blocks left by the White Paper had been disposed of, to push ahead with preparations for the bill which would need to be passed in the 1962–63 Session of Parliament.

Other views on the White Paper

Thus the political situation gave an edge to the events preceding the publication of the Bill and even more to the proceedings on the Bill itself. But there were other factors too which were important in the history of these events. Professional bodies concerned with teaching and the children's service have been particularly mentioned because these services were the focus of attention. Other professional bodies, however, were not slow to offer the Government views and advice on the White Paper, particularly directed towards influencing the detailed provisions of the forthcoming Bill. Planning was one function in which professional views were strongly expressed. This was partly because of the importance of the function in the proposed new structure and partly because the White Paper had left the precise distribution of powers between the GLC and the boroughs somewhat uncertain.

The Town Planning Institute played a prominent part in putting forward proposals both in the period following the White Paper and again after the London Government Bill had been produced. As on previous occasions they stressed the need for effective regional planning for an area at least as large as that of the Abercrombie Plan.[66] Within this limitation they strongly supported the Government's proposal to make the Greater London Council responsible for the preparation and review of the development plan; but they wanted to strengthen the GLC's powers in development control, in particular by giving them power to prescribe categories of development for which the boroughs were to refer applications to them for decision. These included applications which involved departures from the development plan. Unlike the Herbert Commission, the TPI did not think that the boroughs should be left to decide whether an application did involve a departure from the development plan. They welcomed the Government's proposals for fewer boroughs, although they still thought that there were too many boroughs in the central area. All these questions raised by the TPI led to significant discussions and controversy in the course of the Bill's proceedings and, in some cases, subsequently.

The Royal Institution of Chartered Surveyors was another body which had definite views on the White Paper, although on the whole these were expressed in more general terms than were those of the TPI.[67] On planning, for example, they wanted the GLC to have power to ensure that a regional planning policy was implemented; and on traffic control they thought that the existing detailed control by the Ministry of Transport should be avoided.

Thus although the political argument and debate was most evident in the period between the White Paper and the publication of the London Government Bill, the Government had in addition a number of difficult practical problems to settle in preparing the Bill. On some of these problems they received advice from outside bodies such as the TPI; on others the views of affected local authorities were expecially important. But in these events, it must be remembered, the contestants, though important, were few in number; the political parties, the local authorities, some professional bodies, a handful of academic observers – these were the people who were interested and participated in the events of those two years. But the proposed reforms were designed to bring benefits to a much larger number of people by way of improved services and the strengthening of local democracy.

They conspicuously failed to arouse much interest in the general public. As the Conservative MP for Beckenham (Mr Goodhart) said in the debate in the Commons on 20 February 1962:

'I have been impressed by the lack of interest shown in my area . . . Since the beginning of this month I have received more letters about the inequities of the discrimination in the taxation on greyhound racing than on this topic.'[68]

8

The Metropolitan Water Board: the New Boroughs

Proposed abolition of the Metropolitan Water Board

Several important issues faced Dr Charles Hill in the spring and summer of 1962 before he could finally determine the contents of the Bill to reform London government. There was the need to settle the number and boundaries of the new London Boroughs; there were decisions and, in some cases, consultations to be made about the precise responsibility for a number of functions which had been left unsettled by the White Paper; and there was the need to consider the administrative machinery and the problems which would arise in making the transition from the old to the new system of London government – especially questions of staffing. All these problems had to be examined against a background of opposition to the whole plan of reform.

Before much progress had been made on any of these issues, however, Dr Hill himself made a fresh proposal which had not been mentioned in the White Paper and had not even been considered by the Herbert Commission. This concerned the future of the Metropolitan Water Board. It will be recalled that the Government had not included water supply in the terms of reference of the Herbert Commission on the grounds that over the greater part of the Commission's area this was not a local government function but had left it 'for separate consideration'.[1] On 4 April 1962 Dr Hill wrote to the board and to the ninety local authorities represented on it telling them that he had come to the provisional conclusion that the Board should be abolished and its functions transferred to a committee of the proposed Greater London Council. He gave the Board a month in which to comment on the proposal which, said their spokesman, 'came as an utter bombshell'.[2]

What was surprising about this was not what was proposed but the way in which the proposal was made. Many people, including some prominent Labour members,[3] had urged that if there was to be a Council for Greater London it would be appropriate for it to undertake the function of water supply performed by the MWB. It was also clear that the constitution of the MWB even if not its existence would need to be reconsidered in any case because of the re-organization of local authorities in the area.[4]

Nevertheless, the Government had given no hint that they were preparing to go as far as abolition of the MWB or even that the question was going to be raised at all. So abrupt was the manner of the announcement that some people began to see sinister motives behind it. This was the time of the Government's attempt to restrain the growth of incomes and shortly before Dr Hill's letter the Board had decided to grant a $7\frac{1}{2}$ per cent increase to its employees against his advice that no more than $2\frac{1}{2}$ per cent was justifiable in the circumstances. Was this 'the only apparent reason'[5] for the Minister's action?

There is probably a simpler explanation which is nearer the truth. The White Paper made no reference to water supply simply because it was left aside as something of lesser importance which could be dealt with later. When Dr Hill came to consider it he found the Ministry's arguments for making it a GLC function convincing. The arguments were convenience and the desirability for local government of having responsibility for this service linked with responsibility for other services affecting Greater London as a whole.[6] The arguments were strong. But the fact that Dr Hill, an experienced politician, made no attempt to pave the way with the MWB for his announcement is surely a further indication that his interest in the reform programme was limited. He may have argued that although the Board themselves would certainly resist their own dissolution nobody else would be likely to spring to their defence. Nevertheless, if he had moved more diplomatically by first suggesting the possibility that the MWB might come under the GLC and inviting discussions he might have taken some of the sting out of the board's opposition. The latter were after all in a weak position; they themselves claimed that 'by far the greatest number' of the local authorities represented on the Board were 'utterly opposed' to its abolition from which they drew the conclusion that the changes 'are not wanted by London in general'.[7] But apart from the dubious assumption in this argument, the authorities whose support they claimed were themselves due to be superseded in the proposed reorganization and were therefore hardly to be expected to take an unbiased view of the situation.

One factor which may have influenced Dr Hill was that of timing.

If the MWB and other questions were to be settled in time for a Bill in the autumn, he may have felt that there was no time for lengthy to-ing and fro-ing; and that it was better to be swift and brutal. Nevertheless, it cannot be said that this incident was very skilfully handled by the Government.

Subsequent events, however, gave an ironic twist to the Government's plans. The Board reacted to the Minister's letter of 4 April by sending a deputation which was received on 9 May and which among other things urged that there should be an independent enquiry. This was rejected. The Board then proposed a further meeting with the Minister which took place on 30 July with Sir Keith Joseph who had by then succeeded Dr Hill. At this meeting they produced a variety of arguments but their central theme was that since nobody had accused them of either inefficiency or failure there could be no reason to suppose that a change would produce a better service.

The Minister's reply (in a letter of 21 August) was in cutting terms and barely within the bounds of the normal civilities of this kind of situation. He was 'altogether surprised' at the stress laid by the Board on some of what he called 'light-weight' arguments; on the main argument of the Board he said simply that he did not 'see anything essentially inconsistent in recognizing the achievements and not accepting that a Board must necessarily continue'. He dismissed the plea for an inquiry on the grounds that it 'would simply be irrelevant. It is not a question for technical demonstration, but a matter of opinion about the right form of organization. I have been required to form an opinion and have done so, with regret for what it will mean to the Board but without any doubts about what should be done.'[8]

With the door so firmly shut in their faces there was little the Board could do except register their protests. Yet four years after the GLC assumed its duties the Board is still in existence. What saved them in 1962 was a technicality. Sir Keith Joseph's expressed intention to make provision in the London Government Bill for the transfer of the Board's powers to the GLC met the lawyer's argument that to do so would transform the Bill from a Public into a Hybrid Bill, that is, one which in part affected private or limited interests. Such a Bill would have to go before a Select Committee which would enable petitioners against the Bill to engage in legal argument against it.[9] The probability of delay to the Bill's progress if this happened was so great that the Government could not afford to run the risk. Rather than that they dropped the proposal and instead announced their intention of introducing at some future date separate legislation to deal with the MWB issue.

But once the London Government Bill had got under way this became an issue of much less urgency and it is not surprising that a year later in October 1963 Sir Keith was tacitly admitting that the Government were unlikely to find time for the necessary legislation in the 1963–64 Session. The change of Government in October 1964 provided further reasons for shelving the question, and although there has been no overt change of policy, clearly the abolition of the Metropolitan Water Board has now a very low priority. One effect of the reorganization of London government was, however, to make changes necessary in the constitution of the Board. Lengthy discussions went on between the Board and the Ministry of Housing and Local Government, the main point of disagreement being the Ministry's desire to reduce the number of members of the Board from the existing eighty-eight to about forty. The Board argued that a membership of sixty would be more appropriate. The Ministry, after consulting the new London Boroughs, rejected their view, and from 1 November 1965 the Board has consisted of thirty-nine members.[10]

The new London Boroughs – the four town Clerks

The Metropolitan Water Board was, however, a side-issue, unlike the determination of the number and boundaries of the new London Boroughs which was a necessary and integral part of the reorganization. It was complicated by the fact that no final decisions could be taken until the outer boundaries of Greater London had been settled.

It has already been pointed out that the Ministry of Housing and Local Government's Circular of 16 December, 1961 which put forward suggestions for borough groupings claimed that these groupings were based on certain criteria although it was not always clear how these criteria had been applied in each case.[11] The Circular also said that the Minister intended 'to invite authorities in the London area to join discussions' in the spring of 1962 about the pattern of London Boroughs.

The curious expression 'to join discussions' was amplified by a circular letter of 26 January 1962 in which the Ministry disclosed that the intention was to hold a series of conferences to be conducted by invited town clerks from outside London; terms of reference were suggested and comments invited from the local authorities and their associations. This was the proposal referred to by Dr Hill in his speech in the debate on the White Paper on 19 February.

There are two other points of some significance in the proposals as put forward at this stage. First, there was a suggestion that the town clerks' conferences might also deal with the question of the peripheral authorities and the outer boundary of Greater London. This suggestion was soon dropped in view of the political implications which the whole question raised.[12] Secondly, the Ministry went out of their way to stress that these conferences would be in no sense public enquiries, but more informal in their proceedings.

This last point throws a good deal of light on the choice of procedure. The Ministry were well aware of the time-consuming nature of the kind of enquiry which generally preceded such changes as the extension of a county borough's boundaries. But lengthy procedures of this kind had to be avoided if the Minister's plans for the introduction of a Bill were not to be upset. They therefore hit on the ingenious formula outlined in the circular letter of 26 January.

They had precedents to guide them: conferences of an informal kind formed part of the procedure of the Local Government Commission set up under the Local Government Act 1958 in formulating draft proposals, although more formal public enquiries were held before final proposals were made.[13] Again, the ill-fated Local Government Boundary Commission of 1945–1949 had held numerous informal conferences with local authorities and these had been conducted by town clerks and others, designated as assistant commissioners.[14] Thus the Ministry could claim that they were merely adapting to a new situation a recognized and convenient administrative procedure. Moreover, they could argue that the situation did not call for elaborate enquiries; the decision had already been made on the changes which were required in the size of authorities. The problem now was essentially the secondary, though still important task of deciding how existing authorities could be amalgamated to form the required pattern.

From the Ministry's point of view this was all very reasonable. What is perhaps more surprising is that the local authorities were content by and large to accept the situation. Some of them, it is true, made it clear that they remained opposed in principle to the Government plan and some did argue for a more formal enquiry.[15]

In this connection it is worth recalling too that the Royal Commission had suggested that there should be 'a simple and expeditious procedure' for enquiries to be made after the passing of general legislation on London government,[16] and had been reluctant to make specific suggestions for borough groupings on the grounds that they were not a Boundary Commission.

Some authorities may have felt that since the Government had made the decision to have larger boroughs than the Royal Commission had recommended there was little point in arguing much about how these were to be created. But the great majority of authorities either disagreed strongly with the Government's proposed groupings or at least thought that they could suggest something better for their own particular area. Most of them seem to have resigned themselves to making the best of the opportunity presented to them by the Government's suggestion for town clerks' conferences.

Discussions continued during February and March on the precise terms of reference for the town clerks. On 23 March the Minister announced the agreed terms and the names of the town clerks who were to conduct the enquiries.[17] He also announced that the first three conferences, to be concerned with borough groupings in the LCC area, were to be held on 9, 10 and 12 April. It will be noticed that the announcement was made before the deadline of 31 March which Dr Hill had given the authorities to comment on the proposed borough groupings. This is an indication of the urgency with which this problem was viewed. Yet, ironically enough, conferences to cover the remaining parts of Greater London could not yet be arranged. Since the determination of the outer boundaries was no longer to be entrusted to the town clerks, the pattern of groupings in the outer area awaited the minister's decision on which areas were to be excluded and, this, as has been seen, did not take place until the middle of May.

An important element in the town clerks' task was the need to devise a pattern for the area of Greater London as a whole. It might be thought, therefore, that it was a premature step to examine the LCC area in isolation before there was any chance of looking at the remaining parts. In practice, there were practical limitations on what the town clerks could recommend. The existence of a different local government system in the LCC area from that in the outer areas made it practically certain that they would not recommend joining a Metropolitan Borough with a County District outside because of the

F

complication in the administrative problems which would result. And this was reinforced later by the Government's decision to retain the LCC area intact for education purposes.

Furthermore, the Government's need to get the question of borough groupings settled quickly in order to have legislation ready in time for the next session of Parliament meant that it was impossible for the town clerks to carry out extensive enquiries of their own. They were therefore practically bound in making suggestions to follow the boundaries of existing authorities. Although, as in the Ministry Circular of 16 December 1961 there were specified criteria for them to work to (lines of communication etc) time and the administrative problems involved ruled out any attempt to draw boundaries completely afresh in accordance with these criteria.

In practice, therefore, the first part of their terms of reference was bound to have considerable influence on their recommendations; and where the authorities concerned were agreeable to the groupings proposed by the Government there was strong incentive to the town clerks to leave well alone. As they put it:

'it seemed to us that an extraordinarily good case needed to be made [for any counter-proposals] if they were to prevail over an agreed grouping, for such agreement clearly provides a good augury for the future'.[18]

To a large extent, therefore, the town clerks saw their job as being to consider alternative proposals put up by the authorities and then, within the limitations of the terms of reference, to see how far they could produce a pattern which reconciled these proposals.

Altogether eight conferences were held. One town clerk was present at and presided over each conference when a group of proposed boroughs was discussed. The last of these conferences, concerned with the Surrey districts and Croydon, was not held until 5 June. After that the town clerks had to consider their proposals, discuss them among themselves and prepare their final reports. These went to the Ministry on 18 July and were subsequently published. On 2 August before publication of the Report the Minister (Sir Keith Joseph) announced the Government's acceptance of their recommendations *in toto*.[19]

Although it has been suggested above that there were precedents for the kind of enquiry conducted by the town clerks, it nevertheless was an unusual feature of the London government reorganization. It is worth considering some of the general points raised and how the town clerks dealt with them. The first conference was held on 9 April at Lambeth Town Hall under the chairmanship of Mr Young to consider the boroughs proposed for the LCC area south of the Thames. It started on an acrimonious note with several Metropolitan Borough representatives (especially Lambeth, Camberwell and Southwark) protesting at the 'indecent haste' with which the Conference had been convened. In addition a number of them (eg Bermondsey and Camberwell) were so firmly opposed to the Government's entire programme that they were not prepared to make any comments at all on the proposed groupings. On the other hand, the largest of the boroughs, Wandsworth, which was Conservative controlled,[20] had very decided views on the proposals and the problem of how to fit Wandsworth into the pattern of boroughs south of the Thames not only dominated this conference but provides an interesting example of the way the town clerks set about their task.[21]

The Government had proposed to split Wandsworth, one of only four major splits of existing authorities which they proposed and by far the most important.[22] The main reasons were that it was very large (347,000 population); and an awkward shape. Moreover, its neighbour, Battersea, was small (106,000 population). It seemed an obviously sensible proposal, therefore, to add part of Wandsworth to Battersea. This the Government had suggested, but unfortunately the result was to leave the remainder of Wandsworth as a separate borough 'without municipal buildings or any other of the basic equipment of public administration'.[23]

This practical disadvantage of the Government's proposal seems to have been the main reason why the town clerks suggested a different borough grouping, but in doing so they rejected the views of both boroughs. Wandsworth did not want to be divided and Battersea simply wanted to take in as much of Wandsworth as would bring it up to the required population size. 'The proposal,' claimed the town clerks, 'would no doubt have had all the virtues that Battersea suggested but it would make worse all the disadvantages affecting Wandsworth.'[24]

To solve the problem they suggested adding most of the eastern part of Wandsworth (ie Clapham and Streatham) to Lambeth, leaving the rest of Wandsworth to be joined to Battersea. The criteria they put forward for the first part of this proposal seemed to be that of service centres and lines of communication: 'most people living in these parts of Wandsworth must be much more familiar with

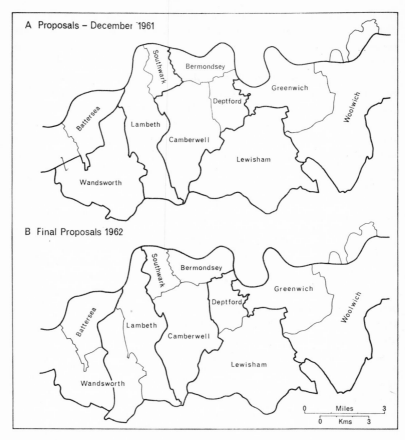

Figure 2. Proposed Borough Groupings: LCC Area South of the Thames.

Brixton, the most important centre of inner South London, either because they go there to shop or because they pass through Brixton on their way to central London'.[25]

However, the consequence of this suggestion was that there had to be a wholesale recasting of practically all the other boroughs in the area. In the government proposals, for example, Lambeth was to have been joined with Southwark. Now a new home had to be found for the latter. 'Fortunately' said the report 'there is an equally strong case and perhaps stronger case for grouping Southwark with

Bermondsey and Camberwell.'[26] In all only one borough south of the river (Greenwich and Woolwich) remained unchanged and there were four suggested new groupings in place of the five put forward by the Government.

Mr Young's colleague, Mr Littlewood, had an easier time north of the Thames. The Conservative Metropolitan Boroughs such as Westminster and Hampstead were not only more forthcoming than the southern Labour Boroughs in putting their views, but on the whole they were also more ready to accept the Government's proposals. Chelsea, however, came out with an ingenious proposal for combining Chelsea, South Kensington and Fulham together with the Knightsbridge area of Westminister. Since none of the other boroughs would look at this suggestion and since it would also have meant splitting existing local authority areas, the town clerks rejected it.[27] Five of the Government's recommended groupings for this area were retained and there were only two suggested new groupings.[28]

An illustration of another type of very difficult problem is provided by the Middlesex conferences which were held on 23 May and 4 June under the chairmanship of Mr Plowman. The Government proposal to amalgamate Wembley and Willesden was fiercely opposed by both councils and on much the same grounds – that the two areas were quite distinct in character, and physically sharply divided. Underlying this was the unspoken fact of political division; in particular, the fear of Wembley's Conservative majority of being swamped by the Labour majority in the much larger Borough of Willesden if amalgamation were carried through.

The difficulty here was to reconcile the different criteria set out in the terms of reference. The physical criteria (present and past associations, lines of communication etc) did not favour the union nor did the views of the authorities themselves. On the other hand any alternative was likely to bring additional problems, particularly in creating the overall pattern of boroughs. Wembley, with a population of 125,000 was too small to stand on its own; it had therefore either to be enlarged or to be joined to another borough – and that meant either Harrow or Willesden.[29] Willesden, on the other hand might conceivably have stood on its own as a small borough of just over 170,000, or would have to be enlarged either by taking parts of neighbouring authorities or by being joined to Wembley. These alternatives were opposed by the authorities affected.

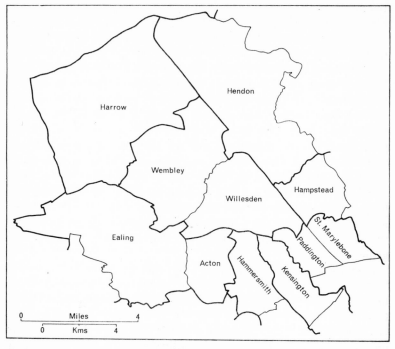

Figure 3. Proposed Grouping of Wembley and Willesden in relation to adjoining areas.

The town clerks rejected all suggestions for change, and came down firmly in favour of the Willesden/Wembley merger. They conceded that the boundary between them might well have been regarded as a barrier to amalgamation but there were 'exceptional circumstances' in this instance. These were not specified, but the hope was expressed:

'that the new borough will in due course become a very effective unit'.[30]

These three examples indicate the difficulties and limitations under which the town clerks had to work. However sensible the Chelsea proposal was, it went too far beyond the scope of what the town clerks were asked to do for them to be able to examine it in detail. It would have been appropriate for consideration by a boundary commission with wide powers, but the town clerks enquiry was designed to avoid the need for such an investigation.

Both the Wandsworth and the Wembley/Willesden examples show how the town clerks were restricted by the need to have regard to the overall pattern of boroughs. In the case of Wandsworth, they were compelled to make a change in the Government's proposal because of a practical difficulty. But the effect of making one change was to cause a rearrangement of the whole pattern of groupings in the LCC area south of the Thames. Fortunately, they were able to do this without doing violence to the criteria specified in their terms of reference.

It seems likely, however, that but for the practical difficulty which faced the proposed new Wandsworth, the town clerks would have been inclined to leave the groupings south of the river as proposed by the Government, and as indeed they did with the Wembley/Willesden proposal. In the latter instance, they were faced with strong grounds for suggesting changes. Not only had both authorities made counter-proposals, but in terms of some of the criteria specified in the terms of reference (eg present and past associations, lines of communication) there was little justification for joining Wembley and Willesden. No changes were proposed because of the exceptional circumstances. These exceptional circumstances were very largely the fact that any change in the Wembley/Willesden grouping would involve repercussions over a number of adjoining groupings which it would be difficult to resolve as easily as had been proposed in the case of London south of the river.

The truth is that it was very difficult for the town clerks to depart very much from the Government's proposals. These formed the starting-point of their enquiries. Moreover, they had to work within the limitations both of the minimum size of borough laid down by the Government and of the need to create an over-all pattern of boroughs within Greater London. They were also restricted by the time factor mentioned earlier. The opportunity for making changes was greatest where there was a reasonable degree of agreement among the local authorities concerned of the need for change and of the changes which might be made; and where these changes could be made without too many consequential changes in other groupings and with a reasonable degree of conformity to the criteria laid down in the terms of reference. These conditions were not often fulfilled.

The results of the town clerks' deliberations can be summarized in terms of the changes which they suggested from the Government's proposals:

County	Borough groupings suggested by the town clerks showing no change from the Government's proposals.	Borough groupings suggested by the town clerks differing from the Government proposals.
* London	6	6
Middlesex (and Hertford-shire)	4	4
Essex	1	4
Kent	–	2
Surrey	2	3
	13	19

This summary exaggerates the extent of change if it is borne in mind (i) that three changes were consequential on the Government's decision to exclude certain areas from Greater London following the issue of Circular 56/61; (ii) that some changes, such as the transfer of Shoreditch already referred to, were relatively minor. Furthermore, the effect of consequential changes has to be remembered. Four of the six changes in the County of London, for example, resulted from the decision to split Wandsworth in a manner different from that proposed by the Government.

Thus, the final pattern of groupings recommended by the town clerks and accepted by the Government did not differ markedly from that originally proposed in the 1961 Circular.[31] The main area of change, apart from the County of London south of the Thames, was in north Middlesex and the adjoining parts of Essex and even this was in part due to the Government's decision to exclude Cheshunt and most of Chigwell from Greater London. It is difficult to avoid the conclusion that the Government regarded the town clerks' enquiries as in the nature of a safety-valve. They offered the opportunity for authorities to argue against the Government's proposals and for

* Thirteen boroughs suggested by the Government were reduced to 12 in the town clerks' proposal.

relatively minor adjustments and improvements to be made. The town clerks did their job conscientiously and well; but in the nature of the case they could not satisfy more than a few of the local authorities who put forward views to them.

Furthermore, from the Government's point of view, there was probably little else which could have been done if the time-table for the forthcoming Bill was not to be put in jeopardy. No doubt ideally there should have been full-scale investigation to determine meaningful areas without regard to existing boundaries. This would have taken years. It was rejected – if indeed it was ever considered at all – for much the same reasons as had applied to previous re-drawings of the map of London. The Metropolitan Boroughs of 1899 were formed out of the existing parish units of that date purely as the most convenient method which lay to hand. In 1962 the London Borough boundaries were drawn to form the most convenient administrative units out of the existing conglomeration of County Boroughs, Metropolitan and Municipal Boroughs, and Urban Districts. An attempt was made to do this with as much regard for criteria such as lines of communication and the location of service centres, as was possible given the limitations of size, of the need to amalgamate whole areas and above all, of time within which the operation was carried out. But when all is said, many of the groupings which finally emerged must be regarded mainly as marriages of administrative convenience. East Ham and West Ham; Hornsey, Tottenham and Wood Green; Ruislip-Northwood, Uxbridge, Hayes and Harlington and Yiewsley and West Drayton – they may form workable patterns for running education, welfare or public library services but it would be hard to find any consistent reasons for the particular amalgamations which were finally accepted. Within the limits imposed on them the town clerks did their job well. But interest must lie mainly in those limitations and the reasons for them.

It remains briefly to note that the immediate Government acceptance of the town clerks' recommendations did not mean the end of agitation by authorities seeking to get the groupings changed; nor did it mean the end of agitation by those authorities who still hoped to get out of Greater London altogether. But they had little hope of success by this stage, even though later the remainder of Epsom and Ewell did indeed manage to keep in Surrey and out of Greater London.[32]

9
Preparations for the London Government Bill

Much detailed preparatory work necessarily had to go on behind the scenes if a London Government Bill was to be ready by the autumn. This was a particular pre-occupation of the Ministry of Housing and Local Government during the summer of 1962, although other central departments were also concerned in it. They now had to settle the precise content of the Bill covering the distribution of functions between the new authorities, their constitution and electoral arrangements, and questions of staffing and financing. To make progress on these questions the central departments and especially the Ministry of Housing and Local Government needed to be in close and constant touch with the local authorities and their associations not only for discussions but also to get information necessary to deal effectively with the detailed administrative problems once policies had been settled.

The LCC's refusal to co-operate

The situation called for a reasonable degree of co-operation on the part of the local authorities. However opposed to the Government's plan some authorities might be, self-interest could be expected to be a strong inducement to co-operate in making the plan workable. It was likely, after all, that many members and officers of existing authorities would be called upon to operate the new system. But the attitude of the LCC, the largest local authority in the area, was somewhat different. Reference has already been made[1] to the fact that at the end of a long session on 13 March 1962 the Council had resolved to send a deputation to the Prime Minister. This deputation, ten strong,[2] was received by Mr Macmillan and Dr Hill on 6 April, and duly presented its case for the alternative (Surrey) plan and its opposition to the Government's plan. On 24 April the Prime Minister replied to the points raised in a letter to Sir Isaac Hayward; the

LCC's points were simply dismissed and the Prime Minister remarked that what was necessary was to 'try to devise something that looks to the future rather than to the past'.[3] The letter concluded with an appeal to the LCC to take a 'full and constructive part' in preparing for the changes, and to allow LCC officials to take part in discussions to clarify the many matters of detail which needed to be settled.

On the 15 May, following the Government's announcement that, at least for the time being, the LCC education service was to be retained, Sir Isaac replied, 'Over seventy years of devoted work' he claimed, was to be thrown away 'for the sake of some theoretically better arrangement'. He asked for a committee of enquiry to look, for example, at the possibility of doing for other services what was now proposed for education, and he wanted the Prime Minister to receive a further deputation. The letter ended with an assurance that 'the Council is fully aware of its responsibilities for co-operating with the Government in the preparation and implementation of legislation. The officers have in fact been authorized to provide the Government departments with factual information which may be asked for and the Council will be prepared to express its views about any other matters arising during the course of any preparatory work.'

The Prime Minister's reply to this on 24 May was (and was intended to be) as discouraging as it is possible to be with this kind of semi-diplomatic exchange. 'I hope you will not mind,' he said, 'if I say that I cannot find in your letter anything which throws a new light on this question . . . I am afraid that I cannot hold out any hope that my colleagues and I can be persuaded that our view of the matter is wrong.' Another deputation would simply go over familiar ground and a further enquiry would only create further delay and uncertainty, and in any case the whole matter had already been 'exhaustively examined' by the Royal Commission. The letter concluded:

'I am grateful for what you say in the final paragraph of your letter. We shall certainly be looking to the Council for help in settling the details.'

Faced with this point-blank refusal, the Council, at its meeting on 29 May passed a resolution profoundly regretting the rejection of the suggestion for an enquiry.

There are thus two complementary threads running through the exchanges between the LCC and the Government. First, there is the disagreement in principle and the failure of the LCC to get the

Government's plan changed or even delayed; secondly, there is the very distinct possibility (or threat from the Government's angle) of the LCC's opposition being taken to the extreme point of refusal to co-operate in the necessary preliminary discussions to the introduction of legislation.

That the LCC was determined to persist in its opposition was evident from other events. In May it issued a pamphlet entitled *The London County Council – Why Destroy it?,* the cover showing a picture of County Hall with a large green question mark overshadowing it, and the text designed to show that the Government's plan would be disastrous for London.[4] 200,000 copies of this pamphlet were produced as 'a popular summary of the views of the LCC.'[5] Other Councils were, however, as strongly opposed to the Government's plan. Only in the case of the LCC was opposition carried to extreme lengths.[6] The issue came to a head in July. On 15 June the Ministry of Housing and Local Government had written to the LCC and other local authorities affected by the proposed reorganization inviting them to attend meetings to discuss important questions of staffing and finance. The LCC were not represented at these meetings on 10 and 20 July.

The General Purposes Committee claimed:

'The Council has made perfectly clear its disapproval of the Government's proposals, and we think that no useful purpose can therefore be served by the Council's being associated with the Government in any attempt to implement them.'[7]

This apparent hardening of attitude since Sir Isaac Hayward had told the Prime Minister that the Council was aware of its responsibilities was challenged by the LCC Opposition party. The Chairman of the General Purposes Committee (Mrs Freda Corbet) claimed that Sir Isaac had not been giving an undertaking but making a statement of fact. She went on:

'The disintegration of the Council's services proposed by the Government would be so disastrous to the interests of the people of London that the Committee have no hesitation in regarding as their over-riding responsibility that of opposing the plan at all stages.'[8]

This claim was rejected both by Sir Percy Rugg, the Conservative leader of the opposition, who claimed that there had been a 'flagrant breach' of the Council's duties[9] and by Sir Keith Joseph, the newly-appointed Minister of Housing and Local Government, who said that the Council's decision not to co-operate

> 'falls below the standards which responsible local authorities observe in matters of this kind; but I hope that even at this late stage wiser thought will prevail.'[10]

As he also pointed out, all the other County Councils concerned were giving 'every assistance'. Middlesex indeed although strong in their opposition to the Government's plan and destined, like the LCC, to disappear altogether, had at an early stage indicated that they would be prepared to co-operate fully in the final solution.[11]

This attitude carried dangers for the LCC that decisions would be taken without proper regard being paid to the LCC's own point of view in matters which were of concern and interest to it. This posed particularly difficult problems for the LCC's senior officers. On the one hand they were bound by the Council's decision not to co-operate; on the other, they realized only too well that if, as seemed likely, the reorganization went through they would have the problems and burdens of trying to operate it, a task which would be made easier the more they were involved in the making of the detailed decisions. In the period until the introduction of the Bill there were undoubtedly informal contacts between LCC officials and the central departments, but they were very restricted in scope and did not go beyond the spirit of the Council's decision. The situation changed once the Bill had been introduced into parliament. On the one hand the LCC's opposition in principle now had to be translated into positive amendments to the Bill; on the other hand, the need for securing that the LCC's views should be taken into account and their interests safeguarded in any reorganization now became more urgent. The effect was to transfer to the Committee stage of the Bill some matters which otherwise would have been dealt with earlier.[12] And as will be seen later LCC officials began to take positive steps towards arranging for the orderly transfer of functions to the new authorities to be set up under the Bill.

From the Government's point of view, the LCC's attitude was more a source of irritation than a serious threat to their programme. It made life a good deal more difficult for those civil servants who were actively involved in preparing the legislation; and if the other County Councils had adopted similar attitudes there might, indeed almost certainly would have, been severe disruption of the time-table. Since this did not happen, the LCC's refusal to co-operate may be regarded almost as a symbolic gesture. Sir Isaac Hayward, the veteran leader of the Council, had asserted in March:

'I believe that it is so bad that it cannot happen.'[13]

It was a view which he held consistently throughout. The LCC's refusal to co-operate was an act of defiance in keeping with this view.

Staff anxieties and the idea of a staff commission

The staff who were going to be affected by the Government's plan were anxious to know as soon as possible just what place each of them individually would have in the new organization of local authorities. At least as important was the general question of how appointments were to be made to the new authorities and what safeguards there would be against redundancy or down-grading of posts. At the same time a number of outside observers and professional bodies were concerned with the effects of the proposed reorganization on the staffing and operation of particular functions. Thus although staff matters were not by any means the only problem which needed attention in the period between the White Paper and the Bill, they were a significant part of the whole preparatory phase. They form the focus of the following discussion of the administrative preliminaries to the Bill, in which the Ministry of Housing and Local Government, the staff associations and the local authority associations played major roles.

The publication of the White Paper in November 1961 led immediately to the voicing of misgivings about the likely effect of the Government's proposals on local authority staff in Greater London. An ex-LCC officer writing anonymously in *Public Service,* the monthly journal of the National and Local Government Officers' Association, suggested that these misgivings might be allayed if there were established some body comparable to the Civil Service Commission to supervise the arrangements for appointing staff to the new authorities.[14] In January 1962, *London Town* advocated 'a properly organized system of allocation of staff through a central bureau'.[15] This idea, in many different forms, was one of the main themes of the staff associations in the following months.

An immediate difficulty of the staff position was that the associations did not speak with one voice. There was, in particular, the division between the LCC and other authorities. The staff grading and structure of the LCC differed from that of other authorities; correspondingly, the national Whitley Council local government negotiating machinery did not include the LCC which had its own quite separate machinery. This was to create difficulties both in the transfer of LCC staff to the boroughs, and in the quite separate question, raised at a later date, of whether GLC staff should be brought within the national negotiating machinery.

Sensing these difficulties, *London Town* suggested 'the creation of a unified body' of all local government staff associations in the Greater London area: 'the security of your employment, your pay, prospects and conditions of service may depend upon it'.[16] This call was not taken up by the associations apart from the LCC Staff Association. Nevertheless, it is an indication of the seriousness with which the LCC staff viewed the proposed reorganization.

By February the LCC Staff Association had adopted and elaborated the idea of a central bureau and made a number of other points about the proposed reorganization; these included suggestions for 'full compensation' for those not offered employment on terms as favourable as those of their existing posts, and a request that local government staff should participate in setting up and in working the administrative machinery for the change-over. On their central point they claimed that only a body of 'overriding authority' to allocate staff to the new authorities could fairly tackle 'this complex operation'. But they recognized the real difficulties of giving such bodies power to determine service conditions and fix establishments for the new authorities since this would conflict with a cherished prerogative of local authorities.[17]

But what exactly were the fears and worries which the LCC Staff Association plan was designed to meet? There was first, the possibility of redundancy. Taking the broad view the Minister of Housing and Local Government was no doubt right to point out in the debate on the White Paper that by and large there would be no less need for the services of local government officers in Greater London.[18] But there were clearly going to be fewer posts of certain kinds – fewer town clerks, fewer medical officers of health, fewer borough engineers – and it was no comfort to men in these positions to know that there were going to be more children's officers and more chief education officers. But apart from the fear of redundancy, there was a very natural apprehension about where they would find new posts and what status they would have. A medical officer of health of a small borough, for example, might find that he could get a post in one of the new and enlarged London Boroughs but only as second or third in rank and not as chief officer. Above all, officers wanted some assurance that they would have a fair chance for the new posts. Again, this partly affected those from the smaller authorities, who might find themselves in competition with officers from much larger authorities in the same borough grouping eg Coulsdon and Purley being joined to Croydon. But it also affected those who because of a transfer of functions were liable to move from a large existing authority to a smaller new authority eg health and welfare staff going from the LCC to the boroughs, education staff transferring from Middlesex to the boroughs.

As against all this it must be borne in mind that for a great many of the staff affected changes were likely to be small. Dustmen working for St Pancras would become dustmen working for Borough No. 2 (later named Camden); clerks in the health department of Wimbledon could look forward confidently to becoming clerks in the health department of Borough No. 22 (later named Merton); and firemen of the Croydon brigade must have assumed that they would automatically become firemen under the GLC. Even so, psychologically speaking, there was need for reassurance.

The Minister of Housing and Local Government (Dr Hill) in the debate on the White Paper referred to the need to safeguard the interests of the staff and said merely 'we shall consult the employers and employed'.[19] By the time of the Lords Debate in March the idea of some impartial body to supervise in some way the transfer and allocation of staff was being actively canvassed. Several speakers referred to the staff problem and two of them (Viscount Mersey and Lord Lindgren, a former parliamentary secretary of the Ministry of Town and Country Planning) brought up the LCC Staff Association's suggestion for a commission or other body to look after the transfer. The Government spokesman, Earl Jellicoe, parliamentary secretary to the Ministry of Housing and Local Government, referred to this merely as 'a very interesting suggestion' which the Minister would pursue. He also tried to minimize the effects which the reorganization would have; he did not think that there would be 'any great disruption', or that the problem of redundancy 'is going to be such a big one in practice as it may now in theory appear'.[20]

In March the National and Local Government Officers' Association also added their voice to the proposition that there should be consultation about the administrative machinery but without putting forward any positive proposals.[21] Shortly afterwards in April the Ministry of Housing and Local Government began informal soundings on the idea of a special body to consider the problems connected with the transfer and allocation of staff. But it was not until June that a formal invitation went out to the local authorities, their associations and the various negotiating bodies in which the staff associations were concerned inviting them to attend a conference to discuss a number of matters connected with the reorganization including the possibility of setting up a special body.[22]

The invitation expressed no opinion on the merits of the proposal but merely drew attention to the matters which would need further study, including the membership of the body and, most importantly, how its proposals could be made binding.

This conference was held on 20 July and as a result of it a working party was set up to examine staff questions with representatives of all the main interests affected. It was on the basis of this working party's suggestion that the Ministry circularized local authorities and local authority associations with a memorandum on 10 October 1962 setting out the suggested form a staff commission (as it was now referred to) should take, and what its terms of reference should be. From that point onwards the history of the staff commission is largely a part of the history of the various administrative arrangements which were made to ensure the transition between the old and the new systems of local government. This is dealt with in more detail below.[23]

The fairly lengthy period which elapsed between the floating of the original idea of some kind of impartial body and the decision to incorporate in the Bill a provision enabling the Minister to establish a staff commission indicates two things. First, there was the difficulty of reconciling the desire of the staff associations, and particularly the LCC Staff Association, to have a body which could effectively influence appointments and safeguard staff interests with the traditional and jealously defended prerogative of local authorities to select and appoint their own staff. Secondly, the Ministry of Housing and Local Government seem to have adopted a neutral stand, at least in the earlier part of the period, and seemed unwilling to be drawn too closely into the discussion; no doubt this was partly because of unwillingness to appear to be interfering in matters which were primarily the responsibility of individual local authorities, and partly because there was at this stage a feeling that the problem would not prove to be as great as the staff associations feared – an approach which was reflected in ministerial pronouncements.

Planners and architects – and other problems

The gradual recognition that there was a need to provide some mechanism for safeguarding staff interests was reinforced by fears of the effects of uncertainty and delay.

When, for example, a number of the LCC's top planning officers left for other posts[24] there was a certain amount of press comment, speculating on how far these moves were due to uncertainty arising from the reorganization plan. Even if this was not the whole explanation,[25] it served to reinforce the fear that experienced professional teams, especially of architects and planners, which had been built up over the years, were likely to be broken up under the Government's plan.

The argument was that the Government had failed to make clear whether and if so how such teams were to be preserved, and that this uncertainty contributed to the general uncertainty of the staff and hence to the search for posts elsewhere. Once again it is notable that this point was raised chiefly in relation to LCC staff, and especially the group of architects there. In February, the Professor of Architecture at Edinburgh University and a former LCC chief architect, Mr (now Sir) Robert Matthew, urged the Government to ensure that the LCC architects were transferred to the new Greater London authority by giving the latter building as well as planning powers.[26] He returned to the point in May, this time widening the plan to include 'the transfer to the Greater London Council of the remaining architectural and planning staffs of the LCC and Middlesex County Councils which will be required for a continuing programme of housing and planned redevelopment'.[27] In July the *Guardian* published a lengthy article by another architect, Diana Rowntree, entitled 'The achievement of LCC architects' which laid even more stress on 'the creative organisation' which had been developed.[28]

In reinforcement of this case, both the Town Planning Institute and the Royal Institution of Chartered Surveyors in commenting on the White Paper,[29] urged that the GLC and each of the boroughs should have separate planning departments under a chief officer. The former argued that it would be 'nothing short of a tragedy' if existing planning teams were dispersed. The RICS also urged the setting up of a commission on the lines of the Civil Service Commission during the period of the transition.

It was true, of course, that both the GLC and the boroughs were likely to have a good deal of planning and architectural work. What lay behind the views expressed was uncertainty about how exactly the new system would work. The precise extent of the powers to be given to the GLC and the boroughs had not been laid down in the White Paper. It was not until August 1962, for example, that the Ministry of Housing and Local Government issued a circular specifying how housing powers were to be divided. And in the even more difficult field of planning the delimitation of powers was a continuing process which was not complete by the time the London Government Bill was prepared.

It was not simply a case of government departments failing to make up their minds with reasonable speed. For everybody concerned, including the central departments, the reorganization presented unknown hazards. This was particularly true in planning where a completely new organization and division of functions was proposed and where it was difficult to predict in advance just what kind and number of staff would be required. Nevertheless, some authorities took steps to prepare for the new system. In October 1962, for example, the Metropolitan Borough of Lambeth for the first time appointed a borough architect; he was Mr Edward Hollamby one of the LCC's senior housing architects.[30] Lambeth were clearly anticipating the day when they would form part of a London borough with greatly increased responsibilities in this field.

On many matters the central departments established contacts with the local authority associations which were to become particularly important during the long passage of the Bill through Parliament. In July 1962, for example, following the two conferences with local authorities, an inter-departmental working party was set up with the local authority associations to consider questions of finance and this body remained in being for two years. In August the Home Office and the associations set up a joint working party to consider general problems of warding in the new authorities.[31] In general, as is usual in such situations, the departments preferred to take informal soundings in the hope of getting a fair measure of agreement on the details of the proposed legislation. But some questions, and not always the most obvious ones, provoked a good deal of disagreement which could not be resolved by the time of the Bill's introduction and gave rise to debate at the Committee stage of the Bill. Typical of such disagreements was the question of audit. The Ministry of Housing and Local Government proposed that the new London boroughs should all be subject to district audit.

The Association of Municipal Corporations disagreed mainly on a point of principle that some of the existing authorities, as municipal corporations, had exercised their right to choose professional rather than district audit and that it would be wrong to take this right from them. The AMC with some reluctance, acquiesced in the Bill's provisions on this point but this did not prevent further lengthy discussion both in the Press and in the Lords' debates on the Bill.

The main impression, therefore, is of a good deal of activity, especially during the summer of 1962, with the Ministry working against time to get a Bill prepared for the autumn. On the whole there was good-will and co-operation between the central departments and the local authorities and their associations. It was after all in the interests of both sides that this should be so once it had become clear that the Government intended to go ahead with their plan. Most of this activity was, however, carried on in the background. It is the unexciting, bread-and-butter hard work of administration. So far as the general public were concerned – or at least that small minority of them which was actively following the progress of the Government's plans – it appeared that these plans were meeting increasingly bitter opposition, and not simply from the LCC and the Metropolitan Boroughs.

The Committee for London Government

Towards the end of June 1962 the formation of a new opposition body was announced. On 25th June the Committee for London Government, under the chairmanship of the Earl of Longford, came into being. 'We go into battle', he claimed,[32] 'under the title Let London Speak. We shall strive by every constitutional means to make it morally impossible for the Government to proceed'. Its first declared statement of plans included the organization of a petition with a target of no less than 500,000 signatures.

The primary object of the Committee according to its chairman, Lord Longford, was to co-ordinate the various protests made against the Government's plan and to 'present these views as forcibly as possible'. He made it clear that opposition was the mainspring of the Committee's activities and that they were less concerned about putting alternatives to the Government's plan. He stressed the non-political nature of the Committee.[33] A council of patrons had been formed which included Mr John Betjeman, Sir William Holford, Sir Stanley Rous, Sir John Summerson and Lord Beveridge, as well as politically committed opponents like Lord Alexander of Hillsborough. Sir William Holford was vice-chairman and Lord Beveridge the treasurer.

The *Guardian's* London Letter found this development encouraging 'because it shifts the arguments away from the entrenched devotions of County Hall and puts anxieties on a professional rather than a party basis'.[34] It hoped that the Committee would provide a focus of well informed opposition for those who did not wish to be identified with the LCC's rather narrow self-defence and who thought that something should be done about London's government but not on the drastic scale intended by the Government.

There can be no doubt that this anonymous comment of the *Guardian* reflected how the organizers of the Committee hoped that people would view it. In other words, it was ostensibly an attempt to get a broad front of opposition to the Government's plan which might conceivably cause the Government to change its policy or at least to delay and modify its proposals. A prime question therefore is how far the Committee succeeded in gaining the broad support of other persons and bodies who were opposed to the Government's plan. To examine this effectively it is necessary to look first at the people behind the Committee and the way in which it set about the task.

There can be little doubt that the idea originated among leading Labour members of the LCC. This does not necessarily mean that they were inspired solely by the desire to try, even at this late stage, to preserve the LCC intact. But a large element in their thinking was that since the LCC's own campaign against the Government proposals was not achieving much success, there was every advantage in trying to broaden the opposition front. However, there was perhaps some ambiguity behind the aims of the Committee. Was it to campaign mainly on the threat to destroy the LCC or to comprehend the whole reorganization plan? Was it to be mainly a vehicle of Labour opposition or genuinely non-party?

The Chairman of the Committee was of course a Labour peer and ex-Minister. He was not, however, identified in any way with local government in London although he had a well-known interest in the social services, particularly education, and was to take a prominent part in the debates on the Bill on this subject. If he was not non-party he was at least fairly non-partisan at this stage. The Committee did indeed include a fairly wide variety of interests from Sir John Wenham, a Conservative ex-chairman of Surrey County Council to Sir William Holford, the architect. But a study of the literature and tactics of the Committee suggests that its most active members were committed Labour Party men, like Mr Michael Stewart, who led the parliamentary opposition in the Commons and Mr Robert Mellish, MP for Bermondsey and chairman of the London Labour Party.[35] The secretary of the Committee, Mr L. French, was a retired LCC official and there is little doubt that the Committee's closest links were with the LCC Labour Group, the London Labour Party, and the Parliamentary Labour Party.

From the start the emphasis was on defence of the LCC. 'Let London Speak', the pamphlet put out by the Committee to explain its aims and invite support was almost wholly concerned with what was to happen to the LCC and its services. 'The Government' it said:

'has announced that it will introduce a Bill to do away with the London County Council. The social services will be broken up and spread among thirty-four new boroughs that will take the place of the present ninety-three local authorities.'[36]

The pamphlet quoted the views of various people, including the president of the London Teachers' Association and the chairmen of the Metropolitan Juvenile Courts, who were exclusively concerned with LCC services. The pamphlet ended with an appeal to 'every Londoner' to protest to his MP and to join the 'monster petition to parliament' being organized by the Committee.

The Committee might argue that the main concern of those who disliked the Government's plan was with the proposed break-up of the LCC.[37] There was some truth in this, but it was certainly not the main concern of some of the strongest opponents of the plan – in Middlesex, in Surrey and in Croydon, for example. By starting off on a markedly pro-LCC tack the Committee made it more difficult for themselves to attract the wide support of the various opposition groups. Even the 'monster petition' forms had different columns for residents in the LCC area and those outside.

Furthermore the Committee's activities had a distinctly Labour Party tone, despite the non-political claims of its launching. Pictures of Lord Longford and Mr Michael Stewart handing out petition forms,[38] the list of mayors present when the petition was eventually handed in at the House of Commons,[39] the people and bodies among whom the Committee had found strong opposition to the Government's proposals[40] – these all indicated clearly where the real strength of the Committee's support was to be found. Again, the councils which gave most support to the Committee and helped to promote the petition were predominantly Labour councils within the County of London. Only a few Conservative councils, such as Wimbledon, where there was particularly strong feeling against the Government plan, co-operated fully but in others, such as Croydon,[41] the strong feeling was tempered by a dislike of association with what was seen as a pro-LCC Labour organization. Again, although the Committee was supported financially by a number of individual donations, some as large as £500, the bulk of its support seems to have come from traditional Labour Party sources, such as the trade unions, although no public disclosure of either the amount or the source of the Committee's support has ever been made.[42]

It seems clear, therefore, that there was some ambiguity in both the aims and the tactics of the Committee. On the one hand, by presenting a common front of the opposition to the Government plan, the aim or at least the hope might be to delay the plan and to get modifications made in it by showing that the opposition was much stronger and more determined than the Government had allowed for. On the other hand it might be seen as a tactical advantage for the more bitter Labour opponents of the Government plan, particularly those on the LCC, to shift the emphasis away from an exclusively pro-LCC argument to what could plausibly be represented as a much broader opposition.

This division and ambiguity between those who genuinely looked to a broadening of the basis of the opposition and those who saw this only as a tactical move in the fight to retain the LCC was fatal to the success of the Committee. *De facto* it became primarily a body fighting for the preservation of the LCC, and because of this and because of its Labour associations it failed to do what it was ostensibly set up to do. It did not attract the really wide support which it needed, did not make the case for opposition to the Government plan as a whole, and did not make clear what positive alternative plan it supported.

On the public launching of the 'monster petition' Lord Longford announced that the aim was to get 500,000 signatures. This represented one in sixteen of the entire population of Greater London, an astonishingly ambitious target particularly in view of the fact that the Committee's main support was likely to be in the LCC area. The petition which was presented to Parliament in February 1963 contained over 171,000[43] signatures, a remarkable achievement in itself but inevitably judged by others as a failure when set against the target.

Once the Government had introduced the London Government Bill the scope for the Committee's activities was somewhat reduced. Any concessions which could be wrung from the Government now depended on the efforts of the Parliamentary Labour Party. Although it continued in being for some time after presenting the petition[44] and acted to some extent as a channel for presentation of amendments in the standing committee on the Bill, it faded away rather than died with the retirement of the secretary, Mr French, in the spring of 1963.

The Labour Party's undertaking

The Committee for London Government failed principally from a misjudgment of the situation and of the scope which existed for carrying forward effective opposition to the reorganization plan. This misjudgment almost certainly goes back to the attitude of those LCC leaders who, as has been suggested, found it hard to believe that the LCC would in fact disappear after over seventy years' existence. There remained the alternative of seeking to commit the Labour Party to repeal any legislation passed by the Government.

As early as March 1962 the London Labour Party was pressing particularly in the person of Lord Morrison of Lambeth, its retiring treasurer, for the Labour Party to declare that it would repeal any legislation based on the White Paper.[45] At the Labour Party's annual conference in October the LLP and the Surrey Federation of Labour Parties put forward a motion calling on the National Executive and the Parliamentary Party to give an undertaking that if a Labour

Government were elected before April 1965 it would repeal any legislation based on the White Paper. The motion was approved although Mr Skeffington, on behalf of the National Executive, displayed some doubts about such an absolute commitment at that stage.[46]

But by April 1963 when the Bill received its third reading in the Commons, the party had arrived at an explicit policy:

'if the change of Government occurs this year, we shall repeal the Bill. If the change of Government occurs after the new borough councils are elected, we shall halt the transfer of functions and the break-up of the social services which the Bill seeks to effect. One or other of those steps, according to time, will be necessary, and will be taken so as to reserve to a new Government the right and the power to recast the government of London in a manner truly in accord with the needs of the time.'[47]

At the time there was a real possibility that the next general election would be held in 1963 and that Labour would be returned to power. From the point of view of Sir Isaac Hayward and his colleagues there was thus a hope that the LCC would be preserved. Even so, it was a slender hope, largely because of the question of timing. After an autumn election in 1963 it would just have been possible for a newly elected Labour Government to have rushed through a measure repealing the London Government Act. After that point the risks of confusion and chaos were likely to increase greatly if any attempt were made to introduce fundamental changes.

Sir Keith Joseph becomes Minister of Housing and Local Government

In all these uncertainties and difficulties for the Government, a political event totally unconnected with the preparations for the London Government Bill yet had a considerable significance for the political struggles which lay ahead. In July 1962 the Prime Minister, Mr Harold Macmillan, decided on a wholesale reconstruction of his Cabinet. In the process no less than seven cabinet ministers, many with long records of service to the Macmillan and previous Conservative administrations, resigned in favour of younger men. Thus Mr Selwyn Lloyd the Chancellor of the Exchequer and Sir David Eccles, the Minister of Education, departed and Mr Reginald Maudling and Sir Edward Boyle were promoted in their place.

Dr Charles Hill, the Minister of Housing and Local Government, was one of the ministers who resigned. At fifty-eight he could not be regarded as old, and indeed as Viscount Hill of Luton he was later to demonstrate his vigour first as chairman of the Independent Television Authority, and then as chairman of the Governors of the BBC. Nor in his brief spell at Housing and Local Government had he conspicuously failed in his task. His departure was rather a sign of the general Macmillan policy than a mark of failure.[48] The point was brought home by the appointment of Sir Keith Joseph to replace him. Fourteen years younger than Dr Hill and a member of parliament only since 1956 his rapid rise to cabinet rank was notable.

From the point of view of the Government's London Government Bill, the change was fortunate. Dr Hill had seemed curiously aloof from the Government's London policy. Sir Keith Joseph had no such inhibitions. Whatever the reasons for the Government's original commitment to the reform of London's local government, he seemed to be in no doubt that the London Government Bill was a radical, reforming measure and ought to be supported for that reason. From the Government's point of view the timing of his appointment could hardly have been better. In July 1962 the Bill was in an advanced stage of preparation. What was needed was someone who could get it through the tough parliamentary battles which lay ahead. Sir Keith took up the task with enthusiasm. This coupled with a great capacity for hard work, enabled him to sustain the initiative throughout the long debates and disputes on the Bill. *The Times* was right to regard the Bill as the 'main legislative battlefield',[49] for the 1962–63 Session. With the appointment of Sir Keith Joseph the Government acquired a formidable protagonist on that battlefield.

10
The London Government Bill

A lengthy and complex measure

The London Government Bill which was introduced on 20 November 1962 was not only the major piece of legislation of the 1962–63 Parliament. The scale and length of the proceedings on it were reminiscent of some of the controversial post-war nationalization measures introduced by the Attlee Labour Government.

Some idea of the length of the proceedings may be gained from the following. After the normal two-day Second Reading debate in the Commons for an important Bill, Clause 1 and Schedule 1[1] were taken in Committee of the whole House; two days were spent on this but failed to complete it. The Government then introduced an Allocation of Time Order (the 'guillotine') under which a further two days were spent on this part of the Bill. The remainder of the Bill was then referred to a Standing Committee which spent twenty-one sittings on it, the Allocation of Time Order requiring the committee stage to be completed by 21 March 1963. Two days were then allotted to the remaining stages of the Bill.[2] The Bill then went to the Lords where the proceedings were also lengthy although not as prolonged as in the Commons. A supplementary Allocation of Time Order was made on 25 July 1963 to limit debate in the Commons on the Lords Amendments to one day. The guillotine had only once before been applied to consideration of Lords Amendments, on the Transport Bill of 1953 when there were seventy Amendments. On the London Government Bill there were 280. As the leader of the House (Mr Iain Macleod) pointed out, 'twenty per cent of the time which we have taken in legislation on the floor of this House has been spent on this Bill, and that is not to mention the twenty-one Committee sittings upstairs'.[3] Altogether, the Bill was in progress for over seven months.[4]

At first sight it may seem surprising that the Bill should have had such a lengthy and tortuous course. London government hardly seems the kind of issue to arouse political passions in this way. The first and major reason for this situation lay in the Labour Party's commitment to make this a major political issue, inspired by their twin beliefs that local government services would suffer if the LCC were broken up; and that the Conservatives were mainly motivated by a determination to end the long period of Labour control at County Hall. Nevertheless, although this basic political issue is bound to form the centrepiece of any discussion of the London Government Bill, two other points were of considerable importance in determining the nature of the parliamentary proceedings on it. In the first place, it is a mistake to think of the Bill as presenting a cut-and-dried blueprint of the new system of London government. Rather it was one stage in the lengthy process of creating the new authorities and defining their responsibilities. Secondly, by its very nature the Bill was inevitably complex and liable to give rise to many detailed problems of drafting and interpretation.

The London Government Bill was concerned with an entirely new structure of local authorities in Greater London, involving changes in both areas and functions. Ideally no doubt the Bill should have defined precisely what the various authorities in the new system were to do. In many matters it did, but in many others, including some of the most important, the position was left uncertain or subject to determination by ministerial order. Furthermore, the very novelty of many of the proposals meant that there could be significant argument about the precise role of different bodies or about the nature and constitution of the new authorities even within the general framework of the Government's plan as set out in the White Paper. All this was a legitimate subject for differences of view and argument in the course of the Bill's passage through Parliament.

The second point is connected with but distinct from the first. Perhaps the most important reason for the complexity of the Bill was the fact that numerous Acts of Parliament dealing with the activities of local authorities had to be applied to the new and changed situation in Greater London. Hence there were many provisions in the Bill itself and in the numerous detailed Schedules modifying and amending a large number of Acts. No doubt the vast majority of these provisions were legal trivialities, such as the insertion of 'the council of a London borough or the Greater London Council' in a definition of highway authorities[5] or substituting 'London boroughs' for 'Metropolitan Boroughs' as authorities responsible for duties under section 1 of the Prevention of Damage by Pests Act, 1949.[6] But not all these provisions were simply consequential upon the major division of functions provided for in the Bill. In some cases questions arose about how best to apply the provisions of other Acts to London, in other cases it was a question of whether and if so how existing provisions relating specially to London should be applied in the new Greater London situation. Again, in some matters the Bill omitted to include certain provisions which ought to have been included. All this meant that the Bill had to be closely scrutinized since all these points would affect the powers and duties of the new local authorities. It was also an important factor in the large number of Government amendments which were put down during the course of the Bill's passage through parliament.[7]

Distribution of functions

From what has been said earlier about the attitude of the LCC's Labour leaders, it might be expected that the Labour Party would adopt two main lines of attack. One was to try to secure the retention of existing services provided by the LCC and the other counties; the other was to try to delay the operation of legislation to reform London government. Both these approaches were made. The London Government Bill was, however, particularly controversial in its proposals for the division of functions, not only between the GLC and the boroughs[8] but also in the role assigned to the central departments. The anxieties, particularly of those with a professional concern in different local government services, about whether the Bill would lead to an improvement in the provision of those services frequently coincided with the Labour Party's approach and served to reinforce the opposition to some of the Government's specific proposals.

A straightforward example concerns the children's service. Both the Association of Child Care Officers and the Residential Child Care Association disliked the Bill's proposals to transfer this service to the boroughs and they advocated that at least the LCC service should be preserved on the lines of what was proposed for the education service. This coincided exactly with the Labour Party's view.

There was a more complex situation in the Bill's provisions dealing with the major services which were to be shared between the GLC and the boroughs, especially planning, traffic and highways, and housing. Here the issue, as seen by many professionally involved in these services as well as by outside observers, was whether the GLC would have sufficient powers to enable it to carry out adequately its strategic role in the government of Greater London. Since a major reason for changing the structure of local government was the need for an effective Greater London authority this was a critical issue. Its understanding requires a brief reference to the Bill's provisions in these functions.[9]

In planning, the Bill made the GLC the planning authority for Greater London as a whole and the boroughs the planning authorities for their own areas. The effect was to make both the GLC and the boroughs responsible for the preparation of development plans. The GLC's plan, to be known as the Greater London Development Plan (GLDP), was to 'lay down considerations of general policy with respect to the use of land in the various parts of Greater London, including in particular guidance as to the future road system'.[10] The borough plans were to be prepared subsequently to the GLDP and within the framework provided by it.

A different division of powers was proposed for development control. Here the boroughs were to receive all applications for planning permission with complete freedom to decide them with one important exception: for development 'of such a class in such area of Greater London as the Minister may by regulations prescribe' the boroughs were to have no function other than the transmission to the GLC of planning applications which they received and decisions on these applications were to be made by the GLC.[11]

Under the Bill's provisions there was a three-fold division of responsibility for roads. Existing trunk roads were to remain the responsibility of the Ministry of Transport; a new class of roads, to be known as 'metropolitan roads', was to be the responsibility of the GLC and for remaining roads the boroughs were to be the highway authorities. Metropolitan roads were not defined but listed in a Schedule to the Bill; generally speaking they were the important traffic-carrying routes other than trunk roads.[12]

Powers in relation to traffic were, under the Bill's provisions, largely shared between the GLC and the Minister of Transport. The GLC had a general duty to secure 'the expeditious, convenient and safe movement' of traffic, but did not have the exclusive power to make traffic orders dealing with such matters as one-way streets. Not only did the Minister retain the power to make orders concerning trunk roads, but he could revoke or vary any order made by the GLC; and he could direct the GLC to make an order or could prohibit them from making an order.[13]

In housing, the GLC was to have powers for building outside Greater London, eg under the Town Development Act, 1952. Within Greater London they could only build with the consent of the borough concerned, or, failing that, with the consent of the Minister of Housing and Local Government.[14] Important transitional provisions allowed the GLC to inherit the LCC's powers (notably in slum-clearance) and stock of housing. It was intended that both should in due course go to the boroughs, who were in general to be the housing authorities in Greater London.[15]

To some people the Bill seemed to confirm their fears that:

'this new authority seems all too likely to find itself ground between the millstones of 'borough primacy' and close Government supervision. Will the Greater London Council really be able to initiate major new policies, or will it function as a sort of ghostly middleman between town hall and Whitehall?'[16]

It is hardly surprising that the Town Planning Institute should have found the Bill's proposals inadequate; they particularly criticized the planning provisions as not giving the GLC adequate powers to safeguard the GLDP 'against proposals which may be prejudicial to its main objects'; and they thought that it was wrong that the Minister of Transport should retain control of trunk roads.[17] But their criticisms were widely voiced by many others.

The Greater London Group of the London School of Economics saw the development plan proposals as diluting the effectiveness of the GLC as the over-all planning authority and as likely to lead to as much friction between the boroughs and the GLC as was found under the existing system; similarly they thought that the 'dual control' of highways and traffic management with the Minister and the GLC exercising concurrent powers would 'seriously inhibit' the latter from 'realizing its true potentialities'.[18] The Royal Institute of British Architects saw the prospect of 'interminable correspondence' between the GLC, the boroughs and the Minister in the Bill's planning proposals; and wanted better means of ensuring that the GLC could effectively integrate highway planning with the other elements in the development plan.[19] *The Times*, too, which consistently supported the reform of London government argued that the GLC needed stronger planning powers and that the retention of powers by the Minister of Transport 'makes nonsense of the GLC's responsibilities'.[20]

Proposals aimed at strengthening the GLC's powers were, therefore, put forward by a number of bodies. They were also set down in the form of amendments to the Bill by the Labour Party at the Committee stage. At first sight, this seems surprising if, as has been suggested, a major aim of the Labour Party was the preservation of the existing system and, particularly, of the LCC. In part, it may be explained as a tactical move, to throw the weight of the official opposition behind some of the strongest criticisms of the Bill; in part, it reflected a pragmatic view of the situation. Although the Party argued that a GLC was unnecessary, nevertheless, they had to consider what the practical consequences would be if the Bill were passed. From that point of view they tended to favour a strong GLC taking as their model the strong LCC in the existing system.[21]

The government, on the other hand, for a number of reasons were reluctant to see too strong a GLC. In part this reflected departmental caution, as in the Ministry of Transport's desire to retain concurrent powers in the traffic field. In part, it was bound up with a fear that if the GLC were made too powerful this would weaken the aim of making the boroughs the primary units of local government for the performance of functions. This was not simply a question of Conservative philosophy favouring the small authority,[22] but was connected with the Government's view of the kind of reform which they had undertaken.

It was an essential element in the Government's plan that the GLC was not to be a superior authority in the sense that in the existing system the counties were the superior authorities in relation to the county districts. The boroughs were to be viable and effective units in their own right. Thus not only should they be fully capable of performing the functions which were exclusively assigned to them, but they should also have a well-defined sphere of responsibility in those functions which of necessity had to be shared between the GLC and the boroughs. The compromise plan over education had already weakened the first of these aims; hence Mr Brooke's attempt to limit the area of the central area education authority and his successor's insistence on a review of the arrangement in order to give the boroughs more say in education. To the extent that more powers were given to the GLC at the expense of the boroughs, this element in the Government's plan would be weakened further. It was likely, therefore, that in looking at the precise distribution of functions the Government would incline towards strengthening the powers of the boroughs.

Conversely, the Opposition viewed the strengthening of the GLC not only as providing a better means of dealing with certain problems, but also as further serving to cast doubt on the effectiveness of the Government's plan. It must not be forgotten, however, that the fundamental question was what was the right division of powers between the central departments, the GLC and the boroughs which would enable the new authorities most effectively to deal with London's local government problems. There was not necessarily a single or indeed a simple answer to this question. But around it revolved much of the debates on the London Government Bill.

In considering now in more detail some of the main issues which were raised in those debates, attention will be drawn not only to the party political battle but also to the influence of other bodies who sought amendments. Three main groups of bodies were involved: the local authorities and their associations; the professional bodies such as the TPI and the RIBA; and the staff associations. As is usual with a major Bill they used various means of persuasion to publicize their views and, if possible, get them accepted as amendments to the Bill. They issued memoranda, circularized members of parliament, had correspondence and discussions with the government departments, and sent deputations to ministers.

One other group played an important part in the Bill's proceedings. This consisted of a number of Conservative back-benchers who in varying degrees disliked the Government's proposals; some, like Sir Cyril Black and Mr Frederic Harris, were so opposed to the proposals that they voted against the Government on a number of occasions; others mainly sought to modify the Bill so far as it affected their own area.[23]

The new authorities

Right from the start the Opposition indicated that they would seek to delay the Bill. When the Order for Second Reading was made on 10 December 1962 Mr Mitchison sought a ruling from the Speaker that this was a Hybrid Bill;[24] the effect of such a ruling would have been to subject the Bill to a lengthier procedure than that of a Public Bill. His arguments were rejected by the Speaker.[25]

Again, when the Bill proceeded to the Committee stage, the first amendment moved by the chief Opposition spokesman, Mr Michael Stewart, was on the relatively trivial question of whether charters

G

should be granted to the new inner London Boroughs to be formed from the Metropolitan Boroughs. Labour members kept the debate going for a whole hour and then forced a division on the amendment.[26]

But there were a number of issues connected with the constitution of the new authorities which aroused controversy; on some of them Conservative back-benchers were almost as critical of the Government proposals as the Opposition. One was the number of borough councillors. The Bill limited each borough to a maximum of sixty councillors. The Government had secured the agreement or at least the acquiescence of the local authority associations to this proposal,[27] but it was heavily criticized in the House both because it would reduce drastically the number of councillors and because it would make it difficult for the boroughs to deal adequately with their functions.[28]

Although Sir Keith Joseph argued that it was right to limit the size of councils since, as policy-making bodies they should not be too large,[29] the Government's majority on two amendments on this point fell to twenty-eight and twenty-six although their overall majority at the time was over ninety. Two Conservative members (Mr Frederic Harris and Mr Ronald Russell) voted against the Government and a number of others, including Captain Litchfield (Chelsea) and Dr Alan Glyn (Clapham), abstained. It was a test case, not only of the Opposition's determination to fight but of the strength of feeling of some of the Conservative back-benchers. As Mr Harris put it: 'Everything which has been said this afternoon supports my view that this is a bad Bill.'[30]

The Government seem to have been surprised by the strength of opposition on this issue. More predictable were the many debates which took place on the question of borough groupings. These provided opportunities for both Conservative and Labour members to deploy familiar arguments either for different groupings or for the exclusion of their own areas from Greater London altogether. On the latter the Government stood firm until the very end;[31] on the former, Sir Keith Joseph was in something of a dilemma. On the one hand he must have been under pressure from his own cabinet colleagues to make some concessions to try to placate the Conservative back-bench critics; on the other he had little room for manœuvre if he was to preserve the essential pattern of London government laid down in the Bill.

A good example is Wandsworth. Sir Hugh Linstead, the Conservative member for Putney, consistently pressed the Metropolitan Borough's claim to keep its identity intact as a London Borough under the new system rather than be split as proposed in the Bill. Sir Keith Joseph went to some lengths in trying to find a way of reconciling this claim with those of the neighbouring Boroughs of Battersea and Lambeth, even though it was evident from the report of the town clerks that it was practically impossible to achieve what Wandsworth wanted and still maintain a satisfactory pattern of boroughs in South London. In the end, therefore, no change was made.[32]

On most other issues concerning the constitution of the new authorities the Government had an easier passage. Under the Bill, both the GLC and the boroughs were to be constituted much like other local authorities. The GLC was to be much like a County Council, although with some special features deriving from the LCC[33]; the London Boroughs were to be Municipal Corporations. Consistently, the Government retained aldermen in both authorities,[34] although pressed by some members (eg Mr Eric Lubbock, the Liberal spokesman) to take the opportunity for reconsidering the traditional local government pattern.[35] In a similar way, the Government resisted suggestions that GLC councillors should be paid, on the grounds that this was a general local government issue and not specific to London.[36]

Several difficulties arose over the arrangements for elections to the new authorities. Some of these involved a straight political challenge to the Government and were resisted for that reason. In particular, there were Opposition arguments for postponing the first elections of the GLC and the boroughs from spring 1964 to some specified later year such as 1965 or even 1967. Given the political realities of the situation in 1963 when these questions were debated, the effect could well have been to delay the elections until after a Labour Government had gained power, with the possible consequence that the whole reorganization programme would then have been drastically modified or abandoned altogether. The Opposition argued that there was not enough time to have properly organized elections by the spring of 1964 and also that the Government had no mandate for the reform proposals.[37] Sir Keith Joseph chose the occasion of a debate on one of these amendments to attack the Opposition's general attitude: 'Here we are embarking on what is an old project to improve local government in London and we find the most backward-looking, retrograde, ossified resistance at every turn.'[38]

There were however other points on the elections which gave rise to more widespread doubts. It was, for example, proposed in the Bill that the first election for the GLC should be on 9 April 1964 and for the boroughs in May; and that the second election for both the GLC and the boroughs should take place in 1967, and possibly on the same day;[39] all the existing councillors were to retire. This raised the question whether triennial elections (as for County Councils) were to be preferred to the annual elections found in boroughs, with one third of the councillors retiring each year. More importantly, it raised the question of whether the difficulties of holding both GLC and borough elections on the same day outweighed the advantages. This was not a party political issue as such, although clearly it was an issue in which the political parties had a close organizational interest. But it turned essentially on whether the electors were more likely to be confused than to have their interest stimulated by simultaneous elections for the GLC and the boroughs. The Opposition moved an amendment in the Lords which would have had the effect of postponing the second GLC election to 1968 to avoid having Borough and GLC elections in the same year and *a fortiori* on the same day. This however caused some confusion since in the Commons amendments had been moved to postpone the second election for both GLC and Borough councillors from 1967 to 1968 on the quite different grounds that the three-year term should be taken as beginning on 1 April 1965 when the first councillors were to take over their full responsibilities.[40] On all these points the Government stood firm on their original intentions.

Traffic and highways

The rather different character of the debates on Part II of the Bill dealing with road traffic, highways and motor vehicles was indicated by the tone adopted by Mr Mellish, one of the principal Opposition speakers, who said:

> 'It has been conceded by all, even those of us on this side of the Committee who did not want to see a Greater London Council come into being, that one good thing that could come out of such a body is that it would have ultimate responsibility for traffic and highway management.'[41]

However, it soon became apparent that on the crucial question of the respective powers of the Ministry of Transport and the GLC there was a sharp difference of view. The Opposition pressed amendments which would have had the effect, first, of limiting the minister's powers to make traffic regulation orders to cases where the GLC had failed to perform their functions;[42] secondly, of transferring responsibility for trunk roads from the Minister to the GLC. In both cases they were closely following the views of the LCC.

It was not only the LCC which thought that the Bill did not fulfil the intentions of the White Paper that

'ultimate responsibility for traffic management and main roads should be placed on the Greater London Council.'[43]

As has been indicated, a number of professional bodies, and independent observers with such widely varying outlooks as the Royal Institute of British Architects, *The Times* and the Greater London Group had seen the two questions raised by the LCC as major weaknesses in the Bill's provisions.

The Government had gone a little way towards meeting these criticisms. They had put down an amendment specifying that the Minister of Transport's powers to give directions to the GLC or himself to make traffic orders were not to be exercised

'unless he is satisfied that circumstances exist which make it necessary for him so to do in order that the matters aforesaid may be secured, or may be secured only, in a manner and to an extent which is proper.'[44]

But the obscurity of the language[45] reflected the Government's dilemma. Although willing to entrust powers to the GLC they hesitated to entrust 'ultimate responsibility' to a local authority. Mr John Hay, parliamentary secretary to the Ministry of Transport, did not disguise this. 'It is true', he said,

'that the Greater London Council will be a big local authority, the largest in the country, but I remind the Committee that it will still be only a local authority. It will, however, be a new local authority, and it will obviously take time to acquire experience and knowledge in this new field of traffic management. . . . It is inevitable . . . that in this field of traffic management one makes mistakes, and if mistakes are made, as they probably will be by the Greater London Council, it is right that the Minister of Transport should have the power to intervene if necessary.'[46]

This reflected the cautious attitude of the Ministry of Transport in the face of the new situation provided by the creation of a new kind of urban authority. This was most evident on the other major point discussed on this part of the Bill, the question of trunk roads. Mr Mellish, in his forthright way had urged for the GLC:

'let us give it some real authority and make it the highway authority in every sense of the word.'[47]

In reply Mr Hay agreed that

'it may well be that in the course of time entirely different arrangements will be made. . . . As the local authorities are reorganized it may well prove highly unsatisfactory, and indeed, illogical, to leave the trunk roads unchanged.'

But he gave two reasons why it was not proposed to make changes under the Bill. The first was that it would be wrong to make such changes under the Bill when there were adequate general powers for doing so under the Highways Act, 1959. The second and more substantial reason was that it was necessary first to carry out 'a comprehensive review' of the position of trunk roads in London; this would have to await the results of the London traffic survey; furthermore, 'it is important that the views of the Greater London Council itself should be known here', not least because of the financial implications.[48]

Housing and planning

On housing and planning powers the Government were much more positive in their approach. The main question here was how powers should be divided between the GLC and the boroughs.

In housing, slum-clearance powers provided a classic illustration of the Government's dilemma over conceding that the boroughs could not adequately perform functions which had been assigned to them.[49] The bill gave these powers to the boroughs.[50] The Opposition argued that in some boroughs the problems were so great that they would require the GLC's help. The Government replied that this was unnecessary and that the boroughs would have adequate resources for this purpose.[51] The Opposition's argument owed a good deal to the strong views expressed by the LCC.[52] There was, as the Lords' debate best indicates,[53] a clear-cut difference of view here. But influencing both sides in the debate were the unspoken thoughts about the effect on the plan of reform of altering the balance of powers between the GLC and the boroughs.

Planning powers raised even greater difficulties. The first amendment argued at length by the Opposition would have deleted the provision in the Bill making the boroughs local planning authorities, but would have required the GLC, as the planning authority, to delegate certain planning powers to the boroughs. This amendment had been suggested by the LCC which saw the proposed division of responsibility in the preparation of development plans as 'inefficient and bound to lead to conflict and delay', and feared that the boroughs' powers to deal with most planning applications would deprive the GLC of the means of ensuring that its plans were effectively carried out.[54] In this amendment the Opposition had a good deal of support from outside bodies.[55]

Mr Skeffington, the Labour spokesman, in arguing for this amendment, spoke of the need for having the GLC as the 'major partner' in planning and particularly urged that it should have the power to 'call in' planning applications which were important to the carrying-out of the development plan.[56] In his reply Sir Keith Joseph referred to the difficulties of delegation, as suggested in the amendment, but staked his main argument on a question of principle:

'we conceive the Greater London Council not as a higher authority but as a wider authority than the London Borough. We see the London Borough not as a lower authority, but as an authority with narrower powers.'[57]

In other words, although the Government recognized that the GLC's strategic planning role would require it to take a wider view than the individual boroughs, they were not prepared to give the GLC power to over-rule the boroughs. In the all-important matter of planning control, for example, only certain specified types of application (to be detailed in regulations), were to be referred by the boroughs to the GLC for decision,[58] and for the rest the boroughs were to have complete discretion to decide applications in the same way as planning authorities in the rest of the country.

Perhaps the Government's underlying philosophy appeared most clearly in relation to another planning problem which had aroused a good deal of concern. The central area of London with its unique status as political, administrative, commercial and cultural centre posed planning problems which differed in kind from those of other parts of Greater London. Under the London Government Bill, responsibility for planning, other than in the broad terms of the Greater London Development Plan, was to be split between the City of London and several boroughs.[59] A number of professional bodies had expressed alarm at this prospect, among them the RIBA[60] and the TPI.[61] Common to these criticisms and of others who shared the viewpoint of these professional bodies[62] was the idea that the central area should be planned as a whole, whether by the creation of a single borough for the area[63] or by making the GLC the planning authority for the area.

This was certainly no party political issue; the argument for unified planning of the central area was put in the Commons by Sir Hugh Lucas-Tooth, Conservative MP for Hendon, a former junior Minister and a staunch supporter of the Government on the Bill. But it was in the Lords that the arguments were most fully deployed, and here the Government had to face the challenge of Lord Conesford[64] and Lord Salter,[65] both Conservative peers, as well as Lord Silkin, the former Labour Minister of Town and Country Planning. The Government's answer was in effect to argue that the Bill made adequate provision for the GLC to

'control and guide the main lines of development in London'

and that they had got the balance between the GLC and the boroughs 'about right'.[66] As in the case of housing, the government's inclination towards giving the boroughs rather than the GLC powers made them stand firm on planning, even though there was a considerable body of opinion in favour of strengthening the GLC.

Children, health and welfare

The most sustained attempt by the Opposition to have the Bill modified occurred on Clause 48 which made the boroughs the children authorities in Greater London. An Opposition amendment to set up an inner London children authority to correspond to the Inner London Education Authority[67] occupied practically two whole sittings of the Commons Standing Committee. The arguments were familiar and had already been thoroughly aired.[68]

There were three important elements in the situation. First, there were fears and doubts about what would happen to the children's service under the Bill's proposals. They had been voiced earlier by the chairmen of the Metropolitan Juvenile Courts and were now increasingly being voiced by professional associations, such as the Association of Child Care Officers, which circularized MPs on the subject.[69] Secondly, these doubts were particularly concerned with what was to happen to the LCC Children's service, and the LCC itself pressed strongly for its retention on a similar basis to education. At the same time, there were also arguments put forward in favour of retaining the Middlesex service.[70] Thirdly, what gave impetus to the arguments against the Government's proposals was that no strong positive case was made out for the contention that the London Boroughs would make more effective children authorities than the existing Counties and County Boroughs.

This last point needs to be elaborated. Government spokesmen certainly argued that there were advantages in having smaller units for the children's service and, more particularly, that close links with other borough functions, particularly health, welfare and housing, were desirable. But they seemed to be very much on the defensive. Miss Mervyn Pike,[71] for example, argued not that the new system would necessarily be any better but

'we are going to have this problem solved, if not as well as under this present centralized system, at least as satisfactorily as can humanly be done.'[72]

In the Lords Earl Jellicoe argued at somewhat greater length the case for the boroughs and especially the advantages of linkage with other borough services. But the emphasis was rather that 'given the over-all pattern of this Bill' it was right that the children's service should go to the boroughs.[73] Similarly, Miss Pike stressed 'The Bill is not about children; it is about good government.'[74] The reasons for the Home Office's attitude and for the Government's resistance to preserving the LCC children's service have already been discussed.[75]

The opposition did not argue for retention of the existing personal health and welfare services. It was common ground between the Government and the Opposition that the boroughs were capable of running part at least of these services.[76] Indeed, the LCC had in 1955 itself put forward proposals for devolving certain of the personal health services on the Metropolitan Boroughs.[77] The claim which was now put forward by the Opposition based on the strongly expressed views of the LCC,[78] was that more time was needed for the transfer of these functions. They therefore proposed that the GLC should remain responsible for these services in inner London but should prepare a scheme of delegation of powers to the boroughs for the period 1965 to 1970 and of outright transfer to the boroughs on 1 April 1970. But behind the Opposition's concern 'that there should be reasonable time so that this can be done smoothly and without loss of efficiency'[79] lay the fact that had the Opposition succeeded in postponing the transfer of these services to the inner boroughs, it would have been easier for them to halt the reform plan if the next general election brought them to power, to the extent of maintaining intact the London County Council.

This political fact was implicit in the amendments put down by the Opposition which would have left the transfer to the outer boroughs to take place on 1 April 1965. If there was a case for delaying the transfer in inner London there was also a case for doing so in outer London. Admittedly it was less strong since the Metropolitan Boroughs, unlike the boroughs in outer London,[80] did not take part in the existing administration of the health and welfare services. But this was only a matter of degree.[81]

Education

The Government had to contend with two difficulties over their education proposals; to justify the different systems in inner and outer London, and to explain the nature and object of the review of the Inner London Education Authority[82] which was to be held by 1970.

The Opposition first tried to get the inner London system extended to the whole of Greater London. The effect of their amendment would have been to make the GLC responsible for education but acting through five separate, specially constituted area committees.[83] Appropriately enough, this amendment was introduced by Mr Pargiter, Labour MP for Southall and a long-standing member of Southall Borough Council and Middlesex County Council.[84] During discussion of the amendment, which occupied more than a whole sitting of the Standing Committee, the Opposition made it clear that what they were seeking was to have education in outer London handled by authorities larger than the boroughs, and not necessarily for precisely the areas indicated in the amendment.[85]

The Government spokesman, Mr Chataway, Parliamentary Secretary to the Ministry of Education, admitted that both the Minister

(Sir Edward Boyle) and his predecessor (Lord Eccles) had seriously considered a scheme on the lines of that put forward by Mr Pargiter. Lord Eccles himself, speaking in the Lords on another amendment, indicated that he favoured larger education authorities.[86] The amendment was supported by the County Councils Association; indeed the Opposition spokesman in the Lords, the Earl of Longford, disarmingly conceded that much of the argument he was putting had been supplied by the CCA.[87] But, significantly, there seems to have been little pressure from teachers or other bodies to have the Bill amended in this way. The London Teachers' Association, for example, had won the most important part of what they wanted in the proposal for an ILEA; teachers elsewhere in Greater London were neither as well organized nor as single-minded in their aims. Some fears were expressed about the difficulties of allowing free movement of pupils among twenty education authorities and a memorandum on this subject of the Catholic Education Council was freely drawn on by speakers in the debates.[88]

Nevertheless, on educational grounds, as Mr Chataway had admitted, it was a matter for argument whether the outer boroughs were large enough to be effective authorities. For the Opposition, this question assumed greater importance because of its implications for the Government's whole reform plan. One Conservative member, a former junior minister (Dame Patricia Hornsby-Smith) claimed that the amendment was a Trojan horse 'designed to wreck the whole purpose of the Bill'.[89] What she had in mind was what Mr Brooke had had in mind in resisting Sir David Eccles' attempts to preserve the LCC education service. The Government's original plan had been weakened by the admission that, for special reasons, the boroughs in inner London were not suitable units for running education services. It would be weakened still further if it were conceded that none of the boroughs was suitable. This lent added significance to the debates on the amendment which the Government were bound to resist.

The proposal in the Bill for a review of the administration of education in inner London was attacked by the Opposition who moved an amendment to delete it. In this they were following the views of the LCC and of those who had originally argued for the retention of the LCC education service.[90] Apart from the fact that it created uncertainty, the proposal aroused suspicion that it was merely a delaying tactic allowing the Government an opportunity at a later date to break up the LCC education service. The wording of the Bill did not allay that suspicion.

Clause 30 (5) began:

'The Minister of Education, shall carry out, and not later than 31st March 1970 lay before Parliament a report on, a review of the administration of education in the Inner London Education area for the purpose of determining to what extent, in what part or parts of that Area, and subject to what conditions, if any, all or any of the functions of the local education authority relating to education should be transferred to, or to a body including a member or members appointed by, the appropriate council, that is to say, as respects the City the Common Council or as respects an inner London Borough the council of that Borough.'

On the face of it the wording implied that the review would only be concerned with the transfer of education functions to the boroughs, and excluded the possibility of retention of the ILEA. When pressed by the Opposition on Second Reading,[91] Sir Edward Boyle went to some length to try to dispel this implication, first by claiming that the wording had been misinterpreted and that the words 'if any' should be taken as applying to the phrase 'to what extent' as well as to the following phrases, and secondly by arguing that it was mistaken to suppose that

'there must be a presumption that education will itself become a borough service after the review. . . . It will be perfectly open to the Government of the day to advise Parliament in 1970, if they so decide, that the balance of advantages lies in retaining a single local education authority in the inner London area . . . this decision, when the time comes, will be taken purely on educational grounds on the basis of what is best for education in inner London.'[92]

This explicit statement seemed to be at variance with what Dr Hill had said in originally announcing the review that it was to be about 'the arrangements for borough participation in education administration'.[93] Moreover, it was only on the Report stage and after strong pressure that the Government agreed to amend the wording of the Clause to read:

". . . for the purpose of determining *whether, and if so* to what extent, in what part". . . . etc.

and this became the wording of the act.[94]

On the same day as Sir Edward Boyle made his explicit statement, Mr Enoch Powell, the Minister of Health, wound up the debate for the Government. He had this to say about the review:

'The review will relate to the question whether the inner London Boroughs will be able in future to participate more fully or directly in the administration of the education service. It would be wrong that we should at this stage close our minds entirely to the possibility that we can find some effective way of bringing the boroughs who will be administering all the other human and personal services, still more closely into contact with the administration of education.'[95]

Mr Powell's emphasis was much more in line with what Dr Hill had said than with what Sir Edward had said.

These differences reflected differences of view within the Government. Sir David Eccles and his successor, Sir Edward Boyle, would have preferred, on educational grounds, to see the ILEA retained permanently. The review was a concession to the views of Mr Brooke[96] and his successor, Dr Hill, who disliked the ILEA because it did not fit into the system of local government which they had devised, and in which they had already conceded, largely on education grounds, that there should be larger boroughs. Sir David Eccles saw the review as a means of considering how best, from an educational point of view, to organize education in inner London. Dr Hill saw it largely as a way of trying to end the anomaly whereby the boroughs in inner London had scarcely any say in education.[97]

In Committee the Opposition pressed an amendment to delete the review provision. The Government were able to resist this pressure although Mr Chataway was given an uncomfortable time, particularly over the question of whether the review was to be undertaken only on educational grounds. As the Opposition pointed out, this was the only part of the London reforms which was to be subject to statutory review. Even some Conservative members were critical and two of them, Mr Compton Carr (Baron's Court), a member of the LCC Education Committee, and Dr Glyn (Clapham) abstained when the amendment was put to the vote.[98]

Staffing

Two important provisions in the Bill related to the terms of transfer of officers and to the establishment of a staff commission. The staff associations, and in particular the LCC Staff Association, sought to have both these provisions strengthened. In the original Bill the Minister had power to make orders dealing with transfers containing 'provisions for the protection of the interests of such persons'.[99] The association tried to get an amendment[100] which would ensure that the terms and conditions of the new appointment 'shall not be less favourable' than those held immediately before the transfer.

The Government themselves put down an amendment conceding this request in relation to conditions of service; as regards salaries, however, transferred officers were to receive salaries not less than they were previously receiving only if they were to be engaged 'in similar duties' to those which they had had before. Sir Keith Joseph argued that compensation arrangements would be available for those transferred to jobs which were not comparable to those previously held.[101] He also indicated how far the Government had gone in trying to meet the wishes of the staff associations, both by the proposal to set up a staff commission,[102] and by going a long way towards ensuring that officers employed by any of the authorities affected should have continuity of employment.[103]

The LCC Staff Association had a particular interest in trying to ensure that the GLC, like the LCC, maintained distinctive arrangements for negotiating salaries and conditions of service. The LCC was not a party to the Whitley Council machinery under which other local authorities and staff associations negotiated. Instead it negotiated directly with the LCC Staff Association and other associations representing LCC staff. As a result both the grading structure and salary scales of the LCC differed from those of other local authorities. The LCC Staff Association induced the opposition to put down an amendment which would have given the GLC staff the same terms and conditions of service as LCC staff had from 1st April 1965 until new terms and conditions had been negotiated.[104] Although the amendment would not have committed the GLC to an LCC-type negotiating machinery as a permanent arrangement, it would have tended to strengthen the LCC Staff Association's hands, to the evident fear of the National and Local Government Officers' Association who were anxious that this question should not be prejudged.[105]

The LCC Staff Association also sent a deputation to the Minister, Sir Keith Joseph, but he resisted the amendment largely because he was unwilling to be drawn into this particular argument between staff associations, or to seem to be taking sides. Nevertheless, the amendment was carried against the Government at the committee stage in the Commons, two Conservatives (Mr Jenkins, the member for Dulwich and Dr Alan Glyn, the member for Clapham) voting with the Opposition. A number of other Conservatives, including Mr Barter (Ealing N) and Captain Walter Elliott (Carshalton) abstained. This somewhat surprising result seems to have been the result more of lack of appreciation of what lay behind the amendment[106] than a deliberate attempt to change government policy. The amendment was deleted from the Bill on Report stage.

This incident illustrates the limits to which the Government were prepared to go. Nevertheless, there is no doubt that they were willing, indeed anxious, to meet the staff associations' points as far as possible. In the Lords one of the chief opposition spokesmen, Lord Latham[107] said:

'I should like to express my gratitude [on behalf] of the staff for the reasonable and sympathetic way the Government are dealing with this question of transfer.'[108]

Sir Keith Joseph, in particular, seems to have gone out of his way to be conciliatory. In part, this was because he appreciated that the successful accomplishment of the reorganization depended on the willingness of the staff; in part, because he recognized that there was a strong case in equity for ensuring fair treatment for staff involved in a considerable upheaval. After the Bill was passed, he continued these efforts by addressing both the LCC Staff Association and NALGO, the latter at a remarkable mass meeting in the Royal Albert Hall.[109]

Statutory appointments of chief officers brought the Government a different set of problems. The Bill required the GLC and the boroughs under general local government legislation,[110] to appoint a clerk, a treasurer, and a surveyor; and the boroughs also a medical officer of health and public health inspector. In addition the GLC was required to appoint a director of traffic.[111] The anomalies of this situation led to claims for other statutory appointments to be made. The Town Planning Institute, for example, urged that the GLC should be required to appoint a chief planning officer.[112] The Royal Institute of British Architects wanted boroughs to appoint architects.[113]

Surprisingly the RIBA succeded in convincing Sir Keith Joseph. In introducing an amendment, he stressed the importance of the development work which the boroughs would have to undertake, and the necessity that this work should be under the charge of an architect. But, as Mr Skeffington pointed out, it was difficult to see why architects were thus singled out when housing managers, for example, were not.[114] Sir Keith conceded that this was indeed 'a slippery slope' and did not make an altogether convincing case for the amendment which was nevertheless accepted.[115]

However when Sir Hugh Lucas-Tooth later moved an amendment to include a planning officer among the appointments which the GLC were to make, Sir Keith argued that it was better to leave the GLC discretion in the appointment of chief officers, apart that is, from the traditional statutory appointments. Mr Mellish pointed out that in that case it was clearly illogical to have included specifically in the bill statutory provision for a director of traffic. Sir Keith could do little more than promise to reconsider the whole matter.[116]

The 'first fruit', as he called it, of this further consideration was an amendment at report stage to delete the obligation on the GLC to appoint a surveyor, leaving the clerk and the treasurer as the only general statutory appointments required to be made. In this way, he avoided the pressures to make statutory appointments of a chief architect or a chief planner. This amendment was accepted.[117]

It seems clear that Sir Keith Joseph also put some pressure on his Cabinet colleague, Mr Marples, to get rid of the provision relating to the GLC's director of traffic which now appeared even more anomalous. In this he succeeded, at least to the extent that the Government moved an amendment in the Lords which substituted a requirement that the GLC should 'make arrangements to the satisfaction of the Minister of Transport' for discharging their traffic functions.[118]

The result of these various changes in the Bill was that it left the requirement on the boroughs to appoint an architect as the only 'non-traditional' statutory appointment. But Sir Keith Joseph, having yielded to the persuasiveness of the RIBA, could not be induced by all Lord Morrison's eloquence to get rid of this anomaly and take the provision out of the Bill again.[119]

Financial arrangements

The Government ran into further trouble with their own supporters over some of the financial proposals in the Bill, particularly the arrangements for transitional assistance from the GLC to the counties of Essex, Hertfordshire, Kent and Surrey. The Bill proposed that if in these counties the additional rate burden resulting from the re-organization exceeded a 6d rate in 1965–66 the GLC was to meet this excess additional cost on a sliding scale viz the whole cost in 1965–66 tapering to one-fifth in 1969–70. Surrey County Council found a sympathetic ear in some of the Conservative members of the Committee on the Bill for their view that these proposals were not sufficiently generous to the affected counties. Sir John Vaughan-Morgan[120] moved amendments which would have obliged the GLC to meet the whole additional cost falling on the counties and not merely that in excess of a 6d rate; and which would have tapered the payments over twelve instead of five years on a diminishing scale. The opposition took the argument still further by proposing that these payments should fall not on the GLC but on the Exchequer on the grounds that the whole reorganization was something imposed on the local authorities by the Government.[121]

The Government spokesman, Mr Corfield, stood firm on the general principle that 'this is essentially a local government expense',[122] and that therefore there was no question of these expenses falling on the Exchequer. But clearly he (and Sir Keith Joseph) felt the need to make some concessions, particularly as he frankly admitted that neither the figure of 6d nor the period of years had been carefully worked out. He therefore promised to look at both again, but with the important reservation that the Government were not prepared to abolish the rate bar altogether, only to consider reducing it. This did not at all satisfy Sir John Vaughan-Morgan who voted against the Government and threatened to raise the matter again. Despite his protests, a Government amendment to reduce the 6d to 5d and extend the number of years of the tapering process from five to eight was agreed without a division on Re-committal of the Bill.[123]

One other financial issue which was raised caused the Government more trouble than perhaps they had expected. This was the question of audit. Before the Bill was introduced the Government had met strong pressure from the Association of Municipal Corporations to maintain the right of boroughs to choose either the district audit system or audit by a member of one of the recognized bodies of the profession.[124] In resisting this and providing in the Bill that the London Boroughs should come under the general local government system for district audit, the Government had apparently satisfied the AMC that this carried no implications for the future of borough rights in the rest of the country. The question was not, however, left there. It was raised in *The Times* in a letter from the president of the Institute of Chartered Accountants urging that the London Boroughs be given the same freedom of choice as boroughs elsewhere. It was also raised in the Lords by such formidable figures as Viscount Colville of Culross and Lord Reith. But the Government were not prepared to yield.[125]

Both these financial questions illustrate the difficulties of carrying through a scheme of municipal reform affecting so many different interests. So too did another problem which the Government must have regarded as of comparatively minor importance until it found itself subjected to pressure from the British Medical Association. This was the problem of future executive council areas in Greater London. These areas usually corresponded to the areas of local health authorities ie Counties and County Boroughs. The BMA was strongly opposed to the creation of thirty-two EC areas and pressed the Minister of Health to say specifically that there should be only five or six, each covering the area of more than one London Borough.[126] On the Commons report stage of the Bill a rather lengthy debate took place, although there was no real disagreement between the Government and the BMA on the principle that there should only be a limited number of EC areas, and subsequently the boroughs were grouped in five such areas.[127]

Metropolitan Police

Among the questions which had been excluded from the Herbert Commission's terms of reference was responsibility for police. The Opposition made sure that this question would be debated by putting down amendments, the effect of which would have been to transfer responsibility for the Metropolitan Police from the Home Secretary to the GLC.[128]

The Opposition's argument was essentially that since elsewhere local authorities exercised powers in relation to the police, to make the GLC responsible for police in Greater London would be 'a logical, practical, common-sense and sound administrative step'.[129]

The Government resisted this proposal largely on the grounds that the Metropolitan Police differed from other police forces in having special responsibilities and national functions which justified the Home Secretary's having responsibility for it.[130] These were familiar arguments. They had indeed been recently presented by the Royal

Commission on the Police which had concluded that there were 'overriding advantages in a unitary system of control over the police in the metropolis and also that, in view of the exceptional police responsibilities in London, control should be in the hands of the Government'. They did not see proposals for the reorganization of local government as a reason for changing this view.[131] Whatever the merits of the arguments advanced for change, the Government were clearly unwilling to embark on further lengthy and controversial discussions on an issue which, thanks to the Royal Commission on the Police, they were content to regard as closed.

Epsom and Ewell

Nothing perhaps sums up the nature of the tortuous and controversial proceedings on the Bill better than one small incident which occurred at a very late stage indeed. It has already been pointed out that the Government had to fight a number of troublesome battles with their own supporters as well as the Opposition over the areas of the new authorities. There were long rearguard actions fought mainly by Surrey Conservatives to try to secure the exclusion of a number of fringe areas, such as Coulsdon and Purley, and Epsom and Ewell. Dr Hill, it will be recalled, had decided that the latter was to be cut in two, the northern part being in Greater London, the southern to remain in Surrey. This decision had not been well received by the borough council, and there was a considerable amount of local feeling and agitation to have the northern parts of the boroughs also retained in Surrey.

An amendment was proposed by Mr Chuter Ede[132] on the Committee stage in the Commons and again by Lord Auckland in the Lords, to take the remainder of Epsom and Ewell out of Greater London. These amendments, like all similar amendments, were resisted by the Government; they could hardly do otherwise since no new facts or arguments were put forward to support them and the situation had not changed since the lengthy discussions of early 1962.[133] Once again on the Report stage Lord Auckland, supported by Lord McCorquodale of Newton, a former Conservative MP for Epsom, pressed the same amendment; once more Earl Jellicoe rehearsed the Government's arguments against it. But on this occasion the combination of dissident Conservatives and Opposition Peers was just enough to turn the vote against the Government.[134] The

Government could have reversed this decision when the Commons came to consider the Lords' amendment in July. They did not do so. The weariness and strain of months of argument and counter-argument got the upper hand. They decided to let Epsom and Ewell remain outside Greater London.

Conclusion

On 31 July 1963 the London Government Bill received the Royal Assent, and the reform of London government entered a new phase, the phase of translating the Act's requirements into a practical organization ready to take effect from 1 April 1965. Although many amendments were made to the Bill during its passage through Parliament, the London Government Act as it emerged did not differ fundamentally from the original Bill. But two parts received important modifications. In the part relating to highways and traffic functions some clarification and re-definition of the respective powers of the GLC and the Ministry of Transport was introduced, and in the part dealing with the position of the staff stronger safeguards were introduced. The debates did, however, serve to emphasize not only the nature of the political disagreements about the Bill's purpose, but also the extreme difficulty of reconciling different interests and viewpoints to produce a satisfactory local government system within the general framework of the Government's plan.

11
The Transition to the New System

The first elections for the Greater London Council were held on 9 April 1964; those for the London Boroughs on 7 May. The new authorities assumed their responsibilities on 1 April 1965. Thus, nearly a year in the case of the GLC and less than eleven months in the case of the London Boroughs was available to the new authorities for taking decisions on important questions such as committee and departmental structure, recruitment of staff and arrangements for the transfer of properties, documents and equipment from the old to the new authorities. The old authorities meanwhile continued in being until 31 March 1965.

But although 1964–65 was the period of most intense activity with the old and the new authorities existing side by side, the transition to the new system took place over a much longer period than this. Well before April 1964 preparations were being made, particularly in relation to staffing and the transfer of functions.

The following account will concentrate on problems arising from the transfer of functions and in staffing. It should be borne in mind that there was a marked degree of continuity in the people who were concerned with the introduction of the new system. Some information on this, so far as it concerned local government officers, is given in the section on staffing, but it was also true that the members elected to serve on the new authorities in 1964 were for the most part also members of the old authorities. Of the 100 GLC councillors elected in 1964, for example, 72 were members of either the LCC (36), Middlesex (18) or one of the other authorities out of which the GLC was constituted. The position was similar in the boroughs; in Tower Hamlets and Westminster, for example, 46 of the 60 councillors were in each case members of the constituent authorities, as were most of the aldermen. Taking councillors and aldermen together it was rare in the boroughs to find less than two-thirds of the members coming from the constituent authorities.

One effect of this situation was that it was very largely the same people who had to keep services going in the old authorities at the same time as they were setting up the new. In an important sense, therefore, these members and officers were, especially in the period 1964–65, a bridge between the old and new system of local government.

It is true that they were frequently faced with new and unfamiliar tasks; councillors in Stepney or Acton, for example, had no experience of running a children's service. Nevertheless they provided an essential link in the transitional period.

The joint committees

The 1963 Act provided[1] that where authorities were to be amalgamated they could set up joint committees to consider the transfer arrangements. The Minister had power to require the setting up of these committees. It was further provided that the borough joint committees might have representatives of the counties as well as of the authorities which were being amalgamated. Under these provisions a joint committee was set up for the GLC and for each of the new London Boroughs formed by amalgamation from existing authorities.

Like all joint committees of local authorities, these bodies had no power to commit their constituent authorities, and their recommendations therefore were only advisory. Moreover, these formal joint committees were not the only means by which negotiations took place between the various authorities concerned. On the transfer of functions, for example, and particularly the transfer of county functions to the boroughs, difficult problems arose which could not be handled by the joint committees alone. In these cases functional committees or working-parties were set up parallel with the territorial joint committees, but presenting their recommendations to them.

Greater London Council Joint Committee. The committee had 27 members, as follows:

London County Council	6
Middlesex ,, ,,	6
Essex, Kent and Surrey County Councils	3 each
Croydon, East Ham and West Ham County Boroughs	2 each

The chairman of the committee was Sir Isaac Hayward, the leader of the LCC and the vice-chairman Mr Horace Cutler, the leader of the Middlesex County Council. The committee was broadly concerned with two questions, the GLC's functions and its organization. Sub-committees were set up to consider each of these questions. The committee was set up immediately after the 1963 Act was passed, and produced a series of reports by April 1964.

With regard to the services taken over from the Counties and County Boroughs, the Committee took the view that there were two stages, assimilation and subsequent reorganization and rationalization. They thought that there would be comparatively few difficult problems in the initial stages of assimilation and that rationalization would have to be undertaken by the GLC in the light of actual experience of operating the services.

Nevertheless, the committee made some recommendations on standardizing existing practices. Often, these consisted in taking the best of these practices as the standard. For example, in the initial training of ambulance staff they suggested that the LCC's eight-week training scheme should be adopted but also including part of Croydon's practical training work.

But among the immediate problems which the Committee felt that the GLC would have to face in taking over these services probably the most prominent was that of shortage of staff. For vehicle licensing, for example, the Committee estimated that 1,100 staff would be needed whereas not more than 700 would be available from the existing authorities. They hoped that the GLC would be able to recruit further staff from these authorities. Again, in the field of traffic management the committee thought that there was likely to be a considerable shortage of staff; to help in meeting this they suggested that arrangements should be made with the Ministry of Transport for seconding staff for a period as well as for recruiting from the London Traffic Management Unit.

The sub-committee on GLC organization suggested that initially, when questions of integration were likely to be prominent, ten committees would be needed with twelve members each. With the comparatively small number of members of the authority, it was felt that there would need to be considerable delegation of powers to officers. But even at this early stage it was recognized that there were likely to be many difficult problems in regard to the GLC's committee and departmental structure. A further task of the sub-committee was the drafting of standing orders for the new council.

The GLC Joint Committee, although it did much useful preparatory work, seems generally to have been somewhat tentative in its approach. It held few meetings and on the whole was anxious to leave the new authority to settle the more important questions. This is particularly evident in its insistence on the distinction between the immediate problems of assimilation and the longer-term problems of rationalization in the operation of services.

London boroughs joint committees

There were great variations in the dates at which borough joint committees were set up. In some areas the initiative was taken long before the London Government Act was passed; in others, despite ministerial and other exhortations, committees did not come into being until some time after. Bromley's, for example, was set up in January 1962 but Enfield's not until September 1963 and Newham's in October 1963.[2]

Among the reasons for early action the most obvious was pressure exercised by those, particularly senior officers, who were most conscious of what needed to be done in a comparatively short space of time. The Association of Metropolitan Town Clerks and the Home Counties Branch of the Society of Town Clerks were at an early stage prominent in these moves. In May 1962 they set up a joint working party which produced reports offering guidance on the establishment of joint committees and warding and electoral arrangements. Individual town clerks and other senior officers, however, often had to act in the first place through informal contact with their opposite numbers in the other constituent boroughs as a means of initiating action towards the appointment of a joint committee.

The main obstacle to joint action was hostility on the part of one or other constituent council to the reorganization proposals. This sometimes persisted until well after the Bill was launched on its long parliamentary career. So strong was the feeling against the Government's proposals in some areas that meetings of officers of the amalgamating authorities were held in secret to prepare the ground for what they saw to be inevitable work arising from the reforms.

Warding was one of the first questions which had to be considered by the joint committees and settled before elections for the new boroughs could take place. The number of councillors had to be agreed, within the maximum of sixty laid down by the Act; following this, a scheme of ward boundaries for the area of the new borough had to be drawn up. Proposals on both these matters had then to be submitted to the Home Secretary for inclusion in the charter or incorporation order of the new borough.[3] There were often differences of view, particularly over the question of warding, between the constituent authorities which resulted in compromise arrangements, each of the constituent areas of the new borough having a different ward-basis.[4]

A second immediate issue which also had to be settled for inclusion in the charters or incorporation orders was the choice of a name for the new borough. In a letter to constituent authorities in June 1963 the Minister of Housing and Local Government proposed three conditions: names should be short and simple, should have local associations, and should not be hybrid or composite. Suggested names were to be approved by the minister. In a number of cases and especially where a large authority was amalgamating with a much smaller one there was little dispute (eg Croydon for the amalgamation of Croydon and Coulsdon and Purley; Islington for Islington and Finsbury). But where disagreement did arise it was often prolonged, and in some cases bitter, arousing local passions which were reflected in the columns of the local press. The merger of Chelsea and Kensington was an example, each borough wanting to preserve its own name. The Minister suggested that Kensington might be the most appropriate name for the new borough. 'This' said the Mayor of Chelsea 'has no chance of willing acceptance in Chelsea'.[5] Pictures of shoppers queuing up in King's Road to sign petitions under the headline 'Chelsea on the march: don't scrap name'[6] underlined the point. The borough was finally called 'The Royal Borough of Kensington and Chelsea' a marked defeat for two of Sir Keith Joseph's three principles.

Elsewhere Sir Keith was better able to resist pressures to preserve historic names. Neighbouring Hammersmith and Fulham, for example, after considering twenty suggestions at two meetings of the joint committee were unable to agree but finally accepted the Minister's proposal to call the borough Hammersmith.[7] But it was not until January 1964 that all the names were finally settled.

Apart from these two questions which had to be settled before elections could be held in May 1964, joint committees had the opportunity to examine other questions which would face the new authorities when they had been elected. Committee and departmental structures, staffing requirements, allocation of physical assets and financial arrangements were all matters on which the new authorities would need to take action. Some of these questions were not simply the concern of the joint committees. Staffing requirements, for example, depended in some cases on decisions about how functions were to be transferred from the counties to the boroughs, and also involved the staff commission.[8] Nevertheless, the progress which the joint committees had been able to make by May 1964 depended essentially on the same factors as governed the speed with which they had been set up in the first place. Where constituent authorities were in harmony and not distracted by attempts to oppose the reorganization plan, joint committees were set up early and were able to make considerable progress.

In the Bromley group[9] for example, the joint committee at an early stage asked the treasurers of the constituent authorities to prepare a joint report on the possibility of bringing financial policies and arrangements into line with one another. The possibilities included standardization of accounting systems, of rate levying and collection, and of housing rent policy. After much hard work on the part of the treasurers in examining and analysing the different policies and practices of the authorities, and after intensive consultation and negotiation between the joint committee, committee chairmen of the constituent authorities, and treasurers and other chief officers, agreement was reached on all three of these financial questions.

The transition to the new system was made much easier by agreements such as those at Bromley. Few other joint committees made as much progress. The standardization of housing rent policies throughout the new borough area is an example of a particularly controversial question where joint committees often failed to agree. But this example also illustrates a wider issue. Joint committees were inevitably limited to advice and persuasion. Even if there was agreement on the joint committees, therefore, about what was to be done it did not follow that the new authorities would accept their recommendations. And where the joint committee failed to agree the question was in any case remitted to the new authority for decision.

Nevertheless, joint committees were a vital element in the transitional arrangements. Continuity is again important here. Members of joint committees tended to be leading members of the constituent authorities; they often became as a result of the May 1964 elections, leading members of the new boroughs.[10] It was unlikely in such circumstances that recommendations of joint committees would be rejected out of hand by the new authorities.

Again, even where joint committees had not reached agreement, or where the new authority came to a different conclusion from the joint committees, the latter's work was not necessarily wasted. A great deal of indispensable information was assembled by the joint committees, often on the most basic subjects, such as the amount and location of office accommodation.[11] It has to be remembered that the task of assembling it fell on local government officers, as an addition to their normal duties. Joint committees were indeed a part of the additional burden which the transition to the new system imposed on both members and officers, not only those most directly involved but all down to the humblest clerk who had to search out information. More than one joint committee acknowledged the debt which they owed to their officers in carrying out work, often in their own time.

Transfer of functions

There were three categories of functions subject to transfer arrangements. The simplest category was that of the assimilation of functions common to the merging authorities. At borough level, many of the environmental health services, parks and libraries fell mostly into this category. At GLC level, they included the fire and ambulance services. A second category consisted of functions, such as planning, traffic and highways where the novel division of powers between the GLC and the boroughs gave no precise guide for the administrative and other arrangements which would be needed.

The third category consisted of those functions which were to be transferred from the counties to the London Boroughs and, especially, the personal health, welfare and childrens services, and, in outer London, education.

Problems of staffing loomed large in all three categories and these are, for the most part, considered separately below. Perhaps the most acute problems apart from staffing, arose in the transfer of services from the counties to the boroughs. This was because it is more difficult to divide up a service which has been provided over a wide area than it is to amalgamate services in a larger unit, as has historically been the main trend in local government. An especially difficult problem was how to allocate children's homes. These had been provided on a county basis; the problem was to ensure that each new London Borough had a fair and reasonable share of the available accommodation. An examination of this problem will indicate the nature of the difficulties and the steps which were taken to meet them.

It must first be noted that the difficulties were not the same in each county. London and Middlesex had to arrange a complete transfer of all their homes. The 'severed counties' (Essex, Kent and Surrey) had to balance the needs of the new authorities against their own diminished needs. Even within these two groups there were variations. In the case of the LCC, not only had homes been sited within the county without regard to borough boundaries but some were in other parts of Greater London or outside Greater London altogether; moreover the LCC had a number of very large homes. These facts created greater problems in the County of London than in Middlesex. In Surrey, the distribution of homes between the parts to be included in Greater London and the parts outside was more uneven than in Essex.

The initiative in proposing arrangements was very largely in the hands of the counties. This was inevitable since they alone had the detailed knowledge and experience of the service in their areas. Nevertheless, in London especially the boroughs were not entirely passive; and the Home Office had a close concern[12] both in the principles governing the transfer of the service and in trying to achieve a reasonable balance between an equitable system and one which was administratively easy to operate.

In London, the Metropolitan Boroughs' SJC like the LCC initially refused to assist Government departments in the preparation of the Bill. But once the Bill had been published, the MBSJC authorized the officers to open discussions with the LCC officers on the arrangements which would need to be made. The LCC too although still firmly opposed to the Government's plan had now reached the point where they tacitly accepted the need to plan for the new situation which the Bill created.

From these preliminary discussions the MBSJC in November 1963 circulated to the joint committees of the inner boroughs a memorandum setting out proposals for the transfer of the health, welfare and children's services. At the same time agreement was reached with the LCC that three joint working parties of officers of the LCC and the MBSJC should be set up, one for each service, to prepare detailed arrangements for the transfer. These working parties, meeting frequently from late 1963 to March 1965 not only agreed detailed schemes for the transfer of these functions but produced memoranda setting out the nature of the services, their problems, current policies and likely future development, designed to assist borough members most of whom would probably have had no experience of these services. The MBSJC also sent their memorandum of proposals to the Ministry of Health and the Home Office in October 1963. The November 1963 memorandum included a provisional allocation of residential children's establishments to the twelve inner London Boroughs. The basis of allocation was an estimate of the number of places in these establishments needed by each borough. Each of the establishments belonging to the LCC was then allocated to individual boroughs to give them the required number of places. An exception was made for certain establishments, usually the large children's homes or those providing more specialized accommodation. These were allocated to one borough with provision for a specified number of places to be made available to one or more other boroughs.

As the following summary table indicates, the effect of these proposals was to create a very complicated pattern. No borough's needs could be satisfied simply by the establishments which were allocated to them, and all had a share in accommodation allocated to other boroughs. Furthermore, some of this shared accommodation was situated outside Greater London altogether. One large children's home, for example, with over 350 places and situated in Surrey was allocated to one borough with four others sharing the accommodation provided. Only one borough (No. 6) had all the accommodation which was allocated to it within its own boundaries, and only one (No. 11) had no accommodation allocated to it within its own boundaries. Between these two extremes there was a great variety of arrangements.

Proposed allocation of children's homes and other residential accommodation

Borough	Allocated to Borough				Borough has use of Accommodation		
	Within Borough	Elsewhere in Greater London	Outside Greater London	Total	Within Greater London	Outside Greater London	Total
1 (Westminster)	3	1	7	11	8	6	14
2 (Camden)	2	1	2	5	6	6	12
3 (Islington)	4	0	6	10	7	3	10
4 (Hackney)	1	3	2	6	6	1	7
5 (Tower Hamlets)	2	3	2	7	5	2	7
6 (Greenwich)	10	0	0	10	7	1	8
7 (Lewisham)	4	4	1	9	9	2	11
8 (Southwark)	1	5	4	10	9	1	10
9 (Lambeth)	3	7	1	11	6	1	7
10 (Wandsworth)	8	2	7	17	5	0	5
11 (Hammersmith)	0	2	4	6	7	5	12
12 (Kensington and Chelsea)	1	5	3	9	8	4	12

Names of boroughs are those subsequently agreed for them.

In the other counties allocations were generally suggested by the County Councils to the joint committees or new authorities. The usual basis was a calculation of the number of places needed by each borough from information about the proportion of children in care who had originally come from each borough area. So far as possible, establishments situated in the borough were then allocated to each borough to give the required number of places; if that were not possible establishments outside the borough were allocated to make up the deficiency. In Middlesex, in marked contrast to London, this method resulted in only two boroughs (Ealing and Brent) having homes allocated to them which were situated in another borough. In the counties which were split (the 'severed counties') there was often more difficulty because of the uneven distribution of homes and the need to ensure that both the boroughs and the reduced counties had sufficient accommodation. Merton, for example, formed from Mitcham, Wimbledon and Merton and Morden, inherited only one home within its own boundaries and three in parts of Surrey outside

Greater London with joint-user arrangements for two homes in other London Boroughs formed from Surrey.

Complex arrangements thus had to be devised to give the new boroughs an initial allocation of children's homes. Nor was this the only problem in the transfer of the children's service. The arrangements under which the new authorities should assume responsibility for children who were in care on 1 April; the degree to which continuity of care of these children could or should be maintained by the transfer of field-worker teams as a whole to the new boroughs; what staff would be needed and where they were to come from. These and similar problems had to be resolved during the transitional period.

Again, the health and welfare services provided another distinct set of problems among which the allocation of homes and other premises was prominent. Here after much discussion the Ministry of Health recommended[13] that some (eg maternity clinics and health visiting premises) should be transferred on a geographical basis and some (eg mental health premises, residential accommodation for old people) on the basis of the authority mainly using them, with arrangements for sharing where necessary.

The main difficulty for those, whether civil servants or members or officers of local authorities, who had to find practical solutions to the problems of transferring the health, welfare and children's services was that they had no guide to follow. No transfer on this scale from large authorities to smaller had ever taken place before. Much new information had therefore to be obtained (eg on the extent to which each of the new borough areas would require children's services) and different possibilities (eg of allocation of homes) explored and discussed before an agreed plan could be put forward. Even when the mechanics of transfer had been agreed there was still much to be done in making the new authorities aware of their new responsibilities.[14]

Two things are particularly important about these arrangements for the transfer of functions. The first is that they were successful in enabling the new boroughs to take over the services from 1 April 1965. This after all was the primary and immediate object to be achieved. Whether the best means were devised and what were the implications for the future operation of the services do not concern us here. They belong rather to the assessment of the working of the new system.

Secondly, these arrangements constituted a considerable burden of work, more especially on the senior officers and members who were concerned in them. To begin with, a great many additional meetings of committees and working parties were needed. These involved not only those who attended the meetings but the clerical and other staff who had to service them. The transfer of functions, like the activities of the joint committees, generated an enormous quantity of minutes and memoranda. Moreover, the preparation of these documents was often no simple matter; it involved much internal discussion and provision of information. It is probably no exaggeration to say that every single officer at least among the headquarters staff concerned with these transferred functions played some part in the preparations for the transfer. All this was in addition to the normal work of ensuring that the services were carried on until the date of hand-over. No doubt some activities were curtailed or deferred – 1964–65 was not a year in which the old authorities were disposed to make innovations in these services – but much of the activity of running services such as these is inescapable. Somehow time had to be found and was found for the extra meetings and discussions, the additional calculations, the supplementary memoranda. But the strain was great.

Staffing: Setting up the Staff Commission

An outstanding fact about the arrangements for the introduction of the new system of London government was the seriousness attached by the Government to safeguarding staff interests. In addition to the appointment of a staff commission, the 1963 Act provided that every member of existing local authority staffs should be transferred (on 1 April 1965) to one or other of the new authorities on terms and conditions of service not less favourable than those which he had enjoyed before. The new authority would either offer him a permanent job or declare him redundant; in the latter case (and also if the job offered to him was less well paid than his previous one) he could seek compensation.

Sir Keith Joseph emphasized his personal commitment to staff concerns by accepting invitations from both the LCC Staff Association and NALGO to address meetings and answer questions without having any of his civil servant advisers present.[15] The questions put to Sir Keith were frank and the discussions spirited.[16] The meetings must have been something of an ordeal for the Minister but they achieved their purpose in convincing the staff that a genuine effort was being made to provide reasonable safeguards for them.

As was shown above,[17] the idea of an independent body to oversee the staffing of the new authorities had gradually come to be accepted by the Ministry of Housing and Local Government in the course of 1962. In July 1962 a working party with representatives of the Ministry, local authorities and staff associations was appointed to prepare detailed proposals. These were embodied in a memorandum 'Suggested Establishment of a Staff Commission' circulated by the Ministry on 10 October 1962.

This memorandum was fairly well received by local authorities, although a few of the Metropolitan Boroughs felt that there was no need for such a body, and a good many of the boroughs and urban districts feared that its powers would encroach on the traditional prerogative of local authorities to choose whom they should employ. It was on the basis of the memorandum that the statutory provisions relating to the commission were drawn up. As finally agreed[18] they required the Minister, after consulting local authority and staff associations or individual local authorities, to establish within one month of the passing of the Act a Staff Commission:

(1) to consider and keep under review the arrangements for recruiting staff by the GLC and the London Boroughs, including the transfer from existing authorities;
(2) to consider staff problems referred to them by the Minister;
(3) to advise the Minister on the steps necessary to safeguard the interests of the staff.

The Minister was to have power to give directions to the Commission about their procedure and to local authorities about supplying information and about carrying out the Commission's advice.

These statutory provisions were not agreed without a certain amount of argument. In particular, the staff associations pressed for amendments during the proceedings on the London Government Bill to get the powers of the Commission strengthened. They wanted the Minister to be obliged to give directions to local authorities if so requested by the Commission. Quite apart from the Minister's objection that this would make him 'the mere agent of the Staff Commission', the local authorities would have strongly resisted something which further encroached on their independence of action.[19] The Minister did accept however, that it was essential for him to have

H

the power to require authorities to give information to the Commission.

The membership of the Commission was announced on 2 May 1963, that is, before the London Government Bill had passed through parliament. They began work immediately, an indication of the urgency of their task.[20] Of the three members of the Commission only one had local government experience,[21] a fact which had caused the AMC to argue strongly beforehand but without avail for a fourth member with borough experience.

The question of the Commission's staff also caused some difficulty. Sir Keith Joseph, following the working party's suggestion, said in the course of proceedings on the Bill that it was proposed that they should have a full-time staff 'seconded to them mostly from local government'.[22] The Commission, however, had persuaded the Minister that it would be simpler to have a small secretariat drawn from the civil service; in addition they appointed a single local government adviser, the recently retired city treasurer of Westminster 'who could share fully in our deliberations'.[23]

These preliminaries are not without importance. The Staff Commission was a new kind of body in local government, which had to find a satisfactory organization for the job and at the same time secure the confidence of local authorities and staff associations. But the real test was in how they set about their task.

The staff commission's procedure

Apart from teachers, residential staff and manual workers, about 50,000 staff were involved in the reorganization, and their transfer had to be arranged within a comparatively short period.[24] To determine the principles on which an orderly transfer could take place was an urgent and immediate task. Following informal discussions during the summer of 1963, the Commission on 23 August 1963 issued their first circular,[25] requesting the joint committees to provide estimates of the staffing requirements of the new authorities.

This request for basic information caused some difficulty, particularly in the case of the county services which were to be transferred since the joint committees had very little data or experience to go on.[26] Furthermore, the need for adequate consultation with the staff associations meant that the original deadline fixed by the Commission of the end of November had to be extended to the end of December.

The resulting statistics, inadequate as they were, led the Commission to the conclusion that there was 'little likelihood of redundancy, except perhaps at the higher levels'.[27] Indeed, further investigation during 1964, when the new councils were in a better position to make forecasts, indicated that there were likely to be shortages of staff, especially for services being transferred from the peripheral counties to the boroughs.

These peripheral counties (Essex, Kent and Surrey, and, to a small degree, Hertfordshire) were required to allocate to the boroughs county staff employed on transferred functions. In the Commission's words 'some friction arose' between the county councils and the boroughs because of the counties' own shortage of staff which 'made it impossible for the counties to transfer the numbers of staff which the boroughs considered were necessary to man the services coming to them'.

The Commission concentrated to a large extent on the problems of appointment procedures and deployment of staff. At the same time they set definite limits to their activities; they did not see it as part of their functions to exercise pressure on the counties to make more staff available since this would have gone beyond their role as guardians of staff interests. It would moreover have meant challenging the counties' assessment of their needs. The Commission depended for their effectiveness largely on persuasion. Most of their proposals were arrived at after much consultation with the authorities and the staff associations before being embodied in circulars either issued by themselves or, in the case of more important matters such as the appointment of chief officers, by the central departments.

Their methods and approach are illustrated by the question of filling vacancies in existing authorities. So far as the second-tier authorities were concerned the Ministry and the Commission, following discussions with the AMC and the MBSJC suggested that vacant posts should first be made available to staff in the authorities which were to constitute the borough group; failing this, advertisement should be restricted to Greater London.[28] But later the Commission conceded that in some cases national advertisement would be necessary; they sought however to get local authorities to seek their permission before advertising nationally and to give precedence to London-employed staff.[29]

The local authorities found this procedure irksome and cumbersome particularly where, because of national shortages, there was little chance of recruiting suitable staff locally. After much debate the Commission agreed that for certain specified categories of staff local authorities could advertise nationally without seeking permission but giving preference to candidates from Greater London.[30]

This relatively minor issue showed clearly the kind of difficulties which the Commission were to be faced with and particularly the inherent conflict between fairness to existing staff and the freedom of local authorities to make their own appointments. The conflict arose again in relation to the procedure to be adopted for the appointment of chief officers to the new authorities. Here, the Commission established as a major principle that the field of recruitment should be confined to Greater London except where there were essential reasons for going farther afield.

So far as the Greater London Council was concerned, the method of appointment was relatively simple. For chief officers and deputies first consideration was to be given to staff from the London and Middlesex County Councils and, where appropriate (eg in the fire and ambulance services) to those from the three County Boroughs also. If the GLC were unable to make an appointment on this basis they could advertise but were to give preference to London applicants. They could also adopt this latter method from the outset for posts for which there was no equivalent in the existing authorities (eg head of the traffic department).[31] Similar arrangements were made for staff below the level of deputy, the GLC in certain cases seeking agreement from the Commission to advertise.

In the case of the boroughs the Commission recognized that different circumstances might apply to different chief officer posts. They did not therefore recommend a single method of appointment.

Thus in the case of *clerks, treasurers, surveyors and chief education officers,* councils were to consider first applications from officers within their own areas including county council staff, but were required before making short-lists to consider also applications from elsewhere in Greater London, these latter being channelled through the staff commission. Only if no suitable candidates were found in London could an authority approach the commission for permission to advertise.[32] 28 clerks, 30 treasurers and 26 surveyors came from constituent authorities and the remainder from elsewhere in Greater London; 18 of the 20 chief education officers came from Greater London and 2 from outside.

Medical officers of health. There was a greater problem here in that although all existing authorities had medical officers of health they were responsible in the second-tier authorities mainly for environmental health services, whereas the new boroughs' health services would be largely concerned with the personal health services which were to be transferred from the counties. The BMA argued strongly that each borough should have both a MOH and an associate MOH, one an ex-county officer and the other an ex-borough (or district) officer.[33] The Commission considered it 'inappropriate' for them to recommend this, presumably because they regarded it as encroaching too much on the boroughs' freedom to appoint.[34] On the other hand, the county medical officers were naturally apprehensive that the best jobs would tend to go to the borough and district officers who were on the spot and known to the authorities.

The procedure, recommended by the Commission and agreed by the Ministry of Health[35] gave some safeguard to these county officers. It provided that each borough post should be open to medical officers of health from any part of Greater London (including county officers whose posts would be affected by the reorganization), that applications should be channelled through the Commission and, most importantly, from the county officers' point of view, that independent assessors should assist councils in compiling short lists and interviewing candidates. These assessors were to be medical officers of health from outside London.[36] All the thirty-two borough medical officers of health came from within Greater London, about half being county officers.

A major question in the case of *children's officers* was whether there were sufficient officers of chief officer calibre within Greater London. Boroughs were therefore particularly anxious to widen the field of choice; at the same time the Commission had to safeguard the interests of existing staff. The procedure suggested by them and agreed by the Home Office was a compromise. Boroughs were to consider first candidates from their own area[37] and then, if these did not give a suitable choice, candidates from the remainder of Greater London. Only after exhausting this procedure were the boroughs to apply for permission to advertise. As in the case of MOH the commission acted a a clearing-house for applications. In inner London (ex-LCC area) 10 children's officers were chosen from within Greater London and 2 from outside; in outer London 7 were from Greater London and 13 from outside.

The achievements of the Staff Commission. Recommending procedures for the appointment of chief officers was only a part, although a very important part, of the work of the Staff Commission. Inumerable problems arose over the transfer and assimilation of staff at lower levels; for example, what weight should be given to the preferences for a particular borough area expressed by county staff who were to be transferred; or how to deal with complaints of loss of status on transfer. Elaborate arrangements were devised for hearing appeals against transfer on grounds of hardship although very few appeals were actually made.[38] Redundancy, as has been indicated, was a problem with which the Commission were very much concerned. Indeed, their desire to keep it to a minimum was a major factor in their insistence on imposing restrictions on the field of recruitment of chief officers.[39] Channels of communication were also regarded by the commission as of great importance; they devoted much effort to ensuring that authorities maintained adequate arrangements for consulting staff representatives and keeping them informed at all stages of plans for the reorganization.

In all this, the Commission held quite consistently to their basic view of their task as being 'to maintain confidence during the period of transition, and to demonstrate by the principles we sought to establish that there would be fair play for all'.[40] There can be little doubt that they succeeded, particularly in the eyes of the staff and their associations. It has become an accepted aim of NALGO to press for the establishment of independent staff commissions in similar situations. They attempted this without success in the West Midlands reorganization of 1966, and the idea was put forward again in their evidence to the Redcliffe–Maud Commission.[41] The local authorities, too, who had more reason to be suspicious of the Commission, on the whole accepted that they had not unduly encroached on their right to appoint their own staff, although there were a number of points of disagreement, mainly over the question of how wide a field of recruitment should be permitted. There were also some thorny questions where the Commission trod delicately to avoid seeming to impose their views.[42]

On the credit side, therefore, of the Commission's activities one may put lack of any serious dispute with the staff over the transitional arrangements with a consequent gain in the speed and smoothness of the transition itself. This, after all, had been one of the Government's main aims.

But one must also consider whether the arrangements for the staffing of the new authorities, under the guidance of the commission, were in the public interest in the widest sense. Did the strong emphasis in the London reorganization on protection of staff interests blunt some of the advantages claimed for that reorganization in terms of the services provided? The Government's and the Staff Commission's policies tended to give existing staff individually at least as good terms under the new system as they had under the old, irrespective of the needs of particular services. Furthermore, the restriction of recruitment very largely to the Greater London area, however justifiable on grounds of equity, might not necessarily produce the best people for the available jobs.

The Commission themselves drew a distinction between 'the maintenance of an efficient public service' and the staff interests with which they were concerned.[43] They were no doubt quite right to do so having regard to the terms of the 1963 Act. Nevertheless, the antithesis is surely unfortunate, the implication being that protection of staff interests could be separated from the maintenance of an efficient public service; and that the former required special machinery whereas the latter could be left to the normal processes of discussion and negotiation between central government and local authorities, and to the discretion of local authorities themselves. That staff interests were separately treated in this way is an indication of the Government's view of their importance in assuring the transition to the new system.

But to answer the question whether the arrangements for staffing enabled the best use to be made of the opportunities provided by the reorganization for carrying out services more efficiently and economically would require a detailed examination of the effects of staffing policies on the working of the services under the new system. Even if it could be shown that by adopting different policies, eg throwing open recruitment more widely, it would have been possible to have secured improvement in the services provided, it does not follow that the Government were wrong in pursuing a policy of safeguarding staff interests, a policy which the Staff Commission carried out admirably. Apart from the question of equity, it could well be argued that without such safeguards there was a real risk that some services might have broken down or at least have suffered badly in the period of transition. That this did not happen must be weighed against the possible advantages of any alternative arrangement.

The new authorities appoint their chief officers

Apart, however, from the Staff Commission, one must also consider the action taken by the new authorities themselves, in whose hands lay the selection of staff. Two questions are of particular interest here; first, the speed with which the new authorities made appointments of chief officers; secondly, the controversies which surrounded some of their activities.

The first question is important since without a nucleus of chief officers the authorities could make little progress in settling realistically their staff requirements and other urgent matters. The statutory appointments of clerk, treasurer and, in the case of the boroughs, engineer/surveyor and medical officer of health were generally the first appointments to be made and practically all these appointments had been made by the end of June 1964. Where circumstances were favourable appointments were made earlier,[44] as at Bromley where appointments of clerk and treasurer were made before the end of May 1964.[45] At Croydon the merging of a large County Borough with a much smaller County District (Coulsdon and Purley) made it almost a foregone conclusion that the top posts would go to Croydon officials, and no less than ten chief officers were appointed at a meeting of the council on 27 May. The GLC too, were quick to appoint their clerk and treasurer who had both formerly served the LCC; their director of housing, chief officer of the parks department and chief officer of the licensing department, were also ex-LCC men.[46] At the same time the Middlesex county valuer was appointed the GLC's valuer.[47]

It was in the filling of other chief officer posts that greater difficulties arose. The post of chief planning officer was publicly advertised, as was the post of director of highways and transportation in the GLC, both being new kinds of job; the former was filled by a former chief planning officer of Middlesex, the latter by the LCC's deputy chief engineer.[48] By the end of July practically all the chief officer posts had been filled.[49] There was considerable delay in many of the boroughs in making appointments of children's officers and in the case of the outer boroughs, chief education officers, largely because a number of boroughs wished to advertise some of these posts and had to overcome the reluctance of the Staff Commission before being able to do so. Thus although Croydon made their appointment of a children's officer in June 1964, Kingston upon Thames and Richmond upon Thames did not do so until the end of October, in both cases choosing officers from outside Greater London. Architects and, where they were appointed, planning officers also tended to be late appointments; the latter was not a statutory appointment and under the 1963 Act boroughs had until 1st April 1968 to make the statutory appointment of an architect.[50]

On the whole, authorities were quick off the mark in making their appointments. Many of the boroughs however ran into controversies, which were much publicized in the local press, over the way in which they made them. Thus at Kingston the council were criticized for making the appointments of clerk, treasurer and surveyor at a special meeting of the whole council from which the press were excluded rather than through a special selection committee.[51] But a far more common cause of complaint which was voiced in council meetings was that of unfairness to the officers of particular authorities. At Brent it was alleged that all the best jobs had gone to Willesden officers.[52] There were similar complaints from Southgate that Enfield LB posts were being filled by Enfield and Edmonton candidates.[53]

But perhaps the classic case was the appointment of a medical officer of health for Richmond upon Thames. Here the rivalry between big Twickenham and smaller Richmond and Barnes was increased by the fact that the former authority was in Middlesex, the latter two in Surrey. Allegations that the Twickenham members were 'bull-dozing' decisions through the new council soon began to be heard.[54] Matters came to a head when it became known that the selection committee had recommended the appointment of a deputy MOH from Middlesex CC for the post of Borough MOH in preference to the MOH for Richmond and Barnes. Not only did this cause reverberations in the council chamber and the local press but it also brought a letter of protest from the Richmond branch of the British Medical Association and a petition from a group of Richmond housewives.[55] But the selection was confirmed and the Richmond MOH had to be content with a deputy post elsewhere.

In spite of the charges and counter-charges however, it would be very difficult to show that the selection procedure in general worked less fairly than such procedures normally do in local government. It is not unknown, for example, for members of a selection committee to have a bias, conscious or unconscious, towards 'the local boy', and it would be surprising if this did not sometimes happen in the case of the London reorganization. What mitigated the position from the point of view of the staff in London was the fact that an officer not selected for a chief officer post in a new London Borough might well be appointed deputy at a salary higher than he had previously been receiving.

Financial questions

Among the working parties set up by the Ministry of Housing and Local Government in the middle of 1962 to consider matters relevant to the London Government Bill was one on finance. One of this working party's main concerns was the question of transitional assistance to the counties which were to lose part of their areas to Greater London. This, as has been indicated,[56] was a question debated at some length in the proceedings on the Bill. Among other questions discussed by the working party were: the disposal of the working balances of existing authorities, and the transfer of financial liabilities to the new authorities. These were not big issues. Nevertheless, they illustrate the detailed administrative problems which had to be settled to bring the new system into operation.

The working-party was concerned with general issues of principle affecting all the new authorities. Each of the new treasurers, however, faced a multitude of problems directly arising from the need to create an effective organization for dealing with the accounts and payments of the new authorities from 1 April 1965. Not the least of the difficulties was that the authorities to be amalgamated frequently followed different policies and practices in their accounting and other financial arrangements. Because of the central importance of the treasurer's department these additional administrative problems arising from the reorganization were among the most difficult of those involved in setting up the new authorities.

Apart from these practical financial questions which had to be resolved, the Greater London reforms also raised some wider issues. The financial effects of the reforms, that is, broadly whether the new system has proved more expensive than the old, is extremely difficult to assess accurately. In any case, any assessment would need to be related to other effects of the reforms eg on the quality of services provided. Some actions which were taken are, however, relevant and would need to be taken into account in any assessment.

There were, first some direct costs of changing from one system to another. There was, for example, a good deal of overtime, particularly in clerks' and treasurers' departments. Again, partly as a result of the Government's and the Staff Commission's anxiety to avoid redundancies wherever possible, there were a number of supernumerary appointments of senior staff. Many of these were temporary appointments for two or three years. For example, some town clerks of merging authorities who did not get substantive appointments in the new boroughs were appointed associate town clerks to assist in the task of reorganization. Often they were near retiring age and their experience and help were invaluable in helping to smooth the transitional period.

Secondly, there is some evidence that administrative costs have risen. In submitting evidence to the Ministry in support of 'London weighting' for the rate support grant the GLC and the boroughs produced estimates of administrative costs in three areas formerly in Middlesex which indicated that these costs were about 30% higher in the London Boroughs than in the corresponding areas under the county system. One element in higher administrative costs may well be the difficulties and expense of communication resulting from the dispersal of office accommodation in the new boroughs.

Thirdly, there is the whole question of the salary structure and gradings of the new authorities. Relevant to this is the action of some councils in the transition period in upgrading the whole or most of their establishments.[57] Behind this move was the desire that staff should not be at a disadvantage in the mergers, but since staff under the Act were to be guaranteed the same salary, provided that they transferred to comparable work, the effect may have been to increase the cost of doing the same job.

Much the biggest of these upgradings and most far-reaching in its effects was that of Middlesex County Council. On 1 January 1964 the Council considered and agreed on a proposal from its establishment committee that there should be a general upward regrading of posts except for staff recently recruited. The main reason for this move seems to have been the view that Middlesex staff would be at a disadvantage in the reorganization because, among other things, LCC staff performing comparable tasks were more highly paid than those of Middlesex CC.[58]

These proposals required the sanction of the National Joint Council, the employers' side of which had some doubts. They agreed that Middlesex gradings were low when judged by standards used elsewhere but suggested that Middlesex should be more selective in its approach to upgradings. Middlesex accordingly carried out an analysis department by department, the broad effect of which, however, was to give increased salaries by way of upgrading to the great majority of Middlesex staff.

Apart from its implications for staff costs the Middlesex upgrading had other repercussions. It alarmed the LCC Staff Association who pressed for similar upgradings to maintain the long-standing differentials between LCC salaries and those of other local government officers. Despite calling an overtime ban, the LCC Staff Association were unable to get the LCC to agree to this course. Instead the LCC without the co-operation of the Association, instituted a separate inquiry by Dr W. S. Bristowe, formerly of ICI, who recommended salary increases only for staff earning over £2,400 a year. These were put into effect.[59]

Finally, it was alleged that the new boroughs in some cases bid against one another for scarce staff and paid inflated salaries.[60] Certainly, there were considerable variations in the scales of salaries paid in different boroughs, for example, for child-care officers, although this in itself does not necessarily prove the point. Some variations might well be justified by the differing needs and circumstances of different boroughs.

Thus, there were a number of ways in which the reorganization may have increased the costs of running local government services. How far this was a temporary phenomenon and how far increased costs must be set against improvements in the services are questions which cannot be answered here.

The administrative burden

The period of transition to the new system of local government in Greater London was a period of strain for members and officers alike. The strain arose largely because the same people were to a great extent responsible for continuing to run the services provided by the old authorities at the same time as they were planning for the new. The strain was greatest on senior officers and committee chairmen. Additional meetings – of joint committees, working parties and, later, of the new authorities – took up the time of those who had to attend them. But memoranda had to be prepared for those meetings, information extracted, new calculations made, fresh problems examined. Few people in London local government at that time escaped an additional burden of work and for some the burden was very heavy. Practically everything had to be looked at afresh. It was not simply the big questions, how to organize the old county service in the new boroughs, how to assess the staffing requirements of the new authorities, how to create an administrative structure for the new GLC services. These and other similar questions certainly called for much thought and effort. But there were many more mundane problems which called for attention. How much accommodation would each of the new departments require and where were they to be located? Which system of book issue was the new borough library service to adopt, what should be the period of loan and the hours of opening of the various libraries? What should be done to standardize the various forms used by the constituent authorities, their stationery and equipment?

Given the circumstances of a complete reorganization of areas and functions, the additional work in examining these and other practical problems was inevitable. But it is also necessary to consider whether the burden of work could have been eased by any different methods of procedure. It is relevant to state again here that besides having to operate the old system and prepare for the new, local authority staff were also naturally concerned with their own future prospects. One element in the procedure emphasized by the Government was the need to keep staff anxieties to the minimum. This, to some extent, has to be set against the burden of additional work so far as the staff were concerned. Furthermore, the transition to the new system was carried out with a remarkable degree of success. There was no hiatus or breakdown in local government services.

Perhaps the main question then is whether a different time-table would have brought similar advantages with less strain on those involved. There was a period of twenty months between the passing of the 1963 Act and the assumption of powers by the new authorities. But the period of greatest activity and greatest strain was that in which both old and new authorities were in existence, nearly a year in the case of the GLC, eleven months in the case of the boroughs. This was when the vital decisions were taken, and this was when the double task was most pronounced. Could this period have been extended?

If it is accepted that reorganizations should take effect from 1 April [61] the period could have been extended by one year to 1 April 1966. Quite apart from any political motive which the Government might have had in not wishing to set the change-over date too far beyond the next general election, there were disadvantages as well as advantages in such a proposal. Although it would have meant that there would have been more time to consider the problems of the change-over, it would also have prolonged the period of dual running with an almost certain increase in friction between the old and the new authorities. As it was there is some evidence that the old authorities took decisions which might not have been regarded as in the best interests of the new.[62]

An alternative might have been to set up the new authorities but to leave them, for an interim period, with the existing services provided by the authorities whom they replaced. Redistribution of functions would then have taken place at the end of the interim period. This would have avoided the disadvantages of friction between old and new authorities; it would also have enabled the reorganization of such services as the fire brigade and libraries to take place over a period. It would have had the serious disadvantage that most of the major services would have suffered from a two-stage disruption. For some reorganization of these services would have been needed simply to keep them going. The GLC for example would have had the problems of taking over the children's and other services from Essex, Surrey and the other counties before the final stage of transfer to the boroughs.

It is clear then, that there is no easy answer to the question of what is the most satisfactory procedure in a major reorganization of local government areas and functions. On balance the Government were probably right to stress the advantages of bringing the new structure into operation as soon as possible. But successful as the changeover was even a month or two's extra time would have eased the strain without bringing too many disadvantages. The difficulty was to find a practical means of extending the time.

A Labour GLC and a Labour Government

Apart from the administrative problems which have been discussed, two political events occurred between the passing of the 1963 Act and the 1 April 1965 with a bearing on the transition to the new system. The first was the Labour victory in the GLC election of April 1964, followed in May by the party's gaining control of twenty of the thirty-two London Boroughs.[63] The second was the victory of the

Labour Party at the general election of October 1964 although by a very narrow majority. The first raised the question of what attitude the LCC Labour opponents of the reorganization would adopt now that many of them found themselves faced with the responsibility of running the GLC.[64] The second brought to the fore the Labour Party's commitment to consider making changes in the London Government Act before it came into full operation.

As early as March 1963 Mr Ben Parkin, the Labour MP for Paddington North, writing in *London News*, the official organ of the London Labour Party, was arguing that recent Gallup polls indicated that Labour could win both the GLC and the next general election. Significantly he claimed that this would 'help it [the GLC] do a better job over a bigger area than ever seemed possible when it was first misbegotten as a weapon to be used against us'. Here was a first sign of a change of attitude which became increasingly evident in the months leading up to the GLC election.

As the elections drew nearer, the political commentators speculated on Labour's chances. 'Still Labour's London?'[65] summed up the general view, a view based almost entirely on the relative standing of the two major political parties in the country, and not on the merits of the arguments about London's government. The point was succinctly put by Mr Hugh Berrington:

'Victory in April 1964 will go to the party which enjoys a clear lead in the public opinion polls. Though the race is still four months away, the betting, at this stage, must be on Labour.'[66]

All three parties made extensive preparations for the election. On the Labour side a Greater London Co-ordinating Committee was established with representatives among others of local Labour parties, the London Labour Party and the LCC. This body was under the chairmanship of Mr Mellish. In the event Labour won 64 of the 100 seats and the Conservative 36. the extent of Labour's victory being exaggerated by the multi-member constituencies.[67]

The children's service and the ILEA review

Perhaps the main effect of Labour's victory at the GLC election was to make the party less inclined to halt the reforms, which in any case would have been difficult without risking a complete break-down in London's local government. On the other hand, a Labour GLC and the strong possibility of a Labour Government before the end of 1964 did raise the question of how far they would carry out Mr Stewart's pledge to 'halt the transfer of functions and the break-up of the social services'.[68]

The general election did not come until October 1964 and it provided Labour with only a bare working majority in the House of Commons. Only in regard to the children's service did the Government propose action in accordance with their pledge.

On 3 December 1964 the Home Office issued a circular letter outlining proposals for the direct involvement of the GLC in the children's service.[69] Under these proposals the GLC would have taken over at least for an initial period the more specialized existing institutions and also the LCC's large children's homes; it would have had power to provide reception centres to serve more than one borough and to establish and maintain approved schools; and it would have had a number of other responsibilities (eg for staff training).

The GLC welcomed these proposals on the basis of a report on them by the LCC Children's Committee. But the Boroughs' Advisory Body of Children Officers thought they would not work. Although most of them were still working for the counties, particularly London and Middlesex, until they fully assumed their new responsibilities on 1 April 1965, they were very closely involved at this stage in the administrative preparations for the change-over. Their case against the proposals was essentially that the children's service was a unity and could not be split in the way suggested by the Home Office. They argued, for example, that if the GLC assumed responsibility for reception centres, the boroughs would inevitably meet their need for reception places to be immediately available by using residential homes for this purpose, which was clearly undesirable.

On 2 February 1965 the Minister of Housing and Local Government, Mr Richard Crossman, made an important statement on the Labour Government's attitude to the London reorganization, including the question of the children's service. After rehearsing the Government's opposition to the plan he claimed that nevertheless the general election had come too late for the system to be reshaped in any material way without the danger of disrupting services. For this reason, and also because of the lack of agreement among those involved, the Government did not propose to make any changes in the children's service, although they had seriously considered this possibility.

Mr Crossman went on to say that the Government would keep the working of the 1963 Act under review and 'will not hesitate to introduce amendments at a later date should experience suggest that it is right to do so'. He ended by saying that the Government would specifically consider the requirement in the Act to review the educational arrangements in inner London before 1970.

The reference to the educational review in inner London did, however, provide an important postscript. On 18 November 1965 the Secretary of State for Education and Science, Mr Anthony Crosland, announced that the Government had decided to repeal the review clauses in the 1963 Act, an announcement which delighted the London Teachers' Association. Their president had earlier declared that there was already evidence that teachers were leaving the inner London service because of uncertainty about the future.[70]

However it was not until the end of 1966 that the Government found time to introduce a Bill. The proceedings on the Bill were chiefly notable for once again demonstrating the differences in approach on the Conservative side. On the second reading,[71] for example, Mr Geoffrey Rippon, the opposition's spokesman on local government, made it clear that the main intention of the review had been either to dissolve the ILEA or to make necessary changes in its composition, structure and functions; and he claimed the right in due course to review the activities of the authority even if the review section was struck out of the Act. Sir Edward Boyle, on the other hand, winding-up for the opposition, claimed that the object of the review would be to consider the best pattern of educational administration for the area and could not really be confined to the ILEA area but would have to examine the situation in outer London too.

In the Lords the differences were even sharper – not surprisingly since Lord Brooke of Cumnor and Viscount Eccles were the chief opposition spokesmen, as they had been the chief architects of the compromise plan in the 1961 White Paper. Lord Brooke, in moving an amendment on Committee stage to reinstate the review provisions in the 1963 Act made reference to the unique nature of the ILEA and of the fact that it was 'a marked departure from the Royal Commission's recommendation that the boroughs should be the main units of local government in Greater London'.[72]

This oblique reference to Lord Brooke's leaning towards acceptance of the Herbert Report brought a more explicit statement from

Viscount Eccles. He 'was very much for ILEA at the time' and he went on:

'there was then the question of reviews, and there were some people who wanted reviews in order to have another chance of breaking up the central London authority. I was very much against that, but I pointed out at the time that it might well be that one would wish to have a review in order to enlarge the area of ILEA because I think that the education of the Greater London area is very much all of a piece, and I was rather sorry that we had left it flexibly open in the Bill. Of course my noble friend, Lord Brooke of Cumnor, knew much more about it than I did, and it therefore went through in that form. Are the Government quite sure they do not want a chance to enlarge ILEA?'[73]

The Government, however, were not to be drawn on this question. Nor is it surprising, in view of the almost contradictory statements of different Conservative spokesmen about the nature and purpose of the proposed review, that the Government should have concentrated on removing uncertainty about the future of the ILEA, and their proposals duly became law.[74]

Thus in spite of the formidable practical difficulties the new authorities were able to carry on London's government on 1 April 1965; and in spite of the fierce political controversies the new system which they then began to operate was essentially the system which the Government had first outlined in the White Paper of 1961. The speed and decisiveness of Government action over London government was undoubtedly one of the most marked features of these events. It requires to be examined more fully, above all to see how and why the London reforms came about.

12
A Summing-up

In viewing the events which led to the establishment of the Greater London Council and thirty-two London Boroughs on 1 April 1965 a significant point of reference is the fact of change in the local government structure. Not only did the 1963 Act completely change the structure of local government in Greater London but it represented the first major change in the local government structure anywhere in the country since the system had been established in the late nineteenth century. It is important to make clear what is being asserted here.

There were many changes in local government between 1888 and 1963. New functions were assigned to local authorities; old ones grew or diminished in importance; some were lost to local government altogether. Within local government new County Boroughs were created; rural districts became urban districts; amalgamations of county districts took place; county boundaries were adjusted; functions were transferred from county districts to counties. But these changes took place, in Greater London as elsewhere, within the framework laid down by the nineteenth century Acts of Parliament. The county and county borough structure outside the county of London, and the special structure of the London County Council and the Metropolitan Boroughs, remained unchanged until, under the London Government Act of 1963, a new type of structure was introduced in Greater London.

To the question why this should be a significant development the previous chapters have attempted to give an answer. The historical evidence up to the time when the Herbert Commission reported favoured the view that fundamental changes in the local government structure were unlikely. Some fairly obvious reasons for this have been suggested. They include, above all, the fact that local authorities on the whole did not want change and that governments almost always had been unwilling to adopt changes either because they agreed with the view of local authorities that change was not needed or because they had no other compelling reasons to take action.

In summing up the history which has been recounted in this volume the fact of change will, therefore, be taken as a central point. The main themes to be examined will be how and why change came about. The situation can be viewed from several different angles. There are first the essential factors in the London situation without which there would have been little or no case for change at all. Secondly, there are the different arguments which were deployed both in favour of and against change. Thirdly, there are the reasons which inspired those who were chiefly concerned to take action. All three, it is suggested, are necessary to an understanding of these events, but in the nature of the British political process the third must ultimately take precedence. If change of this kind is to come about it must result from decision and action by the central government. The focus of attention in the end, therefore, must be on the reasons which induced the Government to act.

The London situation

The most significant factor in the Greater London situation to which attention has been drawn is the long continued growth of London itself. This growth provided the setting for the arguments about London's government. In itself the growth of London was not an argument either for or against change in the local government structure. It was rather that growth had certain consequences and provided certain problems. Two problems or rather sets of problems have been identified. First, there were problems in the provision of certain local government services; these problems arose most obviously in connection with traffic and planning. The first of these was a problem simply because the growth of traffic which accompanied London's growth did not confine itself to the existing local authority boundaries. In the case of planning, the question arose of how one could plan for a large urban area which was split between a number of different authorities.

One other consequence of London's growth which has been given prominence here gave rise to problems of a very different nature. This was the urbanization of the areas adjoining the County of London. Middlesex in particular was transformed into an urban county consisting of a series of large boroughs intermingled with a number of smaller urban districts. The consequences seem at first sight to be of less significance than those connected with the provision of services. The large boroughs in Middlesex with their desire for county borough status might create tensions within the local government structure but this would not necessarily affect the provision of services. The problem might be regarded as one to be solved within local government.

The reason why this could not be left as a purely internal local government issue was that it formed part of the county borough versus county controversy which, for a long time, had haunted any question of local government reorganization. Boroughs promoting Bills to achieve county borough status and county boroughs proposing extensions to their boundaries had generally been vigorously opposed by the counties which stood to lose both territory and rateable value. Governments were inevitably involved in these disputes. They might claim to decide each case on its merits, but in Middlesex the consequences of so doing presented them with an exceptionally acute problem. If Ealing and the other boroughs with populations at or above the minimum generally acceptable for county borough status were granted that status, Middlesex would lose over half its population and there would be *de facto* a very considerable change in the structure of local government in Greater London.[1] If county borough status were refused and no other action taken, it would become increasingly difficult to find reasonable grounds for such a refusal. Thus a political problem was inherent in the demands of certain local authorities for county borough status.

A more difficult question is whether a consequence of the situation described above was to create a movement in the climate of opinion in the direction of change. The expression 'climate of opinion' is extremely vague. Nevertheless it has its uses. For example, a comparison of the evidence to the Herbert Commission with that to the Redcliffe-Maud Commission[2] shows a considerable shift of opinion towards acceptance of the idea that some change in the local government structure may be necessary or desirable. Few people would have predicted in 1960 when the Herbert Commission reported that the Association of Municipal Corporations would within a few years put forward a plan for large provincial authorities (even though with limited responsibilities) or that the Government departments would almost with one voice advocate thirty or forty large authorities as the solution to local government's problems. For whatever reasons, the climate of opinion had changed in a few years.

It is admittedly more difficult to identify a movement of opinion of this nature in the Greater London situation before 1957. Nevertheless, recognition of London's problems existed and had been commented on long before the Herbert Commission were appointed not only by outside observers, but in Government statements as well. The question is whether over the course of time there was increasing awareness of the need for at least an examination of these problems. It will be recalled that as far back as 1946 Mr Bevan had said that there was a need for an enquiry into local government in Greater London.[3] The 1956 White Paper[4] had reached the point of recognizing that the conurbations presented special difficulties and this recognition received practical form in the greater freedom given to the Local Government Commission to recommend changes in the conurbations. Although Greater London was largely excluded from these White Paper proposals, one might argue that the White Paper did at least indicate some awareness that the problems presented by the conurbations including London did not grow any easier with the passage of time. But if there was a movement of opinion it certainly did not extend to the view that large scale reorganization was essential. It is rather that one may argue that it was easier as time went on to propose and gain acceptance of the idea that an enquiry into London's government should be undertaken.

The arguments about London government

Nothing in what has so far been said implies that London's growth inevitably required a change in the system of local government sooner or later. All that has been argued so far is that the facts of the situation posed problems which from time to time forced themselves on the attention of the central government. There were three sets of arguments which were important in the history of the events leading to change.

(1) *Functional arguments:* In terms of public discussion both before and after the Herbert Commission much the most important group of arguments concerned the provision of local government services. Whether or not they were the true grounds for taking action or adopting attitudes, debate was almost entirely concerned with the effective provision of services. A major argument put forward by those who advocated changing the system was the need to make effective provision for dealing with problems such as traffic, planning and overspill housing

in Greater London. Conversely, a major argument put forward by those who favoured the retention of the existing system was that it would be wrong to destroy organizations which were providing a good service eg in education and child care. It is also important to note that the major argument put forward for change was strongly disputed and that in the course of lengthy debates it was claimed that these problems could be adequately dealt with either by some arrangement within the existing system or, alternatively, by action on the part of the central government. Naturally, these arguments for and against change were most prominent in the period after the Herbert Commission had reported and still more after the Government White Paper of 1961.[5]

(2) *Arguments about the value of local self government:* An essential key to the understanding of the Herbert Commission's proposals lies in their views about the health of local government. They argued that their plan would not only provide a means for efficient performance of local authority services, but would also reinvigorate local government in London by attracting councillors of high calibre and by increasing public interest in the work of their councils. Specifically, they used this as an argument for not having boroughs which were too large. In the nature of these arguments they could not provide the same precise points of debate as arguments over the provision of services. Indeed, little was heard about either the specific views of the Commission or the wider case for local self government in arguments about the Government's proposals when they were presented. This does not necessarily mean that they were unimportant; they may have been implicit rather than explicit. One difficulty, as Professor W. J. M. Mackenzie has pointed out [6] is that the idea of local self government is an 'extremely vague notion', and involves a 'maze of ambiguities'. He quotes from a Conservative Political Centre Pamphlet which claimed:

> 'the local council whether it be in a parish, rural or urban district, borough or county is an expression of the British genius for self government and is rightly jealous of any encroachments by the Central Government.'[7]

In other words the virtues of local self government are seen not in the size of authority, as was implicitly argued by the Herbert

Commission but in the existence of distinct communities which may be as large as a county or as small as a parish. And from this point of view it could be argued that the creation of the Greater London Council and the London Boroughs represented a strengthening of local government. Thus in so far as arguments about the health of local government formed a part of the events following the Herbert Commission's Report they tended to be invoked both by those who supported change and those who were opposed to it.

(3) *The Political Arguments:* The author of the only major study of the reform of London government has claimed:

> 'While the fight over the Greater London proposals was not solely partisan in its underlying concerns, the considerations of power politics were never far removed from the heart of this controversy.'[8]

From this point of view the London reforms can be treated as a contest in which local authorities, professional bodies, the Conservative Government and the Labour opposition each sought certain specific aims which were reflected in the events preceding the 1963 Act. If political arguments in this sense are the key to these events they represented the underlying motives rather than the overt arguments which were put forward. The only specific political argument which was prominent in those events was the Labour Party's charge that the Conservatives were gerrymandering and seeking a purely party political advantage in destroying the LCC. It was a fact of the situation that on balance the Conservative Party stood to gain from the London reforms and the Labour Party to lose. Largely this was because the LCC was to disappear. After nearly thirty years of uninterrupted Labour control the London County Council could be regarded as a Labour stronghold. It was too an important political prize because of the powers and prestige attaching to the capital's principal local authority. Its disappearance was therefore of greater significance in party political terms than the abolition of Middlesex and the three County Boroughs, and the truncation of Essex, Kent and Surrey. Moreover, the Greater London Council seemed on the face of it to present the Conservatives with a greater opportunity for gaining control than had the London County Council.

There are, therefore, two sets of related arguments involved here; first general arguments about the motivation of different bodies and individuals in terms of power politics; secondly, the more specific arguments about party political advantage.

Underlying motives

In considering the underlying motives of those who were chiefly concerned in the events under discussion, the aim will be, as suggested above, to relate those motives both to the facts of the London situation and to the arguments which developed about London government. Discussion will be concentrated on the two or three key points in the historical narrative. These were first the decision to set up a Royal Commission in 1957; secondly, the Government's decision on the Royal Commission's Report which was embodied in the White Paper of 1961; thirdly, the decision to go ahead with the London Government Bill in 1962 and 1963.

Smallwood in his book on Greater London came to the conclusion that:

> 'One of the most reassuring aspects of the analysis is the fact that the entire story unfolded with a reasonable degree of predictability.'[9]

Another commentator on these events has said that the London Government reforms came about: 'through a series of favourable political circumstances'.[10] The account presented here emphasizes that there was a considerable element of unpredictability about the key decisions which were taken by the Conservative Government, and that 'favourable political circumstances' were certainly an important element in the situation.

(a) The decision to set up a Royal Commission

It was 'a favourable political circumstance' for those who advocated a reform of London Government that Mr Henry Brooke became Minister of Housing and Local Government in January 1957. If Mr Sandys had remained as Minister and the White Paper proposals had been put into effect there would have been, perhaps, some adjustment of powers between the LCC and the Metropolitan Boroughs and, after the Local Government Commission had reported, a joint body of some kind set up to consider problems affecting Greater London as a whole. It is very unlikely, given the circumstances in which the White Paper was produced, that any more substantial changes would have been made in London's local government.

It is easy to argue that Mr Bevan's view in 1946 that an examination was needed of local government in Greater London simply waited eleven years for someone to take the initiative and put it into action. Mr Brooke took that initiative. Therefore one may plausibly argue, the decision to set up a Royal Commission was largely due to his view of the situation. The problem then is why Mr Brooke took a different view from his predecessor.

There is first the question of departmental influence. Mr Brooke might well not have acted as he did if he had not had strong support from his departmental advisers.[11] But this in turn raises two further questions; first, the reasons for the departmental view and whether the Middlesex issue or the wider problems of London's planning, housing and traffic needs were their main concern; secondly, the reasons why Mr Brooke was receptive to departmental advice on the need for a London enquiry, and whether with or without such advice, he would have advocated a Royal Commission to examine London government if he had not had the political stimulus deriving from his years as Conservative leader at County Hall, of wishing to see an end of Labour's long control of the LCC.

None of these questions can be answered with any certainty but the analysis presented in this volume has suggested that Mr Brooke was receptive to departmental advice, partly because he saw the problems of London Government and the inability of the White Paper to deal effectively with them and partly because he himself had an interest in, and knowledge of, local government. The Middlesex issue was the practical stimulus to action, but it is certainly not clear whether either Mr Brooke or Dame Evelyn Sharp saw it as anything more than a symbol of the wider problems of providing local government services which were of Greater London significance. On the other hand, it is reasonable to assume that the case which Mr Brooke put to the other members of the Government was basically the same as the one which he made in the House of Commons:

'It may be impossible to determine what is the right structure of Middlesex except in the context of the Greater London area. The plain fact is that Greater London needs to be looked at as a whole.'[12]

This interpretation might seem to dismiss too easily Mr Brooke's years at County Hall as merely an interest in London government. Surely, it might be argued, a leading Conservative politician, who became Home Secretary, must have had a stronger political motive for initiating action. Certainly, Mr Brooke must have been aware of the political situation in London. This may have consciously inclined him towards a fresh look at London government, or, more in keeping with his character, may have unconsciously influenced his attitude. But it was not an important influence in the decision to set up a Royal Commission. If it had been important, one would have expected it to have influenced the choice of members of the Commission. But there is no evidence that they were chosen because they inclined towards reform of London government. Rather the evidence is that they were uncommitted and chosen to carry out an independent enquiry whose outcome could not be predicted.

Clearly, there was a possibility that a Royal Commission might recommend a Greater London authority and the consequential disappearance of the LCC; the idea of such a body went back at least to the time of the LCC's approach to the Government in 1920. But there was, perhaps, an equally strong possibility that a Royal Commission, faced with the opposition of the large authorities, such as the London and Middlesex County Councils, to any fundamental change, would seek some solution within the existing local government system. The decision to set up a Royal Commission implied no kind of commitment on the part of the Government. Indeed, popular mythology would attribute quite a different significance to the setting up of a Royal Commission, regarding it as an indication of Government desire to shelve a problem. The 1957 decision assumes its greatest importance in retrospect when it is seen as the first stage in a series of events which led to the 1963 Act. It is, therefore, probably fruitless to probe too deeply into the significance of the decision. At the time, the decision aroused little comment, itself an indication that few regarded it as at all startling. Perhaps of greater interest in the long run is the fact that there had been so much reluctance to initiate an enquiry earlier.

(b) *The decision to reform London government*

The Government White Paper of 1961 is much more critical in terms of what ultimately happened. It also provides a much more difficult and complex situation to interpret. Furthermore, we have to consider here not only why the Government decided to go ahead with a plan of reform, but why the plan took the form it did. Most of the argument about the Herbert Commission proposals and those of the Government was ostensibly concerned, as has been suggested, with the efficient performance of local government functions and yet the London Government Bill provoked a most bitter political debate. If one could explain this one would be well on the way to explaining how the White Paper came about.

A simple explanation both of the Government's determination to go ahead and of the violently hostile opposition of the Labour Party might be found in the political situation. The Conservatives stood to gain from the disappearance of the LCC and the creation of a Greater London Council in which the predominantly Conservative outer suburban areas would counterbalance Labour's inner stronghold to give the Conservatives a greater opportunity of securing control than they had in the London County Council.

There is certainly evidence that some Conservatives, at least, were hostile to the LCC. Sir David Eccles, for example, in the debate on the White Paper said:

'I am sorry to have to say this, but I am aware – because they have made me aware of it – that some of my hon. friends feel that the LCC has shown itself so doctrinaire in its educational planning that it would be worth almost any price to hand over its responsibilities to the new boroughs.'[13]

Again, the Chairman of the Housing Committee of the Conservative Metropolitan Borough of Chelsea asserted.

'Some Conservatives cannot wholly hide their glee at the prospect of the disappearance of what they regard as a monument to bureaucracy, extravagance and inefficiency.'[14]

Again the fact that once the Government had committed themselves in the White Paper they went ahead with a long and complex Bill in a remarkably short space of time makes plausible the view that they had a strong political commitment to London government reform.

The important but difficult question is whether these attitudes and political facts were the decisive factor in the Government's decision to go ahead with a plan of reform. The question needs to be seen in relation to the stages by which the plan was agreed. It has been argued earlier that the plan for the reform of London government which was presented by Mr Brooke to the Cabinet for approval was essentially a compromise between what the Herbert Commission had proposed and the educational views of Sir David Eccles. Factors other than the political ones were thus an influence on the kind of plan which was put forward. To consider whether, nevertheless, polical motives were predominant in the Government's decision, it is necessary to examine the pressures which were exercised, both from outside, primarily from local authorities and professional bodies, and from within the Government itself.

The difficulty of assessing the extent of influence of outside pressures is well illustrated by the activities of the London Teacher's Association. The LTA campaigned vigorously against the Herbert Commission's proposals for education and in favour of maintaining intact the LCC education service. The Government's proposals in their final form did just what the LTA wanted. Should one, therefore, argue that the LTA 'scored the first direct bulls-eye in the reorganization contest'?[15]

It does not follow that the LTA's campaign was the only or even the main reason why the Government diverged from the Herbert Commission proposals on education. To assume this implies a great deal about the working of pressure groups in the British parliamentary system and about the influence of the LTA in particular. What one really wants to know is a great deal more about the internal pressures. What advice, for example, did the officials of the Ministry of Education offer to their Minister on the Herbert Commission proposals and what influenced their views? How much was the Minister open to departmental suggestions and what determined his views? Above all, perhaps, what was the balance of power within the Cabinet Committee which had to decide what to do about the Commission's Report?

These questions are raised not merely in a destructive spirit, but to indicate that any view of the reasons behind the Government's decision has to rely a good deal on inference from limited facts. Among the facts which are important are first that the views of local authorities and other bodies on the Herbert Commission's proposals did not lend enthusiastic support to the idea of a reform of London government; secondly, that education was a vital point in the Government's plan as presented in the White Paper and as subsequently modified.

On the first point, it is true that a number of second-tier authorities welcomed the Herbert Commission's proposals. But this hardly amounted to pressure on the Government to put those proposals into effect. No deputations went to the Minister from Harrow or Ealing urging the Government to act. This was in part because the Commission did not give any existing authority, with the exception of the City of London, complete satisfaction. On the other hand, there was plenty of indication that many local authorities were utterly opposed to the Commission's plan. If one is looking for the reasons why the Government decided to take action, the influence of local authorities must, therefore, be largely discounted.

A somewhat similar situation arises over the position of professional bodies. Many of them, like the LTA, were opposed to the Herbert Commission's proposals. Others, such as the Town Planning Institute, were uneasy about specific parts of the proposals. There was, therefore, very little in the way of solid support for the Herbert proposals from outside, except from the organs of informed opinion, notably *The Times*.

One, therefore, naturally looks to the situation within the Government for an explanation of why they went ahead. It has been argued here that the Cabinet had to decide on a plan which resulted from a conflict of two viewpoints, Mr Brooke's desire to see the Herbert Commission's proposals carried out and Sir David Eccles' opposition to the Commission's education proposals. Mr Brooke's role was the more important. If he, as Minister of Housing and Local Government had not been willing to take up the Commission's Report, the whole question might well have been shelved. The first question is, therefore, why Mr Brooke was concerned to see a reform plan on Herbert Commission lines put into effect.

As has been discussed earlier, there are two possible reasons for Mr Brooke's action. There was first the fact that the Herbert Commission's Report presented him with an answer to the problems of London government. Secondly, there is the political motive, that a plan on the Commission's lines might well mean the end of Labour's long control of the LCC. It has been argued earlier in this volume that the first reason was the major one, particularly as it was supported by departmental advice but certainly this does not mean that he was uninfluenced by political motives, only that on this particular issue they were not the dominating factor.

Is there perhaps a third possibility, that although Mr Brooke saw himself as dealing with a problem of London government, the real stimulus to action was provided by his unconscious desire to oust Labour from control at County Hall, a desire which he did not acknowledge even to himself? There are obvious dangers in positing explanations in terms of unconscious motivation. One cannot exclude such a possibility; equally one cannot demonstrate its truth. Ultimately, acceptance or rejection of it turns on what view is taken of Henry Brooke's character. The view taken here is that an adequate explanation of his attitude can be found without the need to suppose that he had this unacknowledged stimulus to action.

In any case, the nature of the compromise plan requires us also to take into account Sir David Eccles' attitude in considering the situation with which the Cabinet had to deal. And he, it is clear, was more concerned with functional than with political arguments. Moreover, his view that on educational grounds the LCC education service should be preserved was strongly held by him personally and did not simply represent a tame following of departmental advice; for that reason, the campaign of the London Teachers' Association was not a major influence on events. So far as the Minister of Education was concerned, they were providing him with ammunition, not converting him to their point of view.

Several consequences followed. The importance of education as a local government service made it essential for Mr Brooke to secure the support of Sir David Eccles to any reform plan which was put before the Cabinet. That support could only be secured for a system of education in Greater London which went counter to one of the main elements of the Herbert Commission's proposals, the disappearance of all the existing major authorities in the area, including the LCC. Hence followed discussions and arguments between Mr Brooke and Sir David Eccles before a compromise was agreed to preserve most but not all of the LCC education service intact. The aftermath of these arguments is clearly seen in the subsequent differences of view over the nature of the review of the Inner London Education Authority when it had finally been agreed to establish the latter body.[16]

The consequence of most importance for the present analysis and one that must be stressed as vital to an understanding of the Government's decision to publish the White Paper is that the compromise plan presented to the Cabinet for decision did not at all appear as a clear-cut issue. Politically, destruction of the LCC might have too high a price if it brought the Government into conflict with their own back-benchers and with influential Conservatives in the counties. Moreover preservation of at any rate a large part of the LCC's education service might lead to pressures, which would be difficult to resist, to preserve other parts of the existing structure.

In functional terms, although there might be a case for a Greater London Council as a planning and traffic authority, did this really justify breaking up existing county services and making the awkward arrangements for education? And would the health of local government be better assured under the proposed modification of the Herbert Commission's plan than under the existing system?

In this situation we have to consider both how Mr Brooke presented the plan to the Cabinet for decision and what reaction he met. If the view presented here is the correct one, Mr Brooke's inclination was to put forward the plan as offering a solution to London's problems; the differences between the plan and the Herbert Commission's proposals would then be seen as a necessary part of the attempt to find a satisfactory solution within the Commission's frame-work. That the plan necessarily involved the disappearance of the LCC and that this had political implications would be obvious to anyone studying the plan.

But many, perhaps most, members of the Cabinet viewed the plan with indifference. It is doubtful whether any of them, apart from Mr Brooke, felt strongly about local government reform. The inclination to do nothing about reforming London government must have been great in the face of the troublesome opposition which could be expected. Moreover, the Cabinet had other more pressing problems to consider in the summer and autumn of 1961: an economic crisis at home, for example, leading to a number of restrictions including the 'pay pause',[17] and a major international crisis over Berlin are likely to have figured prominently on the agenda at this time. It would not be surprising, therefore, if there was considerable reluctance to become involved in the reform plan for London government put forward by Mr Brooke. It may well be that the Cabinet was fairly evenly divided and that the majority in favour of going ahead was small.

Such a view is plausible but speculative. But it emphasizes the point that in this situation it is impossible to say that any one set of arguments or motives was predominant in arriving at the decision. The decision was rather the result of a number of factors among which Mr Brooke's advocacy, functional arguments and political arguments were prominent. It would be difficult to pinpoint precisely the reasons for the Government's decision without conducting an enquiry into the factors which weighed most with members of the Cabinet, individually and collectively. One may argue that without the argument from political advantage it is unlikely that a majority of the Cabinet would have been in favour of reform, given the traditional reasons against involvement in local government reform. But it may be that without the Herbert Commission's well-argued case or Mr Brooke's advocacy there would have been no majority for reform in spite of the political advantages.

There can be no conclusive answer to the question of why the Government committed themselves to the reform of London government. If they had decided not to go ahead, their decision would have caused no surprise, and it would have been assumed that, like previous Governments, they had been unwilling to act against strong local authority opposition. The surprise was that they did decide to go ahead in spite of this opposition. Because they did, it is natural to look for an over-riding motive; and because the decision was a political decision, it is tempting to see this over-riding motive as political. Certainly, political arguments and motives were important, but the argument here has been that there was no over-riding motive and that it gives a truer representation of the situation when Mr Brooke presented his reform plan to the Cabinet to stress the confused nature of the arguments and motives which led to the ultimate decision. It can perhaps be summed up by saying that in the Conservative Cabinet of 1961 there was no very great enthusiasm for London reform, only an inability, in the face of Mr Brooke's enthusiasm, to think of an alternative other than simply preserving the existing system. Great decisions may often be taken for no better or worse reason.

(c) *The decision to continue in the face of opposition*

Once the White Paper was published, the Government's plan was bound to have a certain momentum of its own. Nevertheless, it has been shown that when Dr Hill succeeded Mr Brooke as Minister of Housing and Local Government, he showed distinctly less enthusiasm for the project and made concessions which it is likely that Mr Brooke would have attempted to resist. The reason was quite simply that Dr Hill's interests were not in local government reform but in

ɪ

housing; moreover Mr Brooke had a much more direct personal commitment to the London reform plan.

The third main stage in the implementation of this plan is perhaps of less interest in terms of the fundamental questions raised in this chapter. The form of the Bill and its handling in the parliamentary stages are important, but the question which would need to be considered is whether there was any chance, after the White Paper had been published, that the Government would decide not to go ahead at all or, more likely, would weaken the plan drastically to meet the various criticisms which were made of it.

The fact that even when Dr Hill was Minister, the Government did not concede that the children's service of the LCC should be preserved is perhaps the best indication that the main part of the plan would be preserved intact. The chief reason was the practical one that having committed themselves to reform London government, the Government had no alternative but to stand firm on the children's issue, just as they had to resist some of the pressures from local authorities who wished to be excluded from Greater London. Both Dr Hill and Sir Keith Joseph understood this, though they may have differed in the degree of willingness with which they undertook the task. Sir Keith Joseph's belief that reform of London government was necessary and desirable helped to ensure that the Government's position was maintained against the strong opposition both of the Parliamentary Labour Party and of a number of Conservative back benchers.

In the whole course of these events there were after all only two proposals about London government which made sense; either to preserve the existing structure of local government with some adjustment of functions and authorities within the counties together with the creation of machinery for joint action over Greater London problems (the Surrey plan); or to create a Greater London authority with all the consequences that followed for existing authorities and the pattern of distribution of functions (the Herbert Commission plan). At no point after the Commission had reported was there any suggestion that a workable compromise plan between these two was either possible or desirable. This is why the most important decision taken by the Government was the decision to accept a plan on Herbert Commission lines; this too is why the bargaining between Mr Brooke and Sir David Eccles is not a subsidiary issue but a vital part of the decision. It seemed to point in the direction of a compromise between the two alternatives, but it also made clear that education could not be treated as a precedent for other functions. It represented a weakening of the plan of reform, not a move towards retention of the existing system.

In one sense, therefore, the record of events hinges on the personality of the Minister who played the leading part, Mr Henry Brooke. The precise form of the final plan was due to him and Sir David Eccles. These are simplifications. In reality the situation was very complex and it is probable that no single explanation will fit all the circumstances. This is not surprising. Few people pursue an aim single-mindedly and without inconsistency. It is unreasonable to expect Governments which are subject to many and varied pressures, to do the same. The London reforms appeared very differently to different people. Sir Isaac Hayward saw only what, to him, was an almost incredible proposal to destroy the LCC; Sir Cyril Black viewed it as a needless disturbance of Surrey's efficient local government; Lord Morrison of Lambeth conceived it as a wicked Tory plot to oust Labour from London's County Hall.

At the end of it all one thing remains certain. Once the White Paper had been published the Conservative Government found that it had embarked on a long and politically hazardous course which ended in the introduction of a new type of structure into English local government. Whether they did it reluctantly or with enthusiasm, whether they were primarily concerned with political advantage or with efficient local government, whether they believed that they were strengthening local democracy or that they were dealing with an awkward problem, are in the long run less significant than what they did. Beyond this is one further question: did they do the right thing?

Appendix 1

Chronological Table of Main Events, 1957-1965

1957

18 January   Mr Brooke replaces Mr Sandys as Minister of Housing and Local Government.

29 July   Announcement of proposal to set up a Royal Commission

10 December   Appointment of Royal Commission (Chairman: Sir Edwin Herbert).

1958

17 February   Commission invite evidence from local authorities.

1959

5 March   Commission begin oral hearings.

1960

2 February   Commission end oral hearings.

19 October   Publication of Commission's Report.

28 November   Ministry of Housing and Local Government invite comments on the Report from local authorities.

21 December   House of Lords debate on the Report.

1961

April   County Council elections.

9 October   Dr Hill replaces Mr Brooke as Minister of Housing and Local Government.

29 November   Publication of White Paper *London Government: Government Proposals for Reorganization.*

16 December   Ministry of Housing and Local Government Circular 56/61 issued, showing proposed borough groupings.

1962

January   First borough joint committee set up in Bromley.

19/20 February   House of Commons debate on the White Paper.

12/13 March	LCC debate on the White Paper.
14 March	House of Lords debate on the White Paper.
23 March	Dr Hill announces the names of the four town clerks to investigate borough groupings and their terms of reference.
31 March	Deadline for local authority comments on proposed borough groupings.
4 April	Dr Hill tells the Metropolitan Water Board that they are to be taken over by the proposed Greater London Council.
6 April	LCC deputation to the Prime Minister.
9 April	First conference on borough groupings by one of the four town clerks.
30 April	Dr Hill announces the exclusion of Banstead, Caterham & Warlingham, and Walton and Weybridge from Greater London.
3 May	Dr Hill announces the decision to retain the LCC education service intact, subject to review.
18 May	Dr Hill announces decisions on other areas seeking exclusion from Greater London.
5 June	Final conference on borough groupings.
15 June	Ministry of Housing and Local Government invite local authorities to discussions on the problems of the changeover.
25 June	Formation of the Committee for London Government
13 July	Government changes: Sir Keith Joseph replaces Dr Hill as Minister of Housing and Local Government; Sir Edward Boyle replaces Sir David Eccles as Minister of Education.
2 August	Sir Keith Joseph announces acceptance of the proposals on borough groupings made by the four town clerks.
20 November	First reading of London Government Bill.
10/11 December	Second reading of London Government Bill (House of Commons)

1963

23 January	Beginning of committee stage on the Bill (Committee of Whole House).
29 January	Government move 'Guillotine' motion.
5 February	Bill in Standing Committee.
21 March	Completion of Committee Stage (House of Commons)
1/2 April	Re-committal, Report and Third Reading (House of Commons)

23/4 April	Second Reading of the Bill (House of Lords).
2 May	Membership of London Government Staff Commission announced.
9 May	Beginning of Committee Stage on the Bill (House of Lords).
30 May	Completion of Committee Stage (House of Lords).
24 June	Beginning of Report Stage on the Bill (House of Lords).
2 July	Completion of Report Stage (House of Lords).
8 July	Third Reading of the Bill (House of Lords).
25 July	Commons consider Lords amendments on the Bill.
31 July	Sir Keith Joseph addresses LCC Staff Association.
23 August	London Government Staff Commission issues first circular.
23 September	Sir Keith Joseph addresses NALGO
November	Metropolitan Boroughs' JC circulate memorandum of proposals for transfer of LCC services to inner London boroughs.

1964

13 February	MHLG circular on method of appointment of borough town clerks etc.
9 April	First election for Greater London Council.
7 May	First election for London boroughs.
15 October	Labour victory in General Election.

1965

2 February	Government announce that they do not propose to make changes in the London Government Act except to repeal the provision for a review of the Inner London Education Authority.
1 April	London Government Act 1963 comes into operation.

Appendix 2

Comparison of Proposals in the Herbert Commission Report and Provisions of the London Government Act, 1963

THE GREATER LONDON COUNCIL

	Royal Commission[1]	*1963 Act*[2]
I. AREA	Review area *less* Watford MB, Bushey UD, Chorleywood UD, Rickmansworth UD, Elstree RD, Watford RD (Aldenham and Watford Rural parishes), Hatfield RD (Northaw parish) (Hertfordshire): Potters Bar UD (Middlesex): Waltham Holy Cross UD (Essex): Dartford MB (Kent) (894–921)	As in Royal Commission Report but *excluding in addition:* Most of Chigwell UD (Essex): Cheshunt UD (Herts): Staines UD, Sunbury-on-Thames UD (Middlesex): Banstead UD Caterham and Warlingham UD, Epsom and Ewell MB, Esher UD, Walton and Weybridge UD (Surrey) (2: Sch 1)

II. FUNCTIONS

(i) Education	Responsibility for maintaining standard of education in Greater London. Formulation of the education development plan. Financial responsibility for education service. Ownership of all schools and colleges. Promotion of parental freedom in choice of schools. Training of teachers and	Education authority for inner London (old LCC area) acting through special committee known as Inner London Education Authority. ILEA *consists of:* (a) all GLC councillors for inner London; (b) one member of each inner London Borough

	Royal Commission[1] maintenance of a single service for Greater London. Colleges of advanced technology and regional colleges (799–829)	*1963 Act*[2] Council and of the Common Council. Review of ILEA not later than 31 March 1970. (Subsequently repealed) (30) ILEA and inner London Boroughs to prepare joint schemes for school health service (32)
(ii) Planning	Greater London Development Plan. Applications to be referred by boroughs: (a) departure from Plan; (b) extraction of minerals. Certain applications relating to the 'central area' (to be defined by Minister) (765–778)	Local planning authority for Greater London as a whole; to prepare and subsequently amend GLDP. Applications to be referred by boroughs: as prescribed by Minister. Minister may also prescribe that other classes of application shall be referred by boroughs for GLC to give directions (24–26)
(iii) Highways and Traffic Management	Responsibility for traffic management throughout GL. Planning, construction, improvement, maintenance and lighting 'main roads' (to be defined by Minister, may include trunk roads). Close contact with LTE, BTC (442: 780–784)	Responsibility for traffic management (subject to Minister's consent on trunk roads). Provision of parking places (subject to borough's consent). Highway authority for 'metropolitan roads' (specified). Licensing of motor vehicles and drivers (9–20: Sch 7)
(iv) Housing	Powers to make provision for housing outside GL	Powers to make provision for housing outside

Royal Commission[1]	*1963 Act*[2]
under Town Development Act, 1952. Powers to build within GL (a) large redevelopment schemes; (b) boroughs unable to meet own needs. Houses built within GL to be transferred ultimately to boroughs. Power to co-ordinate borough housing lists (785–798)	GL under Town Development Act, 1952. Powers to build within GL but require borough consent, except: (a) comprehensive development; (b) rehousing persons displaced by GLC activities. Temporary inheritance of LCC housing powers and accommodation. Record of housing needs and facilities for exchanging housing accommodation (21–23: 61)
(v) Personal Health	Ambulance service (836)	Ambulance service (45(3))

(vi) Environmental Health	Refuse disposal (837) LCC and MCC main sewers (839)	Refuse disposal (Sch 11. para. 15) Main sewers in a large part of GL; GLC may propose extension of area (35)
	Certain large open spaces (eg Crystal Palace; Hampstead Heath) (844–5)	Parks and open spaces of LCC and MCC, but GLC to submit scheme to Minister specifying which to be transferred to boroughs (58)
	Land drainage where more than one borough involved (848)	Land drainage authority for major part of GL (Sch 14)
(vii) Research and Intelligence	Intelligence department to be set up for research into problems of GL (758–763)	Research and information organization to be set up (71) Publicity for GL amenities (73).

	Royal Commission[1]	*1963 Act*[2]
(viii) Other Functions	Fire Service (889)	Fire Service (48)
	Cost of administration of justice (865)	Cost of administration of justice.[3]
	Appointment of coroners (866–7)	Appointment of coroners (78)
	Possibly some aspects of civil defence (890)	Certain civil defence functions (49)
	Provision of art galleries, museums and entertainments (concurrently with boroughs) (868–9)	Provision of entertainments (concurrently with boroughs); LCC powers and property in relation to concert halls, museums etc. (eg Royal Festival Hall, Geffrye museum) (57)
	Public control powers, as determined by the Minister (878)	Licensing of theatres and other places of public entertainment (52; Sch 12); licensing of greyhound racing tracks for betting (53); licensing of premises for storing petrol (50). Provision of smallholdings (55)
	Building regulations (881–888)	Building control (inner London) (43). Power to supply boroughs, voluntary organizations, hospitals etc., with goods. (72)

III. FINANCE

Implicit view that Council should precept on boroughs. Clearing house for new type of rate equalization scheme (963)	Power to precept on boroughs (Sch 2, para 22) Minister may make scheme for rate equalization involving GLC (66).
Special procedure for raising loans similar to that of LCC (970)	Power to promote annual Money Bills for raising capital (Sch 2., paras. 25–29).

Royal Commission[1]	*1963 Act*[2]
	Power to establish insurance fund (Sch 2., para 30) Power to establish superannuation fund (77) Transitional payments (up to 1973) to Essex, Herts, Kent and Surrey (70)

IV. CONSTITUTION

One member for the area of each parliamentary constituency in GL i.e. 109.	Two, three or four members for each borough area (total 100) as interim measure; ultimately one member for each parliamentary constituency.
Triennial elections at same time as borough elections. Aldermen a national issue (850–857)	Triennial elections, ultimately on same day as borough elections. 16 aldermen (one-sixth of councillors). (Sch 2., paras 1–9).

THE LONDON BOROUGHS[4]

I. AREAS[5]	52 Greater London Boroughs (922–945).	32 London Boroughs (Sch 1)

II. FUNCTIONS

(i) Education	Management and maintenance of schools.	20 outer London Boroughs to be local education authorities (30). 12 inner London Boroughs (and City) to be 'minor authorities' eg for purpose of appointing managers of primary schools (31(10)). Joint schemes by ILEA and inner London Boroughs (and City) for provision of school health service. (32)
	Appointment of managers and governors. Administration of youth service and youth employment service. Appointment of teachers. School health service (829)	

	Royal Commission[1]	*1963 Act*[2]
(ii) Planning	Primary authorities for considering and deciding applications, *except* for those to be referred to GLC (see under GLC above) (766)	Local planning authority for preparation of borough development plans. Reception of planning applications and decision on all except those referred to GLC (see under GLC above) (24–26)
(iii) Highways and Traffic Management	Construction, improvement, maintenance and lighting of all except main roads (731)	Highway authorities for all except trunk and metropolitan roads (16) Provision of parking places (13)
(iv) Housing	Housing authorities, including ancillary functions, eg improvement grants (786, 787, 797)	Housing authorities for all purposes. No provision of housing outside GL without Minister's agreement (21)
(v) Personal Health, Welfare and Children's Services	All services except ambulance (830–836)	All services except ambulance. (45–47)
(vi) Environmental Health	All services except those listed under GLC above (837–846; 848–9) City to remain Port Health Authority (847)	All services except those listed under GLC above. (35–40: 44: 54–58: (Sch. 9: Sch. 10: Sch. 11: Sch. 13). City to remain Port Health Authority (41)
(vii) Other Functions	Art Galleries and museums (868) Entertainments (869–70) Libraries (871) Food and Drugs Act (872–4) Weights and Measures (875–6)	Provision of entertainments etc. (57) Libraries (56) Food and Drugs Act (54) Weights and Measures (62(4))

Royal Commission[1]	*1963 Act*[2]
Fertilizers and feeding-stuffs (877)	Slaughterhouses, diseases of animals etc (54)
Shops Act (880)	Offices, Shops and Railway Premises Act (51)
Public control powers as determined by the Minister (878–9)	
Possibly some aspects of civil defence (890)	Certain civil defence functions (49)
Remaining functions wherever possible (892)	Licensing of riding establishments etc. (62)
	Any residual powers of a county borough (4)

III. FINANCE

Rating authorities. Boroughs to make transitional payments to affected counties (964–9)	Rating authorities (63) Authorities to whom general grants payable (64); also rate-deficiency grants (65). Provision for rate equalization scheme (66) Power to establish superannuation fund (77)

IV. CONSTITUTION

As for municipal boroughs outside GL (858)	As for municipal boroughs outside GL, *except* (i) triennial elections; (ii) number of aldermen to be one-sixth of number of councillors; (iii) maximum number of councillors to be 60. (1(4): Sch 4, paras 6, 8).

NOTES

(1) Numbers in brackets refer to paragraphs of the Commission's Report.

(2) Numbers in brackets refer to Sections of the Act: Sch. = Schedule.

(3) Under Administration of Justice Act, 1964.

(4) For details of the composition etc, of the London Boroughs see Appendix 3.

(5) Under the Commission's proposals the City of London was to be a Greater London Borough. Under the 1963 Act the City is specifically assigned each function conferred on a London Borough, but is not designated a London Borough.

(6) See Local Government Act, 1948, section 132.

Appendix 3

The London Boroughs

Greater London Boroughs proposed by the Herbert Commission(52), (Mid-1959 population in brackets)	*London Boroughs proposed by the Government in Circular 56/61 (34) (Census1961 population in brackets)*	*London Boroughs as constituted under the London Government Act, 1963 (32)*	*Names of the London Boroughs and populations (mid-1968)*
1. City of London (4,900)	City of London (4,771)	*City of London	(4,210)
2. City of Westminster (94,640)	1. City of Westminster Paddington Met. B. St Marylebone Met. B. (269,379)	1. City of Westminster Paddington Met. B. St Marylebone Met. B.	City of Westminster (243,960)
3. Paddington Met. B. St Marylebone Met. B. (183,830)			
4. Hampstead Met. B. St Pancras Met. B. (225,510)	3. Hampstead Met. B. Holborn Met. B. St Pancras Met. B. (245,776)	2. Hampstead Met. B. Holborn Met. B. St Pancras Met. B.	Camden (231,680)
5. Finsbury Met. B. Holborn Met. B. Shoreditch Met. B. (98,730)	4. Finsbury Met. B. Islington Met. B. (261,822)	3. Finsbury Met. B. Islington Met. B.	Islington (241,890)
6. Islington Met. B. 223,400)			
7. Hackney Met. B. Stoke Newington Met. B. (213,400)	5. Hackney Met. B. Stoke Newington Met. B. (216,836)	4. Hackney Met. B Shoreditch Met. B. Stoke Newington Met. B.	Hackney (243,180)

Greater London Boroughs proposed by the Herbert Commission (52) (Mid-1959 population in brackets)	London Boroughs proposed by the Government in Circular 56/61 (34) (Census 1961 population in brackets)	London Boroughs as constituted under the London Government Act, 1963 (32)	Names of the London Boroughs and populations (mid-1968)
8. Bethnal Green Met. B. Poplar Met. B. Stepney Met. B. (207,400) 9. Woolwich Met. B. (144,800)	6. Bethnal Green Met. B Poplar Met. B. Shoreditch Met. B. Stepney Met. B. (245,840)	5. Bethnal Green Met. B. Poplar Met. B. Stepney Met. B.	Tower Hamlets (192,250)
10. Deptford Met. B. Greenwich Met. B. (158,630)	7. Greenwich Met. B. Woolwich Met. B. (excl N Woolwich) (230,082)	6. Greenwich Met. B. Woolwich Met. B. (excl N Woolwich)	Greenwich (229,700)
11. Lewisham Met. B. (221,000) 12. Camberwell Met. B. (176,100)	8. Lewisham Met. B. (221,590)	7. Deptford Met. B. Lewisham Met. B.	Lewisham (281,140)
13. Bermondsey Met. B. Southwark Met. B. (142,840)	9. Bermondsey Met. B. Camberwell Met. B. Deptford Met. B. (294,779)	8. Bermondsey Met. B. Camberwell Met. B. Southwark Met. B.	Southwark (293,120)
14. Lambeth Met. B. (223,300)	10. Lambeth Met. B. Southwark Met. B. (309,337)	9. Lambeth Met. B. Wandsworth Met. B. (eastern part)	Lambeth (329,250)
15. Wandsworth Met. B. (part) (222,000)	11. Wandsworth Met. B. 10. (southern part) (240,300)	10. Battersea Met. B. Wandsworth Met. B. (western part)	Wandsworth (321,720)
16. Battersea Met. B. Wandsworth Met. B. (part) (225,300)	12. Battersea Met. B. Wandsworth Met. B. (western part) (212,667)		
17. Fulham Met. B. Hammersmith Met. B. (222,200)	13. Fulham Met. B. Hammersmith Met. B. (222,059)	11. Fulham Met. B. Hammersmith Met. B.	Hammersmith (197,590)
18. Chelsea Met. B. Kensington Met. B. (216,020)	14. Chelsea Met. B. Kensington Met. B. (217,976)	12. Chelsea Met. B. Kensington Met. B.	Royal Borough of Kensington and Chelsea (210,720)

Greater London Boroughs proposed by the Herbert Commission (52) (Mid-1959 population in brackets)	London Boroughs proposed by the Government in Circular 56/61 (34) (Census 1961 population in brackets)	London Boroughs as constituted under the London Government Act, 1963 (32)	Names of the London Boroughs and populations (mid-1968)
19. Chingford MB Walthamstow MB (159,030) 20. Chigwell UD Leyton MB Wanstead and Woodford MB (221,520)	15. Chigwell UD (northern part) Chingford MB Leyton MB Walthamstow MB Wanstead and Woodford MB (355,182)	13. Chingford MB Leyton MB Walthamstow MB	Waltham Forest (236,900)
21. Ilford MB (178,600	16. Chigwell UD (southern part) Dagenham MB (small part) Ilford MB (195,610)	14. Ilford MB Wanstead and Woodford MB Dagenham MB (small part) Chigwell UD (southern part)	Redbridge (246,090)
22. Romford MB (114,800) 23. Hornchurch UD (122,600)	17. Hornchurch UD (northern part) Romford MB (214,506)	15. Romford MB Hornchurch UD	Havering (252,290)
24. Barking MB Dagenham MB (189,180)	18. Barking MB (major part) Dagenham MB (major part) Hornchurch UD (southern part) (206,845)	16. Barking MB (major part) Dagenham MB (major part)	Barking (169,520)
25. East Ham CB (109,900) 26. West Ham CB (164,300)	19. Barking MB (small part) East Ham CB West Ham CB Woolwich Met. B. (N. Woolwich) (264,545)	17. East Ham CB West Ham CB Barking MB (small part) Woolwich Met. B. (N. Woolwich)	Newham (255,130)
27. Bexley M.B. Crayford UD Erith MB (166,800)	20. Bexley M.B. Chislehurst and Sidcup UD Crayford UD Erith MB (252,844)	18. Bexley M.B. Erith MB Crayford UD Chislehurst and Sidcup UD (northern part)	Bexley (215,470)

Greater London Boroughs proposed by the Herbert Commission (52) (Mid-1959 population in brackets)	London Boroughs proposed by the Government in Circular 56/61 (34) (Census 1961 population in brackets)	London Boroughs as constituted under the London Government Act, 1963 (32)	Names of the London Boroughs and populations (mid-1968)
28. Chislehurst and Sidcup UD Orpington UD (163,640)			
29. Beckenham MB Bromley MB Penge UD (166,750)	21. Beckenham MB Bromley MB Orpington UD Penge UD (251,437)	19. Beckenham MB Bromley MB Orpington UD Penge UD Chislehurst and Sidcup UD (southern part)	Bromley (304,230)
30. Croydon CB (249,000)	22. Caterham and Warlingham UD Coulsdon and Purley UD Croydon CB (361,933)	20. Croydon CB Coulsdon and Purley UD	Croydon (329,210)
31. Caterham and Warlingham UD Coulsdon and Purley UD (104,140) 32. Banstead UD Epsom and Ewell MB (106,890)	23. Banstead UD Beddington and Wallington MB Carshalton UD Epsom and Ewell MB Sutton and Cheam MB (281,769)	21. Beddington and Wallington MB Sutton and Cheam MB Carshalton UD	Sutton (165,430)
33. Beddington and Wallington MB Carshalton UD Sutton and Cheam MB (171,700)			
34. Mitcham MB Wimbledon MB Merton and Morden UD (192,280)	24. Mitcham MB Wimbledon MB Merton and Morden UD (188,621)	22. Mitcham MB Wimbledon MB Merton and Morden UD	Merton (184,220)
35. Kingston-upon-Thames MB Malden and Coombe MB	25. Esher UD Kingston-upon-Thames MB Malden and	23. Kingston-upon-Thames MB Malden and Coombe MB	Royal Borough of Kingston upon Thames (144,480)

Greater London Boroughs proposed by the Herbert Commission (52) (Mid-1959 population in brackets)	*London Boroughs proposed by the Government in Circular 56/61 (34) (Census 1961 population in brackets)*	*London Boroughs as constituted under the London Government Act, 1963 (32)*	*Names of the London Boroughs and populations (mid-1968)*
Surbiton MB (147,800)	Coombe MB Surbiton MB Walton and Weybridge UD (252,060)	Surbiton MB	
36. Esher UD Walton and Weybridge UD (100,920)			
37. Barnes MB Richmond MB (81,210)	26. Barnes MB Richmond MB Twickenham MB (181,581)	24. Barnes MB Richmond MB Twickenham MB	Richmond upon Thames (177,130)
38. Twickenham MB (103,600)			
39. Feltham UD Staines UD Sunbury-on-Thames UD (129,370)	27. Brentford and Chiswick MB Feltham UD Heston and Isleworth MB Staines UD Sunbury-on-Thames UD (291,432)	25. Brentford and Chiswick MB Heston and Isleworth MB Feltham UD	Hounslow (205,580)
40 Heston and Isleworth MB (105,000)			
41. Ruislip-Northwood UD Uxbridge MB Yiewsley and West Drayton UD (162,510)	28. Hayes and Harlington UD Ruislip-Northwood UD Uxbridge MB Yiewsley and West Drayton UD (227,913)	26. Uxbridge MB Hayes and Harlington UD Ruislip-Northwood UD Yiewsley and West Drayton UD	Hillingdon (236,990)
42. Hayes and Harlington UD Southall MB (121,570)			

Greater London Boroughs proposed by the Herbert Commission (52) (Mid-1959 population in brackets)	London Boroughs proposed by the Government in Circular 56/61 (34) (Census 1961 population in brackets)	London Boroughs as constituted under the London Government Act, 1963 (32)	Names of the London Boroughs and populations (mid-1968)
43. Acton MB Brentford and Chiswick MB (121,770)	29. Acton MB Ealing MB Southall MB (299,762)	27. Acton MB Ealing MB Southall MB	Ealing (298,720)
44. Ealing MB (182,700)			
45. Wembley MB (126,300)	30. Wembley MB Willesden MB (295,678)	28. Wembley MB Willesden MB	Brent (284,460)
46. Willesden MB (172,800)			
47. Harrow MB (213,700)	31. Harrow MB (208,963)	29. Harrow MB	Harrow (208,220)
48. Hendon MB (151,500) 49. Barnet UD East Barnet UD Finchley MB Friern Barnet UD (165,350)	32. Barnet UD Finchley MB Hendon MB (248,645) 33. East Barnet UD Enfield MB (western part) Friern Barnet UD Hornsey MB Southgate MB Wood Green MB (329,239)	30. Finchley MB Hendon MB Barnet UD East Barnet UD Friern Barnet UD	Barnet (316,240)
50. Hornsey MB Southgate MB Wood Green MB (215,630)		31. Hornsey MB Tottenham MB Wood Green MB	Haringey (245,270)
51. Edmonton MB Tottenham MB (210,520) 52. Cheshunt UD Enfield MB 140,810)	34. Cheshunt UD Edmonton MB Enfield MB (eastern part) Tottenham MB (308,009)	32. Edmonton MB Enfield MB Southgate MB	Enfield (267,830)

* City of London – not designated as a London borough but given the powers of one.

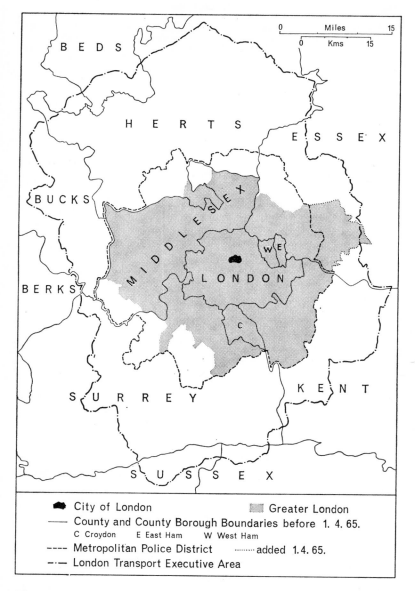

Figure 4. Greater London (as constituted 1st April 1965) in relation to former County and County Borough Boundaries, the Metropolitan Police District and London Transport Executive Area.

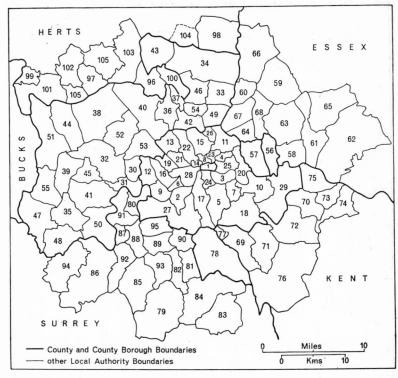

Figure 5(a) Area of Review of the Royal Commission on Local
Government in Greater London, 1957-1960.

KEY TO AREAS IN FIGURE 5(a)

County of London.
1   City of London
2   Battersea Met. B.
3   Bermondsey ,,
4   Bethnal Green ,,
5   Camberwell ,,
6   Chelsea ,,
7   Deptford ,,
8   Finsbury ,,
9   Fulham ,,
10 Greenwich ,,
11 Hackney ,,
12 Hammersmith ,,
13 Hampstead ,,

14 Holborn Met. B.
15 Islington ,,
16 Kensington ,,
17 Lambeth ,,
18 Lewisham ,,
19 Paddington ,,
20 Poplar ,,
21 St. Marylebone,,
22 St. Pancras ,,
23 Shoreditch ,,
24 Southwark ,,
25 Stepney ,,
26 Stoke
        Newington ,,

27 Wandsworth Met. B.
28 City of
        Westminster ,,
29 Woolwich ,,

Middlesex.
30 Acton MB
31 Brentford &
        Chiswick ,,
32 Ealing ,,
33 Edmonton ,,
34 Enfield ,,
35 Feltham UD
36 Finchley MB

Figure 5(b) Greater London Boroughs as Proposed by the Herbert
Commission, October 1960 (see Appendix 3 for Key).

(continued)

37 Friern Barnet UD
38 Harrow MB
39 Hayes and Har-
   lington UD
40 Hendon MB
41 Heston and Isle-
   worth MB
42 Hornsey MB
43 Potters Bar UD
44 Ruislip-North-
   wood ,,
45 Southall MB
46 Southgate ,,
47 Staines UD
48 Sunbury-on-
   Thames ,,

49 Tottenham MB
50 Twickenham ,,
51 Uxbridge ,,
52 Wembley ,,
53 Willesden ,,
54 Wood Green ,,
55 Yiewsley and
   West Drayton UD

Essex.
56 East Ham CB
57 West Ham ,,
58 Barking MB
58 Chigwell UD
60 Chingford MB
61 Dagenham ,,

62 Hornchurch UD
63 Ilford MB
64 Leyton ,,
65 Romford ,,
66 Waltham Holy
   Cross UD
67 Walthamstow MB
68 Wanstead and
   Woodford ,,

Kent.
69 Beckenham MB
70 Bexley ,,
71 Bromley ,,
72 Chislehurst and
   Sidcup UD

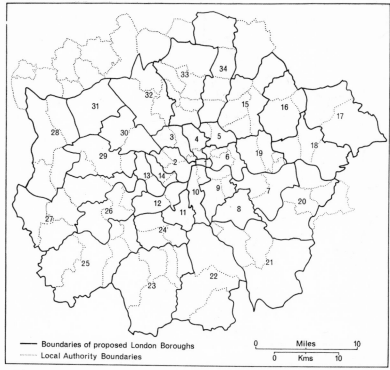

Figure 5(c). London Boroughs as Proposed by the Government, December, 1961 (see Appendix 3 for Key).

(continued)
73 Crayford „
74 Dartford MB
75 Erith „
76 Orpington UD
77 Penge UD

Surrey.
78 Croydon CB
79 Banstead UD
80 Barnes MB
81 Beddington and
    Wallington „
82 Carshalton UD
83 Caterham and
    Warlingham UD
84 Coulsdon and
    Purley „

85 Epsom and
    Ewell MB
86 Esher UD
87 Kingston-upon-
    Thames MB
88 Malden and
    Coombe „
89 Merton and
    Morden UD
90 Mitcham MB
91 Richmond „
92 Surbiton „
93 Sutton and
    Cheam „
94 Walton and
    Weybridge UD
95 Wimbledon MB

Hertfordshire
96 Barnet UD
97 Bushey „
98 Cheshunt „
99 Chorleywood „
100 East Barnet „
101 Rickmans-
    worth „
102 Watford MB
103 Elstree RD
104 Hatfield „
    (Northaw parish)
105 Watford „
    (Aldenham and
    Watford Rural
    parishes)

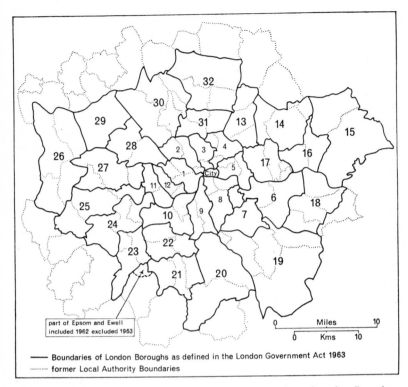

Boundaries of London Boroughs as defined in the London Government Act 1963
former Local Authority Boundaries

part of Epsom and Ewell included 1962 excluded 1963

Miles
Kms

Figure 5(d). London Boroughs as Constituted under the London Government Act, 1963 (see Appendix 3 for Key).

N.B. For key to numbered areas in Figures 5(b) to (d), see Appendix 3, page 255.

Notes

The following abbreviations are used in the notes:

Report: Report of the Royal Commission on Local Government in Greater London, 1957–60 (Cmnd 1164: London, Her Majesty's Stationery Office, 1960).

WE: Royal Commission on Local Government in Greater London, Written Evidence from Local Authorities, Miscellaneous Bodies and Private Individuals (5 vols, London, Her Majesty's Stationery Office, 1962).

ME: Royal Commission on Local Government in Greater London, Minutes of Evidence (Published separately for each day by Her Majesty's Stationery Office, 1959 and 1960).

Mem. Evid.: Memoranda of Evidence from Government Departments (London, Her Majesty's Stationery Office, 1959).

Standing Com. F: Official Report, Standing Committee F (Her Majesty's Stationery Office, 1963).

CHAPTER 1

1   See for example Map 3 in the *Report of the Royal Commission on Local Government in Greater London, 1957–60* ('Herbert' Commission) Cmnd 1164 (HMSO, 1960).

2   W. A. Robson, *The Government and Misgovernment of London*, (London, Allen & Unwin, 2nd edit. 1948), p. 42.

3   Sir Keith Joseph speaking as Minister of Housing and Local Government (HC Deb., 13 February 1963, Vol. 671, col. 1370).

4   Extended by the Metropolitan Police Act, 1839, to a radius of 12–15 miles. The City of London was not included in the Metropolitan Police District and still retains its own separate police force. See Figure 4 for the boundaries of the present Metropolitan Police District.

5   Election of members of the Board was by the 99 parishes in the area acting either singly or in groups.

6   These scandals involved corrupt transactions in relation to a number of building projects (see Robson, *The Government and Misgovernment of London*, pp. 63–4).

7 On this see Robson, *The Government and Misgovernment of London*, pp. 92–96.

8 By the time of the Herbert Commission of 1957 only six English county boroughs had bigger populations than the largest metropolitan borough (Wandsworth).

9 See Figure 4 (p. 261) for the boundaries of Greater London.

10 The area of the Metropolitan Board of Works was the area of the metropolis defined by the Registrar General for the purpose of compiling mortality statistics. (See on this T. W. Freeman *Geography and Regional Administration*, Hutchinson University Library, London, 1968, pp. 151–5).

11 See *Report of Royal Commission on London Government* ('Ullswater') Cmd 1830, 1923, para. 132; also Minority Report of Messrs Donald and Walsh, para 11 onwards.

12 In his memorandum to the Cabinet, the Minister of Health, Sir Alfred Mond, described the LCC's approach and the reaction of other local authorities and added 'I think that a case has been made out for setting up a Royal Commission'. (PRO Papers CP3089 LG45, 29 June 1921).

13 The majority consisted of Viscount Ullswater, a former speaker of the House of Commons and subsequently an alderman of the East Suffolk County Council; Sir Horace Monro, a retired permanent secretary of the Local Government Board; Sir Albert Gray, counsel to the Chairman of Committees of the House of Lords for many years; and Sir Edmund Turton, a London county councillor from 1892 to 1897 and subsequently Conservative MP for Thirsk.

14 Signed by Mr (later Sir) E. Haviland Hiley, a senior railway official and Mr (later Sir) George Talbot, a High Court judge from 1923 to 1937.

15 It was signed by Mr (later Sir) Robert Donald founder of the Municipal Journal and the Municipal Year Book, and Mr Stephen Walsh an ex-miner and Labour MP for Ince who was Parliamentary Secretary to the Local Government Board in 1917–18.

16 'We hold that Greater London is one and indivisible in all the essentials which constitute one great civic and urban community' (para. 231).

17 See *Report* of the Ullswater Commission, paras. 87, 92, 93 and 126ff.

18 Quoted in *Report* of the Ullswater Commission, para. 275.

19 Minority Report para. 112.

20 See PRO Papers HLG9/46 (91002/1/58). A verbatim report of the proceedings was printed by the LCC.

21 See *Report* of the Ullswater Commission, para. 262 and Minority Report, para. 35.

22 For the functions and composition of the London and Home Counties Traffic Advisory Committee see Robson, *The Government and Misgovernment of London*, pp. 149–55.

23 *First Report of the Greater London Regional Planning Committee* (Knapp, Drewett, London, 1929), p. 5.

24 Robson, *The Government and Misgovernment of London*, p. 464.

25 Cmd 6579 (1945) para. 1.

26 Cmd 6579, p. 18.

27 Cmd 6579, p. 19.

28 Under the Local Government (Boundary Commission) Act, 1945.

29 HC Deb., Vol. 417, 20 December, 1945 col. 1646.

30 See HC Deb., Vol. 428, 24 October, 1946, W.A. cols. 1–2.

31 See Commission's Report for 1948 (HC 150, 27 April 1949), p. 7.

32 HC Deb., Vol. 466, 27 June 1949, cols. 758–761.

33 See Map 4 in Herbert Commission Report (Cmnd 1164, 1960) for the relationship of these different areas.

34 Greater London Plan 1944 (HMSO 1945), p. 1.

35 He was also to be chairman of the advisory committee.

36 See page 8 above. The alternatives assume that planning remains a local government function, as indeed the Clement Davies Committee thought it should.

37 The position had been complicated by the introduction of what became the Town and Country Planning Act, 1947 during the course of the Committee's deliberations; among other things this drastically reduced the number of planning authorities. For an account of the Committee's activities by one of the participants, see Robson, *The Government and Misgovernment of London*, pp. 491–7.

38 *Report* para. 326.

39 *Areas and Status of Local Authorities in England and Wales* (Cmd 9831, HMSO 1956), para 12.

40 Cmd 9831, paras 44–47.

41 *Functions of County Councils and County District Councils in England and Wales* (Cmnd 161, HMSO 1957), paras 25, 26.

42 Now Lord Brooke of Cumnor.

43 HC Deb., 29 July 1957, vol. 574, col. 917.

44 His local government career began in 1936 when he was elected a councillor of Hampstead Metropolitan Borough; from 1938 to 1945 he was Member of Parliament for West Lewisham which he represented on the LCC from 1945 to 1946; he represented Hampstead in Parliament from 1950 to 1966 and St George's (1946 to 1949) and the Cities of London and Westminster (1949 to 1955) on the LCC.

45 See below, chapter 7.

46 cf his successor's view of his passion for legislation and of the deep respect felt for him by his civil service staff (Lord Hill of Luton, *Both Sides of the Hill*, Heinemann 1964, p. 214).

47 On the Second Reading of the Luton Bill the Minister (Harold Macmillan) said: 'The time must come soon when we must decide either to deal with county borough Bills such as these on their merits ... or to introduce, or to put a time on the introduction of, a large-scale measure of local government reorganization . . . This is the last time that I hope either I or my successor will ask the House to refuse approval to a Bill giving county borough status to a local authority solely on the ground that a new prospect is just around the corner' (HC Deb., 18 March 1954, 711–2).

48 Ealing, Enfield, Harrow, Hendon, Heston and Isleworth, Tottenham, Twickenham, Wembley and Willesden all had populations of over 100,000.

49 cf the proposals made in the Hiley/Talbot minority report of the Ullswater Commission (above p. 15).

50 *ME.* 68th day, 12 January 1960, Q 15546.

51 He was Director General of the Post and Telegraph Censorship Department from 1940 to 1945.

52 See Appendix to this chapter for a list of members, and the terms of reference of the Commission.

53 Mr Paul Cadbury and Sir Charles Morris.

54 Professor W. J. M. Mackenzie.

55 Local Government Act, 1958, Sections 17–20.

56 An example will illustrate this: the Commission's proposal to make Cambridge a county borough and amalgamate the remainder of Cambridgeshire with Huntingdonshire, the Isle of Ely and the Soke of Peterborough to form a single county, was modified through the strong opposition of the counties to a proposal for two counties (a) Cambridgeshire (including Cambridge MB) plus Isle of Ely (b) Huntingdonshire plus Soke of Peterborough.

57 See Appendix to this Chapter; also Figure 5 (a), p. 262 for the relationship of the Commission's area to other areas and the local authority areas included in the review area.

58 This information was given in answer to a Parliamentary Question (HC Deb., 26 November 1957, cols. 964–5).

59 With the exception of the City of London police and a few fringe areas beyond the Metropolitan Police District; but apart from other considerations which may have affected the Government's views on this, it would have been absurd to consider the City of London police in isolation from the Metropolitan Police.

60 For the later position about water supply see pages 140–3 below. The Prime Minister (Mr Harold Macmillan) reported the discussions over functions in the following terms: 'I was not able to accept suggestions that the scope should be widened so as to cover matters outside the normal field of local government. The draft terms of reference were; however, amended so as to leave the administration of water supply for separate consideration . . . . It is perfectly true that a number of authorities . . . wished that the police functions should be considered in the review, but for the bulk of the area police is not a local authority function.' (HC Deb., 28 November 1957, cols. 1279–80).

61 HC Deb., 28 November 1957, col. 1280.

CHAPTER 2

1 See above, p. 5.

2 Cmnd 1164 (later referred to simply as *Report*), para. 12.

3 See Frank Smallwood, *Greater London* (New York, Bobbs–Merrill, 1965), pp. 171–4.

4 The letter is reproduced as Item 3 of Part II of the Commission's Report (p. 270).

5 *Report,* para 160.

6 See the account in J. A. G. Griffith, *Central Departments and Local Authorities* (RIPA, Allen & Unwin, 1966), pp. 33ff, especially 40–43.

7 We learn, for example, that a public convenience at Hillingdon has, as a special feature 'a central compartment in which the whole of the plumbing and flushing systems are contained and which can be heated if required', that Uxbridge has provided a bird sanctuary and that the number of gas street lamps has been reduced from 869 to 572 since the war.

8 *Written Evidence from Local Authorities, Miscellaneous Bodies and Private Individuals* (5 vols. HMSO 1962) Vol. I, p. 156.

9 *WE* Vol. I, p. 27.

10 *Minutes of Evidence (ME)*, 11th day, 23 April 1959, Q 2393.

11 *ME* 11th day, 23 April 1959, Q 2380.

12 See *Report* para. 178.

13 See London County Council Minutes, 15 July 1958, pp. 487–90.

14 *ME* 37th day, 17 September 1959, Q 8638.

15 *WE* IV, p. 12.

16 *ME* 44th day, 1 October 1959, Q 10 775.

17 *ME* 43rd day, 30 September 1959, Q 10 450.

18 See p. 14 above.

19 It was an essential part of such proposals that the new authority should have only a limited number of important functions, the remainder going to the boroughs.

20 If the Royal Commission had accepted all the suggestions put to them for County Borough status there would have been nearly 30 in all in place of the existing 3.

21   *ME*, 8th day, 10 April 1959, Q 1897.

22   *ME* 19th day, 29 May 1959, Q 4156.

23   *ME* 8th day, 10 April 1959, Q 1686.

24   The population of Wandsworth was a good deal larger than that of East and West Ham combined and even exceeded that of large county boroughs such as Coventry and Hull.

25   See especially *ME*, 1st day, 5 March 1959, Q 99–104.

26   Fulham proposed the extension of the LCC system to the rest of Greater London but freely admitted that the proposal had not been fully thought out (3rd day, 12 March 1959, Q 556).

27   It is significant that the three staunch Labour Boroughs of Bermondsey, Poplar and Southwark were the only authorities in the whole of Greater London who did not consider it worthwhile to give any evidence at all to the Commission and several others (including Hammersmith and Islington) did not give oral evidence.

28   The Local Government Act, 1958, extended delegation in certain county services to urban county districts of 60,000 population or more; this provision did not apply to Greater London.

29   *WE* II, pp. 31–35.

30   *WE* II, p. 40.

31   *ME* 37th day, 17 September 1959, Q 8544.

32   *WE* II, p. 430.

33   Acton, Brentford and Chiswick, Finchley, Southall, Southgate, Uxbridge and Wood Green Boroughs; Feltham, Hayes and Harlington and Ruislip–Northwood Urban districts.

34   *WE* II, p. 657.

35   *ME* 31st day, 10 July 1959, Q 7308–9.

36   Most notably that of Dr P. G. Richards (see below p. 52).

37   *ME* 13th day, 30 April 1959, Q 3702–3.

38   *WE* Vol. III, p. 631.

39   *ME* 15th day, 7 May 1959, Q 3402.

40   See p. 35 above.

41   *ME* 13th day, 30 April 1959, Q 3198.

42   *ME* Q 3224–7.

43   *ME* Q 3228–9. The greater the sub-division of expenditure under individual headings, the less flexibility there was in the system of financial control. Middlesex had 119 headings.

CHAPTER 3

1   *Memoranda of Evidence from Government Departments* (HMSO 1959), p. 23.

2   *Mem. Evid.* p. 66.

3   *Mem. Evid.* p. 89.

4   *Mem. Evid.* p. 110 and 116.

5   *Mem. Evid.* p. 120.

6   *Mem. Evid.* p. 166, 174–5.

7   In fact as a 'specimen exercise' they went so far as to suggest some possible groupings of existing authorities; some of these by chance coincided with the final London Borough groupings (eg Wembley/ Willesden, Hornsey/Tottenham/Wood Green).

8   *Mem. Evid* p. 89.

9   *ME*, 65th day, 6 January 1960, Q14923–27.

10   *ME*, 64th day, 4 January 1960, Q14697–9, 14746, 14855–6.

11   *ME*, 68th day, 12 January 1960, Q15542.

12   *ME*, Q15551.

13   *ME*, Q15601–2.

14   eg they came out fairly definitely in favour of one single authority, or at least a small number of authorities, for refuse disposal (Q 15634).

15   Report and comments on the Evidence of other Authorities and the Government Departments (Middx. CC April 1959).

16   *ME* 16th day, 21 May 1959, Q3466.

17   *ME*, 1st day, 5 March 1959, Q1.

18   *Report*, para. 200.

19   *Report*, para. 202.

K

20 *Report*, para. 199.

21 cf J. A. G. Griffith, *Central Departments and Local Authorities* p 506, and pp. 515–528. The appointment of the Royal Commission on Local Government in England in 1966 did stimulate the departments to make more positive statements on the number and size of authorities which they considered desirable.

22 *Mem. Evid.*, p. 23, Dame Mary Smieton, the Ministry's Permanent Secretary referred to West Ham's reaction in the course of giving oral evidence and somewhat modified the Ministry's criticisms (Q15499–500).

23 *Mem. Evid.*, p. 24.

24 *ME* 64th day, 4 January 1960, Q14693.

25 *ME*, Q14741.

26 *ME* 68th day, 12 January 1960, Q15542.

27 *ME*, Q15602.

28 *WE*, V pp. 253–4.

29 cf *ME* 51st day, 22 October 1959, Q12052.

30 *ME*, Q12144–61.

31 *WE*, V pp. 259–260.

32 *WE*, V, p. 261.

33 *ME* 56th day, 6 November 1959, Q13266, 13277.

34 *ME* 61st day, 26 November 1959, Q14190.

35 *ME* 61st day, Q14190.

36 *ME* 58th day, 12 November 1959, Q13688.

37 *ME*, 59th day, 18 November 1959, Q13849.

38 *ME*, 57th day, 11 November, 1959, Q13338–9, 13356–9.

39 *ME*, 56th day, 6 November 1959, Q13151–7.

40 *ME*, 45th day, 7 October 1959, Q11034–5.

41 *ME*, 46th day, 8 October 1959, Q11097.

42 The Society of Medical Officers of Health, who were invited by the Commission to give evidence, did not do so no doubt in part

because they did not have a common policy on a question of this kind.

43   *WE* V, p. 274.

44   *WE.* V, pp. 289–90.

45   *WE* V, p. 415.

46   The position is all the more remarkable when contrasted with the (1966) Royal Commission on Local Government in England. Here the evidence of, for example, NALGO not only shows a detailed grasp of the problems but also attempts to deal with all aspects of them. In contrast to their evidence to the Herbert Commission NALGO obviously gave a good deal of thought to their evidence to the later commission. It is tempting to see in this the influence of changed ideas on local government reorganization.

47   *WE* V, p. 705.

48   *WE* V, pp. 701–703.

49   *ME* 57th day, 11 November 1959, Q13516–19.

50   *WE* V, p. 748.

51   *Report*, para 21.

52   *WE* V, p. 458.

53   *WE* V, p. 446.

54   cf *WE* V, p. 459 'There can be no serious objection on the grounds of size to the creation of a Greater London authority.'

55   *ME* 55th day, 5 November 1959, Q13055–6.

56   See p. 14 above.

57   ie the twelve authorities concerned in the area of the Abercrombie Plan.

58   *WE* V, pp. 455–6.

59   *WE* V, 457. One curious result of this was that the Regional Advisory Council which had decided in 1958 not to give evidence now changed its mind and submitted a written statement in January 1960. It is true that they denied that this step was solely due to the Group's evidence but its timing and the fact that the main part of their evidence ('The values of the Present System') was a vigorous denial of the group's explicit statements and a rejection of the need for a

Greater London Authority to be responsible for technical education, all point to the Group's evidence being at any rate the major reason for their action (see *WE* vol. V, pp. 354–65 esp 360–4).

60 Among other advantages claimed for this was that it should make for a better political balance. (*WE* V, p. 460).

61 *WE* V, p. 476.

62 *WE* V, p. 469.

63 *WE*, p. 496. They did, however, suggest that there should be urban parishes (of around 10,000–50,000 population) within the London counties, but mainly as debating bodies with little real power.

64 *WE* V, p. 514.

65 D. V. Donnison '*Health, Welfare and Democracy in Greater London*' (Greater London Paper No 5, London School of Economics and Political Science, 1962).

66 *ME* 55th day, 5 November 1959, Q13005.

67 *ME*, Q13031.

68 *ME*, Q13069. An additional statement of criteria for determining minimum population level was later put in to the Commission (see 63rd day, 14 December 1959, pp. 2682–4).

69 See 63rd day, Q14689 and *Report*, para 736.

70 See 63rd day, Q 14685 (p. 2676) and Q14686 (p. 2679).

71 Cmd 9831, para. 17. See *WE* V, p. 642.

72 For example: 'The assessment of specific faults in the distribution and exercise of local government functions . . . is thus an exceedingly complex matter. It has to be based on the kind of thorough and prolonged enquiry which . . . is *beyond the capacity of an academic body such as ours*' (my italics) (*WE*, p. 643).

73 See Smallwood, *Greater London*, p. 197.

74 See *WE* V, p. 679.

75 *WE* V, p. 663.

76 *WE* V, p. 651.

77 *ME* 70th day, 2 February 1960, Q15900.

78 *ME*, Q15922.

79 cf p. 31 above.

80 The Centre were the last people to give oral evidence, on 2 February 1960. This was less than a fortnight according to the Commission's Report, before the Commission met to thrash out their recommendations. (*Report*, para 34.)

81 *WE* V, p. 663.

CHAPTER 4

1 *Report*, para. 743.

2 *Report*, para 743.

3 They dealt with 'Social and Economic Groupings as indicated by a study of service centres and areas' and 'The Delimitation of Greater London' (*Report*, pp. 295–305 and 341–53.)

4 ie excluding the factual memoranda etc. published in Part II of their Report and dealing with such matters as the pattern of educational administration in the review area.

5 *Report*, para. 20.

6 *Report*, paras 287 and 288.

7 *Report*, para. 34.

8 *Report*, para. 352 (2).

9 *Report*, para. 405.

10 *Report*, para. 407. The Commission set out at length the story of two notorious cases (Narrow Street Bridge, Stepney and the Hammersmith flyover) where administrative confusion had led to interminable disputes and delays (Report pp. 323–7).

11 *Report*, para. 442 ('One authority must be responsible for traffic management.)' The general point was, however, further argued (see p. 70 below).

12 They did not devote any attention to relatively less important functions (in terms of administrative structure) such as libraries or weights and measures.

13 *Report*, para. 517.

14 *Report*, para. 518.

15 *Report*, paras 9 and 10.

16 For example, paras. 88 and 748 where it occurs three times. Even the increase in road traffic is claimed as 'a conspicuous example of the Londoner's vitality' (para. 398).

17 *Report*, para. 220.

18 *Report*, para. 220.

19 *Report* para. 240.

20 *Report*, paras 675–94.

21 *Report*, para. 689.

22 *Report*, para. 689.

23 *Report*, para. 694.

24 There was some data on voting figures eg in the evidence of the London School of Economics (Greater London Group) and the Centre for Urban Studies, but it was not very detailed.

25 *Report*, para. 743 (1).

26 *Report*, para. 707.

27 They used both terms (*Report*, para. 723).

28 See above p. 14.

29 See L. J. Sharpe, *Research in Local Government* (Greater London Paper No 10, London School of Economics and Political Science, 1965), pp. 5–6.

30 Report, para. 762–3.

31 Report, paras 850–7.

32 *Report*, para. 748.

33 *Report*, para. 748.

34 *Report*, para. 737.

35 *Report*, paras 87, 88.

36 *Report*, para. 895.

37 *Report*, para. 743 (11). But they rejected any suggestion that boundaries should be drawn so as to give a better political balance (para. 250).

38 *Report*, para. 927.

39 *Report*, paras 744, 931–2.

40 *Report*, para. 950.

41 See *Report* pp. 354–62 for the basis on which the rate burden of the new boroughs was calculated. For children, for example, they calculated the charge to each borough 'by applying the county cost per child to the number of children who were taken into care from the borough'. (p. 356.)

42 *Report*, para. 951.

43 *Report*, paras 953–63. Here too some of their claims are open to question; they claimed, for example, that their proposed amalgamations would even out some of the existing variations in resources, but the table showing £1 rate product per head which they used to support this claim indicated that 16% of the new boroughs would have £1 rate products of under £15 against 19% of existing authorities; on the other hand 13% of the new boroughs, as against 14% of existing authorities would have £1 rate products of £25 or over. These figures do not indicate any very startling reduction in the range of variation.

44 *Report*, paras 844–5.

45 *Report*, para. 754.

46 *Report*, para. 770.

47 *Report*, paras 772–4.

48 *Report*, paras 780–1. Transport in the widest sense was outside their terms of reference and the Commission contented themselves with hoping that some machinery would be devised for effectively coordinating the work of the Ministry, the Council, London Transport and British Railways (para. 784). They thought the question of whether London Transport should be municipalized as 'worthy of study' by some other body. (para. 440.)

49 Including development schemes which were 'too large for the resources of a single borough' (para. 792).

50 *Report*, paras 794–5: there might be an arrangement in the case of ex-LCC houses for the Council to retain the right to nominate a certain percentage of lettings.

51 *Report*, paras 797–8.

52 The idea of a team of domiciliary attendants (doctors, nurses, midwives, health visitors and home helps) under the general guidance

of the family doctor had been put forward by the Ministry of Health as the ideal organization for promoting co-ordination and avoiding duplication of effort. This idea was endorsed by the Commission. (*Report*, paras 595 and 831).

53 *Report*, para. 800.

54 *Report*, paras 801–14.

55 *Report*, paras 801, 817–22.

56 *Report*, para 824.

57 *Report*, paras 740, 741.

58 Smallwood, *Greater London*, p. 196.

59 They might have mentioned, however, that the Ministry of Health had attempted to assess such relevant factors as work-load per officer and the amount of supervision required.

60 *Report*, para. 927.

61 Above, p. 57.

62 The Greater London Group wanted technical education to be a Greater London Council function; this however marked a further difference of view from the Commission who, like the Ministry of Education did not wish to see 'the essential unity of the educational process' split.

63 This point was not in fact dealt with specifically in the Greater London Group's evidence. The assumption was that with large authorities any overall planning (eg for provision of special schools) would be achieved by joint action.

64 Smallwood, *Greater London*, p. 24.

65 *Report*, para. 217.

66 cf *Report*, para. 746.

67 *Report*, para. 738.

68 eg Fulham (popn 113,000) with Hammersmith (109,000); Dagenham (114,000) with Barking (75,000); Tottenham (116,000) with Edmonton (94,000).

69 eg Kensington (167,000) with Chelsea (50,000); Walthamstow (113,000) with Chingford (46,000); Enfield (110,000) with Cheshunt (31,000).

70 *Report*, para. 243.

CHAPTER 5

1 Charles J. Hanser, *Guide to Decision: The Royal Commission,* (Bedminster Press, Totowa, New Jersey, 1965), p. 198.

2 Thus the Government announced plans to implement 'many' of the recommendations of the Royal Commission on Marriage and Divorce ten months after the latter reported in December 1955 and accepted the findings of the Royal Commission on Doctors' and Dentists' Remuneration within 3 months of its report in February 1960; most of what the Royal Commission on the Law relating to Mental Illness and Mental Deficiency recommended in May 1957 was incorporated in the Mental Health Act 1959 (see Hanser, *Guide to Decision*, pp. 99, 138).

3 This had affinities with some parts of the ill-fated Local Government Boundary Commission's proposals (see Report for 1947, HC 86, 1947/48, 11 March 1948).

4 *The Times*, 20 October, 1960.

5 *The Economist*, 21 October 1960.

6 *New Statesman*, 29 October, 1960.

7 Nevertheless, the initial reaction of Mr Pargiter, chairman of Middlesex CC, was surprisingly mild, far more so than the Chairmen of Essex or Surrey (see *Guardian*, 20 October, 1960).

8 See Figure 1, p. 90.

9 See the printed report *Statement of Views by the Surrey County Council* (February 1961), p. 28. There were differences in detail in the proposals made by the LCC and Middlesex.

10 See p. 97.

11 An exception among first-tier authorities was West Ham CB which fully conceded the case for a Greater London authority for overall planning, traffic management, etc.

12 The solidarity was underlined by a meeting of the London Labour Party on 14 February 1961 when those present (including both LCC and Borough Labour Party representatives) agreed unanimously on an opposition line to the Herbert Commission proposals.

13 Meetings were held on 19 December 1960 and 3 February 1961 with all the district authorities (ie not just those directly affected by the

Herbert plan); the county council claimed 'a considerable measure of general support' (*Statement of Views*, p. 28).

14 'The problems of London' said the urban district council in reply to the Ministry's circular 'are not those of Chigwell' – an apt summing-up of this general attitude.

15 See *Journal of the Town Planning Institute*, XLVII, 5 (May 1961), pp. 139–40.

16 See the duplicated memorandum put out by the RIBA in February 1961; also *RIBA Journal* vol 68, No 2 (December 1960), p. 45.

17 See *Technical Journal*, February 1961, pp. 421–2.

18 See their 4-page *Observations on the Report of the Royal Commission* (no date).

19 *The London Teacher*, Vol. 79, No 1279 (November 1960) pp. 67, 69.

20 Smallwood, *Greater London*, pp. 113–115.

21 HL Deb., vol. 227, cols 1040–1, 21 December 1960.

22 HL Deb. vol. 227 col. 1053.

23 Marjorie McIntosh 'The Report of the Royal Commission on Local Government in Greater London', *British Journal of Sociology*, September 1961. She was a Labour councillor on the LCC from 1947–52 and since 1958 had been an alderman and chairman of the Education Committee.

24 See *Statement of Views*, para 30.

25 *Report*, para. 734. ('each representative tends to regard himself as a delegate from his own authority and conceives it his duty to further the interests of that authority and to express its views'.)

26 *Statement of Views*, paras 35, 36.

27 Hertfordshire was very little affected by the Commission's proposals and did not join with the other counties.

28 For a detailed account, see Smallwood, *Greater London*, pp. 207 ff.

29 See above, p. 95; cf Peter Self 'The Herbert Report and the Values of Local Government', *Political Studies*, X, 2 (June 1962) pp. 150–3.

30 *Report*, para. 720.

31 William A. Robson 'The Reform of London Government' (*Public Administration*, Spring 1961, pp. 59–71).

32 L. J. Sharpe, *A Metropolis Votes* (Greater London Paper No 8, London School of Economics 1962), p. 1.

33 *A Metropolis Votes*, p. 72.

34 These lectures were later published as Greater London Papers, Nos 1–7.

35 D. V. Donnison, *Health, Welfare and Democracy in Greater London* (Greater London Paper No. 5), p. 20.

CHAPTER 6

1 Cmnd 1562 HMSO November 1961.

2 Cmnd 1562, para. 8.

3 Cmnd 1562, paras 10–13.

4 Cmnd 1562, paras 19–20. The boroughs were to be called 'London Boroughs' (para. 21) and not Greater London Boroughs as proposed by the Commission. The Government accepted, however, that the boundaries and status of the City of London should remain unchanged (para. 22).

5 Cmnd 1562, para. 15.

6 Cmnd 1562, paras 9 and 38.

7 Cmnd 1562, para. 40.

8 Cmnd 1562, para. 41.

9 Cmnd 1562, para. 24. 'Greater London Council' was the designation which the Government preferred to the Commission's 'Council for Greater London'. It is now frequently referred to simply by its initials as GLC.

10 Cmnd 1562, para. 25.

11 Cmnd 1562, para. 51.

12 Cmnd 1562, para. 14.

13 Cmnd 1562, para. 17.

14 Shortly before the White Paper was published, in October 1961, Mr Brooke was succeeded by Dr Charles Hill as Minister of Housing and

Local Government, but the latter arrived too late to influence the White Paper decisions.

15 See above, chapter 3, p. 41; and ME esp. 64th day, Q14697–9, 65th day, Q14924–8.

16 See above, chapter 3, p. 40;

17 See below, p. 226.

18 But it did disturb the logic of their case conceived in terms of both functional efficiency and the health of local government.

19 See above, p. 46.

20 See above, p. 17.

21 cf Edward Carter *The Future of London* (Penguin Books, 1962), p. 37.

22 He was MP for Chippenham 1943–62; Minister of Education 1954–57 and October 1959 – July 1962 when he fell victim to the 'Macmillan axe' and was created a viscount. He had a strong personal interest in education and educational problems.

23 *Mem. Evid.*, p. 21; cf p. 24.

24 Dame Mary Smieton was appointed Permanent Secretary at the Ministry of Education in 1959 after over 30 years in the Ministry of Labour. Of course Sir David's *original* commitment to large education authorities may well have derived from departmental views.

25 *Mem. Evid.*, p. 24.

26 Smallwood, *Greater London.*, pp. 227–30.

27 As a side light on differences of view over London government we have the admission of Lord Hailsham, Minister for Science, that he had been 'not unattracted' by the Commission's education proposals (HL Deb vol. 238, 14 March 1962, Col. 201).

28 HL Deb., Vol. 248, 23 April 1963, col. 1153. On Lord Morrison's attitude, see below, p. 132.

29 Cmnd 1562, para. 55.

30 *The Times*, 23 November, 1962.

31 Circular No 56/61 of 16 December 1961.

32 See Appendix 3. p. 255.

33 Consisting of Brentford and Chiswick, Feltham, Heston and Isle-worth, Staines and Sunbury-on-Thames (see Figure 5(c), p. 264).

34 Hayes and Harlington, Ruislip – Northwood, Uxbridge, Yiewsley and West Drayton.

35 These included authorities both inside and outside the proposed boundary of Greater London; not only Epsom and Ewell and Ban-stead for example, but also Leatherhead and Reigate (see Surrey County Council, General Purposes Committee Report of 8 January 1962, para. 29).

36 *The Times*, 9 March 1962.

37 *Municipal Journal*, 8 December 1961.

38 Together with Hertfordshire whose representatives refused to at-tend any further meetings on the grounds that they did not endorse the Surrey plan.

39 A further meeting was held on 16 March 1962.

40 No doubt helped by the fact that there were not, as in Middlesex, any powerful districts eager for County Borough status.

41 MP for Wimbledon since 1950. He was a member of Wimbledon Borough Council from 1942–65 and of Surrey County Council from 1943–65; he was chairman of the latter body from 1956–9.

42 *Daily Telegraph* 16 February 1962. A few days later Croydon were also attacked for issuing 75,000 leaflets and 10,000 stickers on the same theme (20 February 1962).

43 *The Times*, 9 March 1962.

44 *Daily Telegraph*, 13 March 1962.

45 *Guardian*, 13 March 1962.

46 On this see below, pp. 154–6.

47 Report of the Local Government Committee of Middlesex CC 7 March 1962.

48 See Report of Local Government Committee considered at a meet-ing of Middlesex CC held on 3 January 1962.

49 Report of the Local Government Committee, 29 January 1962, en-dorsed by the county council meeting on 28 February.

50 See *Evening Standard* 27 February 1962 for reported criticisms of the county council for not resisting the Government proposals more strongly.

51 Hackney and Stoke Newington; Fulham and Hammersmith: Chelsea and Kensington; Merton and Morden, Mitcham and Wimbledon; and the two boroughs to be formed (1) by adding Battersea to part of Wandsworth (2) from the remainder of Wandsworth, although the precise boundary was not the same in the two proposals.

52 See Figure 1 (p. 90 above).

CHAPTER 7

1 See p. 113 above.

2 Smallwood, *Greater London*, p. 241.

3 He had succeeded Mr Brooke in October 1961.

4 HC Deb., Vol. 654, (20 February 1962), col. 243.

5 Of the proposed boroughs to be formed in the LCC area only Boroughs 7 (Greenwich/Woolwich), 8 (Lewisham) and 13 (Hammersmith/Fulham) did not reach the centre of London or close to it. The combined population of these 3 boroughs was only 675,000 out of a total population of over 3 million for the LCC area.

6 HC Deb., Vol. 658, (1 May 1962) col 140 (written answer).

7 HC Deb., Vol. 658 (3 May 1962) cols 154–6 (written answers).

8 HC Deb., Vol. 659 (18 May 1962) cols 156–7 (written answers). The three districts to escape first were Banstead, Caterham and Warlingham and Walton and Weybridge (see below pp. 124–6).

9 Leader in *Guardian*, 9 March 1962.

10 For the latter see report of the presidential address by Mr Pyle to the Association's Annual Conference (*Guardian*, 10 February 1962).

11 Letter to *The Times*, 8 February 1962.

12 See Leaders in *The Times*, 30 November 1961 and 4 May 1962 (which called the Government's decision to keep the LCC education service intact 'wise').

13 *Evening Standard*, 3 May 1962.

14 See below, p. 188.

15 See below, p. 133. For the arguments on preserving the county education pattern intact, see chapter 10, p. 186.

16 This announcement was not made in parliament which was not sitting on that date.

17 Cheshunt, Esher, Staines and Sunbury-on-Thames.

18 Most of Chigwell and the southern part (incl Epsom) of Epsom and Ewell.

19 Romford, Barnet, Carshalton, Coulsdon and Purley, Feltham, Yiewsley and West Drayton.

20 Surbiton, Hornchurch.

21 See Figures 5(a) to (d), p. 262–5 and Appendix 3, p. 255.

22 Only Wandsworth would have been split on their proposals and this as will be seen later, was a particularly difficult area in any scheme of boroughs.

23 HC Deb., Vol. 659, 18 May 1962, cols 156–7 (written answers).

24 Cmnd 1164 pp. 349–353. Later data on commuting appear to confirm the Herbert Commission's inclusions. See Royal Commission on Local Government in England, Research Study No 1 *Local Government in South-East England* by the Greater London Group (HMSO 1968), pp. 428–434.

25 HC Deb., Vol. 654, 19 February 1962, col. 93.

26 HC Deb., Vol. 654 cols 138–46. He was MP for Epsom and later became Sir Peter Rawlinson and solicitor-general 1962–4.

27 The indignation of the Borough Council of Epsom and Ewell at the prospect of being cut in half seems to have been greater than if they had been totally included; and this seems to have coincided with the views of many of the inhabitants of the borough; the idea was mooted of having a referendum of the residents of the northern part of the borough (Reports of the Borough's General Purposes Committee, 24 May and 19 June 1962).

28 'The New London', *The Economist*, 5 May 1962, pp. 425–6.

29 In his memoirs, Dr Hill devoted several pages to housing ('I was desperately anxious to make a success of housing'), to planning, and to Wales, but only one word to London – and that in a quotation of a note from his successor, Sir Keith Joseph! (Lord Hill of Luton, *Both Sides of the Hill*, Heinemann, 1964, pp. 215–29, especially 215, 221).

30 eg Mr G. A. Pargiter; he was MP for Spelthorne 1945–50 and Southall 1950–66; he was mayor of Southall 1938–40 and a member of Middlesex County Council 1934–65, being elected an alderman in 1946 and chairman 1959–60.

31 In the autumn of 1961 the opinion polls indicated that Labour were beginning to overtake the Conservatives. In the early part of 1962 the Government suffered a series of by-election defeats including the celebrated Liberal victory by Mr Eric Lubbock at Orpington in March.

32 *Guardian*, 16 February, 1962.

33 cf the answer given by the Leader of the House (Mr Iain Macleod) to the Leader of the Opposition (Mr Hugh Gaitskell) on 8 February, 1962 (HC Deb., Vol. 653).

34 eg Mr Frederic Harris, Conservative MP for NW Croydon, who had tabled an amendment to reject the White Paper proposals. He voted against the Government as did Sir Cyril Black (Wimbledon) and Commander Kerans (The Hartlepools).

35 HC Deb., Vol. 654, 19 February 1962, col. 44.

36 HC Deb., Vol. 654, col. 48.

37 HC Deb., Vol. 654, col. 43.

38 20 February, 1962, cols. 235–6.

39 col. 240.

40 col. 242.

41 col. 243.

42 col. 246.

43 HC Deb., Vol. 654, cols. 229–34.

44 HC Deb., Vol. 654, col. 310.

45 See pp. 143–53, below

46 *The Times*, 5 March, 1962.

47 HL Deb., Vol. 238, 14 March 1962, cols 170–2.

48 HL Deb., Vol. 238 cols 188–9.

49 HL Deb., Vol. 238 col 193

50 HL Deb., Vol, 238 col 192.

51 See report of his speech to the London Labour Party (*Guardian*, 26 March 1962).

52 One factor influencing this was that in 1955 a scheme had been agreed between the LCC and the Metropolitan Boroughs for a transfer of certain health and welfare responsibilities to the latter; it had not, however, been put into effect because it had not received the approval of the Ministry of Health.

53 At the time of the debate on the White Paper the Government had not of course yet announced their decision to retain the whole of the LCC's education service intact.

54 *Children in Care*, a four-page pamphlet (no date).

55 *The Times*, 17 May 1962.

56 *The Times*, 22, 23, 24 May 1962.

57 *The Times*, 25 and 29 May 1962.

58 *The Times*, 4 June, 1962.

59 HC Deb Vol. 569, cols. 613–5, 10 May 1962.

60 HC Deb Vol. 660, 31 May 1962, cols. 1568–70.

61 See p. 41 above.

62 cf the following exchanges in the Commission's examination of the Home Office Permanent Secretary:
Sir Edwin Herbert: I suppose if we had a Greater London Authority it would have to take over the fire services for the whole of its area.
Sir Charles Cunningham: We should certainly feel that to be the right organization. (ME 65th Day, 6 January 1960, Q15006).

63 See below, p. 185.

64 *Guardian*, 9 March 1962.

65 This culminated in Mr Gaitskell's pledge to fight the London Government Bill 'clause by clause and line by line' (Reported in *The Times*, 2 July, 1962).

66 For their comments on the White Paper see *TPI Journal*, XLVIII, No 4 (April 1962), pp. 101–2; these comments were sent to the Ministry of Housing and Local Government on 19 March 1962.

L

67   See RICS Duplicated Memorandum on the White Paper, dated May 1962.

68   HC Deb., Vol. 654, 20 February 1962, col. 286.

CHAPTER 8

1   See above, p. 22.

2   *The Times*, 5 April, 1962.

3   eg Mr Robert Mellish MP for Bermondsey, and chairman of the London Labour Party (see HC Deb., Vol. 654, 19 February 1962. col. 152). cf also Lord Morrison of Lambeth: "if ever there was a case for anything to go to the Greater London Authority, there is one for the Metropolitan Water Board." (HL Deb, Vol. 227, 21 December 1960, col. 1039). This was in line with the evidence of the London Labour Party to the Ullswater Commission.

4   The board consisted of members appointed by local authorities in its area. It was organized on party political lines with a leader of the board, and a leader of the opposition. Again, one may quote Lord Morrison of Lambeth: 'I think that to try to make politics out of water is one of the hardest things of life. It is not really possible – though I had a good try'. (HL Deb., 21 December 1960, col. 1040).

5   cf Smallwood, *Greater London*, p. 243.

6   cf the Minister's reply to a parliamentary question (HC Deb., Vol. 657, 10 April 1962, WA cols 104–5).

7   'Future of the Metropolitan Water Board', Report of the General Purposes Committee adopted by the Board on 19 October 1962, p. 4.

8   'Future of the Metropolitan Water Board', pp. 6–7.

9   Under Select Committee on Private Bill procedure, which would apply in a case of this kind, both the promoters of the Bill, and petitioners against it are entitled to be represented by counsel and to bring forward witnesses. The procedure is more akin to a court of law than to committee stage on a Public Bill.

10 Apart from the chairman and vice-chairman; 27 members are appointed by the London Boroughs and the City, 6 by the GLC and the remainder by the Essex, Herts, Kent and Surrey CCs, the Thames Conservancy and the Lee Conservancy Catchment Board (1 each). See Annual Report of MWB 1965–66, pp. 8–10.

11 See above, p. 112.

12 Above, p. 125. It is of interest to note however that senior officers of the Ministry held a series of private meetings with peripheral authorities to hear representations from them, and that their reports formed the basis of the Minister's first list of exclusions (Banstead, Caterham and Warlingham, Walton and Weybridge).

13 Local Government Act 1958, s. 21(3) and (4).

14 On the Commission's procedure see especially Report for 1946 (HC 82, 1946–7) pp. 4–5 and Appendix A, p 19. One of their assistant commissioners was Mr Harry Plowman, Town Clerk of Oxford, who also became one of the town clerks to investigate the London Borough groupings.

15 eg the Metropolitan Boroughs Standing Joint Committee 'did not think that town clerks would be suitable for this job' (Lord Jellicoe, HL Deb., Vol 238, 14 March 1962, col 275).

16 Report, para. 744.

17 They were the town clerks of Plymouth (Mr Lloyd Jones); Cheltenham (Mr Littlewood); Oxford Mr Plowman); and South Shields (Mr Young).
The terms of reference were:

    (i) To take into consideration the map showing the possible groupings of boroughs sent to local authorities in the London area on 16 December, 1961 (subject to any amendments to the outer boundary which the Minister may indicate), and the views expressed and any alternative suggestions made by local authorities in respect of this map.

    (ii) To make recommendations (after such consultations with each other and with the department as they may think necessary) for the creation of a pattern of London Boroughs over the whole of this Greater London area (other than the City of London) mainly by the amalgamation of existing local government areas.

    (iii) In making recommendations to have regard to the Government's declared aim of creating boroughs with a minimum population of around 200,000 wherever possible (some boroughs might be substantially larger than this); and also to the present and past associations of existing local government areas, to the lines of communication, the pattern of development, and the location and areas of influence of service centres. (See Report *London Government: The London Boroughs* (HMSO 1962), p. 3).

18   *London Government: The London Boroughs,* para. 14.

19   HC Deb., Vol. 664, 2 August, 1962, WA col. 137.

20   This conference was held before the borough election in May 1962 when Labour gained control of Wandsworth.

21   See Figure 2, p. 148 illustrating these proposals.

22   The other 3 were Chigwell, Hornchurch and Enfield. Minor splits were proposed for Woolwich, Dagenham and Hackney.

23   *London Government: The London Boroughs,* para. 50.

24   *London Government: The London Boroughs*, para. 53.

25   *London Government: The London Boroughs*, para. 56.

26   *London Government: The London Boroughs*, para. 58.

27   *London Government: The London Boroughs*, para. 41–43.

28   These two groupings in fact only involved moving one small borough (Shoreditch) from the Government's proposed Borough 6 to Borough 5.

29   See accompanying map, Figure 3.

30   *London Government: The London Boroughs,* paras. 159–64 and 171–2.

31   See Appendix 3, p. 255.

32   On this, see below, p. 195.
The Minister rejected all suggestions that there should be any machinery of appeal from the town clerks' recommendations on the grounds that final proposals would be incorporated in legislation on which Parliament would make the decisions (See HC Deb Vol. 657, WA cols. 101–3, Vol. 663, WA col 75).

CHAPTER 9

1   See above page 116.

2   It included the leader of the council (Sir Isaac Hayward), the chairmen of all the main committees and the Labour chief whip (Mr Fiske).

3 For these and other quotations from the correspondence, see Minutes of the LCC meeting on 29 May 1962 where the full texts were printed.

4 The pamphlet equated the LCC area with London, eg 'the people of London will suffer'. 'The services of the London County Council . . . are all carefully geared to the needs of Londoners as a whole' etc.

5 This information was given in answer to questions by Sir Louis Gluckstein and Mr Sebag-Montefiore at the LCC meeting on 29 May, 1962.

6 The Metropolitan Boroughs Standing Joint Committee, following the LCC's lead, passed a resolution in July of non-co-operation with the Government, but its practical effect seems to have been rather limited.

7 Report of GP Committee 'Reorganization of London Government' in Minutes of LCC Meeting, 17 July 1962.

8 This was in reply to a question; see LCC Minutes, 17 July 1962.

9 See Report 'LCC in row over London plan' in the *Guardian*, 18 July 1962.

10 HC Deb., Vol. 663, cols 97–8 (written answers), 20 July, 1962.

11 See above, p. 116.

12 cf Sir Keith Joseph's remark: 'had the London County Council come to life earlier, a lot of the clarification that would have emerged from the normal consultation that occurs with Bills of this sort, would have been able to have been put in the original drafting of the Bill.' (HC Deb., Vol. 675, 2 April 1963, cols. 399–400).

13 As reported in the *Guardian*, 13 March 1962.

14 *Public Service*, December 1961; a number of letters from 'representative' contributors were generally pessimistic about the prospects.

15 See editorial in *London Town* (Vol LXIII, No 745): this publication, founded in 1900 was the organ of the administrative, professional, technical and clerical staff of the LCC; it claimed to be independent both of the council and the staff associations.

16 *London Town*, p. 2.

17 See Staff Association News in *London Town*, March 1962, p. 73.

18   cf HC Deb., Vol. 654, 19 February 1962, col. 54.

19   HC Deb., Vol. 654, 19 February 1962, col 54; he also announced improvements in the scales of compensation for loss of office.

20   HL Deb., Vol. 238, 14 March 1962, cols. 292–3.

21   *Local Government Chronicle*, 17 March, 1962.

22   MHLG circular letter on London Government, 7 June 1962.

23   pp. 208–18.

24   The chief planning officer (Mr Leslie Lane) went to the Civic Trust and two of his senior planners (Mr Walter Bor and Mr Graeme Shankland) to Liverpool.

25   eg *The Times* 6 October 1962: *Observer* 7 October: *Guardian* 12 October. The secretary of the LCC Staff Association suggested that they went because they could get higher salaries elsewhere (*Guardian*, 18 October).

26   Reported in *The Times*, 13 February 1962.

27   Letter to *The Times*, 5 May 1962.

28   *Guardian*, 4 July 1962.

29   See above, p. 138.

30   *The Times*, 20 October 1962.

31   Among other questions on the constitution of the new authorities discussed with the local authority associations were the ratio of aldermen to councillors on the Greater London Council; the ratio of councillors to electors for the London Boroughs and whether elections to the latter should be held annually or triennially in the autumn or in May (see replies by Mr Brooke, Home Secretary, and Sir Keith Joseph, Minister of Housing and Local Government, HC Deb., Vol. 664, 2 August 1962, WA cols. 124 and 136).

32   See *Evening Standard*, 25 June 1962.

33   See report in *Guardian*, 26 June 1962.

34   *Guardian*, 26 June, 1962.

35   See the revealing letter by Mr Preston Benson, a former journalist and a member of the Committee in the *Croydon Advertiser*, 17 August, 1962.

36 It was not immediately obvious from this statement that the 34 boroughs and the 93 authorities referred to the whole of Greater London and not simply the LCC area.

37 The pamphlet claimed: 'so many protests have been made by responsible bodies and individuals against the proposals of the Government to destroy the London County Council and to make other sweeping changes' – the order and emphasis indicate exactly the committee's interests and concern.

38 See *The Times*, 18 September 1962.

39 See *Guardian*, 14 February 1963.

40 They included the LCC, the London Labour Party, the Surrey Federation of Labour Parties, the Surrey CC, various professional bodies such as the London Teachers' Association and the National Association of Child Care Officers, and 'eminent members of the Conservative Party' – see Press Note of Committee, 13 February 1963.

41 See letter from Mr Preston Benson already referred to, in *Croydon Advertiser*, 17 August 1962.

42 At an early stage the Committee estimated that its campaign might cost £15,000 (*Guardian*, 25 July 1962).

43 The great majority of the signatories were resident in the LCC area (Committee's Press Note, 13 February 1963).

44 Its most spectacular effort was a river procession along the Thames from Greenwich.

45 See report of Annual Conference of LLP, *Guardian*, 26 March 1962.

46 Nevertheless he quoted Hugh Gaitskell as saying 'we will scrap the present plan when we are returned to power'. (Report of 61st Annual Conference of the Labour Party, Brighton, 1962, p 196).

47 Mr Michael Stewart, HC Deb., Vol. 675, 2 April 1963, col. 399.

48 He had, in any case, let it be known that he was thinking of retiring from active politics, although not quite so soon. (See Lord Hill, *Both Sides of the Hill*, pp. 213–14)

49 *The Times*, 23 November, 1962.

CHAPTER 10

1 These dealt with the areas and constitution of the London Boroughs

2 See HC Deb., Vol. 670, 29 January 1963, col. 764 for details of the motion.

3 HC Deb., Vol. 681, 25 July 1963, col. 1789.

4 That is from the second reading in the Commons on 10 and 11 December 1962 to the Royal Assent on 31 July 1963.

5 London Government Act 1963 Schedule 5, Part I, para. 32.

6 London Government Act 1963, Schedule 17, para. 10.

7 1,250 amendments were put down in the Commons alone, and of these over 450 were accepted, the great majority being Government amendments designed to clarify and rectify omissions from the original Bill (cf the exchanges between Lord Windlesham and Lord Morrison of Lambeth, HL Deb., Vol. 248, 24 April 1963, cols. 1269–70).

8 'Boroughs' here and in the following account also includes the City of London; under the Bill it was to retain its existing powers (eg as a police authority) but to acquire in addition the powers of a London Borough.

9 References (LG Bill) are to the Bill as first printed in November 1962; for a summary of the provisions of the Act as it finally emerged see Appendix 2, p. 247.

10 LG Bill, clause 25(3). More specific details of what the GLDP was to cover were to be laid down in ministerial regulations.

11 LG Bill, clause 24.

12 LG Bill, clauses 16 and 17 and Schedule 7.

13 LG Bill, clauses 9 and 10.

14 LG Bill, clause 21(4). In certain circumstances (eg in a comprehensive development area) the GLC could build within Greater London without needing borough consent.

15 LG Bill, clauses 21 and 23

16 Peter Self, 'The Herbert Report and the Values of Local Government' (*Political Studies X*, 2, June 1962), p. 148

17 See TPI Journal (Vol. 49, No 3, March 1963), pp 76–7. They circularized all MPs on the Standing Committee concerned with the Bill and included a copy of their memorandum on the 1961 White Paper (above, p. 138).

18 Comments and criticisms on the London Government Bill (duplicated memorandum, December 1962).

19 RIBA memorandum 'The London Government Bill' (no date – ? January 1963); early in January Sir Keith Joseph discussed these points at a meeting at the RIBA (HC Deb., Vol. 670, 24 January 1963, col. 322).

20 *The Times*, 6 December 1962.

21 Once the Bill was introduced, the LCC, although never formally renouncing its policy of non-co-operation, turned its attention to proposals for detailed amendment of the Bill's provisions; many of these were designed to strengthen the GLC (See Minutes of LCC meeting, 5 February 1963).

22 On this, see Smallwood, *Greater London*, p. 139.

23 eg Mr Ronald Russell (S Wembley) who urged that Wembley should be joined with Harrow rather than Willesden (HC Deb., Vol. 671, 13 February 1963, cols. 1350–3).

24 On hybrid bills, see Erskine May's Parliamentary Practice (16th ed. 1957), pp 495, 521, 526, 537. The main point is that if it had been held that the Bill was hybrid because it affected private rights over a limited area, it would have had to be referred to a select committee which would have heard petitions against the bill.

25 HC Deb., Vol. 669, 10 December 1962, cols. 37–49.

26 HC Deb., Vol. 670, 23 January 1963, cols. 105–126. The debate was on Clause 1 which was taken in Committee of the whole House.

27 There was a precedent in the London Government Act, 1939, which limited the metropolitan Boroughs also to a maximum of sixty councillors.

28 HC Deb., Vol. 670, 23 January 1963, cols. 129–47.

29 HC Deb., Vol. 670. cols. 153–5; 164–6.

30 HC Deb., Vol. 670 col. 141.

31 See below, p. 195.

32   On Wandsworth see especially HC Deb., Vol. 675, 2 April 1963, cols. 301–14.

33   eg the GLC like the LCC was to have power to promote an annual Money Bill for its capital expenditure needs (Schedule 2 of 1963 Act).

34   The proportion of aldermen was incidentally to be one-sixth of the number of councillors as for the LCC and Metropolitan Boroughs and not one-third as elsewhere.

35   See Standing Committee F, Official Report, 5 February 1963, cols. 4–11; also HC Deb., Vol. 675, 1 April, 1963, cols, 102–113, HL Deb., Vol. 249, 9 May 1963, cols. 945–57.

36   See Standing Committee F, Official Report, 5 February 1963, cols. 25–30; HC Deb., Vol. 675, 1 April 1963, cols 87–99: HL Deb., Vol. 249, 14 May 1963, cols. 1278–88.

37   See, for example, the contrasting speeches of Lord Shepherd and Lord Silkin (HL Deb., Vol. 249, 9 May 1963, cols. 913–20, 923–5). On the question of time, Lord Hastings for the Government pointed out that at the request of the AMC. the date of the elections had been brought forward from autumn 1964 as proposed in the White Paper to spring 1964   (HL Deb., Vol. 249. col. 943, also 16 May, col. 1499). See also HL Deb., Vol. 251, 24 June 1963, cols. 17–30.

38   HC Deb., Vol. 670, 24 January 1963, col 322

39   Strictly speaking the position was rather more complicated. For the 1964 GLC elections each London Borough was to form an electoral area returning 2, 3 or 4 councillors. This was intended as an interim measure. The ultimate aim was, as in the case of the LCC to have single-member electoral areas identical with parliamentary constituencies. This aim could not be achieved until the latter had been revised since some of the existing constituencies were partly inside and partly outside Greater London. The proposal to hold GLC and borough elections on the same day was also linked to the revision of parliamentary constituencies. It was provided in the Bill (and subsequently in the Act) that until this had been carried out the 1964 electoral arrangements for the GLC should continue at subsequent elections and that the date of such elections should be determined by the Home Secretary. This is in fact what happened in 1967. After re-drawing of electoral areas GLC elections would be held on the same day as borough elections throughout

the country, including Greater London. See London Government Act, 1963, s. 1(7), s.2 (4), s. 89 (1) ('relevant year of election'). Sch. 2, para. 2–7 Sch.3, paras 15–18, Sch. 4, para. 8.

40 For this amendment moved by Mr Robert Jenkins (Conservative MP for Dulwich) on behalf of the Association of Municipal Corporations see Official Report, Standing Committee F, 21 March 1963, cols. 980–6. For the Lords debate, HL Deb., Vol. 249, 14 May 1963, cols. 1226–35: Vol. 251, 24 June 1963, cols 91–106.

41 Official Report, Standing Committee F, 12 February 1963, col. 115.

42 And then only after consultation with the GLC (Official Report, Standing Com F, col. 109).

43 Cmnd 1562 para. 36.

44 Official Report Standing Committee F, 12 February 1963, col. 109.

45 This was subsequently improved; see Act, section 9(2).

46 Standing Committee F, 12 February 1963, cols. 113–14. He hastened to add that he thought it 'very unlikely' that there would be a wide divergence between the Ministry and the GLC (Standing Com F, 12 Feb. 1963, col. 115).

47 Standing Com. F, 12 Feb. 1963, col. 162

48 Standing Com. F, 12 Feb. 1963, cols. 163–6. There was a Ministry grant of 100 per cent for trunk roads but of only 75 per cent for Class 1 roads.

49 See above, p. 176.

50 Except that for a temporary period the GLC was to retain powers inherited from the LCC (Clause 21(5)).

51 Official Report Standing Committee F, 14 February 1963, cols 220–241.

52 See Report of Housing Committee, Minutes of LCC Meeting, 5 February 1963; similarly, the LCC wanted the GLC to hold permanently the LCC's stock of housing which the Bill transferred temporarily to it (Clause 23).

53 HL Deb. Vol 250, 20 May 1963, especially cols. 25, 29.

54 LCC Minutes, 5 February 1963.

55 eg The Town Planning Institute (p. 175 above). The Royal Institute of British Architects, also argued that the Bill 'does not ensure that the boroughs plan within the GLC's framework.' (Memo, para. 7)

56 Standing Committee F, 19 February 1963, cols. 315–24.

57 Standing Com. F, 19 Feb 1963. col. 326.

58 Clause 24(4). This provision was, however, somewhat strengthened by a Government amendment providing that (again by regulation) certain other types of application might be singled out for reference by the Boroughs to the GLC who could then give directions on how they were to be dealt with.

59 The exact number depended on the limits chosen for the central area but was not less than 5.

60 Memorandum on Bill, para 8, (cf HL Deb., Vol. 250, 20 May 1963, cols. 76–7).

61 See *Journal of the Town Planning Institute*, March 1963 (Vol. 49, No. 3), p. 77.

62 eg the Greater London Group in their memo; see also W. A. Robson, *The Heart of Greater London* (Greater London Paper No. 9 London School of Economics, 1965) for an elaboration of this view.

63 This was argued forcibly by Mr Lubbock (Liberal MP for Orpington) (HC Deb., Vol. 670, 24 January 1963, col. 423).

64 As Mr Henry Strauss he had been parliamentary secretary to the Ministry of Town and Country Planning in 1943–45; he was also president of the Architecture Club and an honorary FRIBA.

65 As Sir Arthur Salter he had been a Conservative minister; he also served as president of the Town and Country Planning Association.

66 See reply of Earl Jellicoe, Minister of State, Home Office, HL Deb, Vol. 250, 20 May 1963, cols 94–6.

67 See below, p. 186.

68 See above, p. 133.

69 cf Mr Geoffrey Johnson Smith, Conservative MP for Holborn and St Pancras South: 'We have all been deluged with letters and

circulars from people experienced in this work, who would not have so acted had they not had genuine doubts on the subject.' (Official Report, Standing Committee F, 12 March 1963, col. 752).

70 The amendment put down by the opposition would have left it possible for a Middlesex area to be retained (see Standing Committee F, Official Report, 12 March 1963, cols 713–4, also the speech by Mr G. W. Reynolds, 13 March, 1963, cols 773–777).

71 Joint Under-Secretary for the Home Department.

72 Standing Committee F, Official Report, 13 March 1963 col. 805.

73 HL Deb., Vol. 250, 27 May 1963, col. 648.

74 Standing Committee F, 13 March 1963, col. 808.

75 See above, p. 136.

76 The BMA, however, had expressed concern that the boroughs would not be large enough, but did not succeed in gaining any support for their view either from the Government or the Opposition. (See Annual Report of BMA Council 1962–63, para. 239).

77 On this proposal see the exchanges between Mr Braine (Parliamentary secretary, Ministry of Health) and Mr Mellish (Standing Committee F, 5 March 1963, cols. 643–4).

78 See minutes of LCC meeting, 5 February 1963.

79 Mr Albert Evans, Labour MP for Islington SW (Standing Committee F, Official Report, 5 March 1963, col. 626).

80 Through membership of area committees (See Herbert Report, Cmnd 1164, paras 554–565).

81 One Labour member (Mr Pavitt, Willesden W.) did indeed argue as though the amendment applied to the Middlesex Boroughs (Committee, 5 March 1963, cols 627–633).

82 This was the name given to the authority set up to administer education in the old LCC area; formally, it was a special committee of the GLC.

83 The ILEA was to be constituted as a special committee consisting of (a) the GLC councillors elected for the inner London area (b) one member from each inner borough and the City; the Opposition amendment would have constituted four other similar committees for the Middlesex, West Essex, North West Kent, and East Surrey areas.

84 Middlesex CC had passed a resolution in favour of this proposal.

85 cf Mr Michael Stewart, Committee, 26 February 1963, col. 456.

86 See HL Deb., Vol. 250, 21 May 1963, col. 232.

87 HL Deb., Vol. 250, 21 May 1963, col. 182.

88 eg Mr Mellish, Committee, 26 February 1963, col. 423.

89 Col. 438.

90 Immediately before the Second Reading Debate, the Minister of Education (Sir Edward Boyle) on 10 December 1962 met a deputatation of London teachers who expressed their anxieties about the uncertainties to which the review provisions gave rise. There was also a certain amount of lobbying by *ad hoc* parents' and teachers' committees.

91 See, for example, Mr Michael Stewart, HC Deb., Vol. 669, 10 December 1962, col. 76.

92 HC Deb., Vol. 669, 11 December 1962, cols 245–8.

93 HC Deb., Vol. 658, 3 May 1962, WA 154–6

94 See Act, S. 30 (6). (words in italics added).

95 HC Deb., Vol. 669, 11 December 1962, col. 335.

96 Mr Brooke was of course only concerned with the earlier White Paper proposal for an undefined central area authority.

97 The review provision was subsequently deleted by the Labour Government; this led to an interesting statement of views by Viscount Eccles and Lord Brooke of Cumnor (see below, p. 225).

98 See Standing Committee F, Official Report, Tenth Sitting, 28 February 1963, esp. cols. 500–507.

99 Clause 79 (1)

100 This was moved by Mr Skeffington on re-committal of the Bill, the Committee stage debate being restricted by the guillotine.

101 HC Deb., Vol. 675, 1 April 1963, cols. 65–6.

102 See above, p. 161. The Bill provided that the Minister 'may' establish a Commission (clause 79 (3)); the Government agreed to an amendment making this mandatory, as urged by the staff associations and other bodies (eg RICS).

103 HC Deb., Vol. 675, 1 April 1963, cols. 63–5.

104 HC Deb., 2 April 1963, Vol. 675, col. 340.

105 See Sir Keith Joseph, Official Report, Standing Committee F, 21 March 1963, col. 1012, and the speech by Mr Harvey (Conservative Walthamstow, E) HC Deb., Vol. 675, 2 April 1963, cols. 332–6

106 See for example, the speech of Captain Elliott, Official Report, Standing Committee F, 21 March 1963, cols. 1015–16.

107 A former Labour leader on the LCC from 1940–47.

108 HL Deb., Vol. 250, 30 May 1963, col. 1031.

109 See below, p. 208.

110 Local Government Act, 1933, sections 98–107.

111 Clause 9 (3)

112 See Journal of the Town Planning Institute, March 1963 (Vol. 49, No. 3) p. 76.

113 See RIBA memo. on the Bill, para 11.

114 A point made also by the Institute of Housing.

115 Standing Committee F, Official Report, 19 March 1963, cols. 925–930.

116 Stand. Com. F, 21 March 1963, cols. 1004–6.

117 HC Deb., Vol. 675, 2 April 1963, cols 314–18.

118 HL Deb., Vol. 249, 15 May 1963, cols 1407–16.

119 HL Deb., Vol. 250, 30 May 1963, cols. 984–996.

120 Member for Reigate; he was a former member of Chelsea Borough Council and the LCC; from 1957 to 1959 he had been Minister of State at the Board of Trade.

121 Official Report, Standing Committee F, 14 March 1963, cols. 828–41.

122 Official Rep., Stand. Com. F, 14 March 1963, col. 856.

123 HC Deb., Vol. 675, 1 April 1963, cols. 45–53.

124 See above, p. 164.

125 HL Deb., Vol. 249 15 May 1963, cols. 1322–46; also Vol. 251, 24 June 1963, cols. 109–124.

126 On the BMA's views see Annual Report of Council 1962, para. 232; Annual Report of Council, 1962–63, para. 239.

127 HC Deb., Vol. 675, 2 April 1963, cols. 183–200: 252–61.

128 They would also, incidentally, have absorbed the City of London Police into the Metropolitan Police.

129 Lord Stonham (HL Deb., Vol. 250, 27 May 1963, col. 660)

130 cf Earl Jellicoe, HL Deb., Vol. 250, 27 May 1963, cols. 665–6.

131 Royal Commission on the Police, Final Report (Cmnd 1728, 1962) para 223. They also saw no reason for any change in the position of the City of London Police (Cmnd, 1728, 1962, para. 228).

132 The member for Epsom (Sir Peter Rawlinson) was Solicitor-General and could not therefore take part in this discussion.

133 See above, p. 124.

134 By 35 votes to 30. See HL Deb., Vol. 251, 24 June 1963, cols. 66–88.

CHAPTER 11

1 Section 86.

2 Names of the boroughs quoted are those which were subsequently adopted; it was one of the tasks of the joint committees to suggest to the Minister names for the new boroughs (See Appendix 3, p. 255 for a list of the borough names and constituent authorities).

3 London Government Act, 1963, s. 1.

4 In Borough 24, for example (Richmond upon Thames), the Twickenham area elected 3 councillors from each of its 10 wards, the Richmond area 1 councillor from each of its 12 wards and the Barnes area 4 councillors from each of its 3 wards.

5 Letter to *The Times* 8 October 1963, Other *Times* correspondents also joined in; Sir Charles Wheeler, for example, who felt 'outraged at the proposal to erase an image of great significance. Chelsea – the very word has a ringing tone which echoes round the world. . . .' (22 October 1963).

6 *Evening Standard*, 30 October 1963.

7 *The Times*, 8 August, 1963.

8 See below, p. 208.

9 ie Borough No 29 comprising Beckenham, Bromley, Orpington, Penge and part of Chislehurst and Sidcup.

10 At Westminster, for example, 11 of the 12 members of the joint committee became members of the new London Borough; of these 11, two were appointed chairmen respectively of the key committees of General Purposes and Finance.

11 This was a serious problem; the new boroughs inherited anything from 2 to 5 town halls not always ideally situated for serving their area.

12 This concern derived not from any specific powers under the London Government Act but from the Home Secretary's general oversight of the children's service (cf JAG Griffith, *Central Departments and Local Authorities* (RIPA/Allen & Unwin, 1966), chapter 6, esp pp. 364–9).

13 In a circular letter (D/L64/26), 2 September 1964; as with the Home Office and the children's service, the Ministry of Health's powers and responsibilities derived from the general legislation about the health and welfare services and not from any specific provision of the London Government Act.

14 For example, the Ministry of Health held a series of meetings in the London Boroughs for this purpose in November and December 1964.

15 The meeting with the LCC Staff Association was at County Hall on 31 July 1963, that with NALGO at the Royal Albert Hall on 23 September. The former date was that on which the London Government Act received the Royal Assent.

16 See Reports in *London Town*, September 1963 pp. 273–5, and NALGO Bulletin No. 8 *Local Government Reorganization*, October 1963.

17 See p. 161.

18 London Government Act, 1963, S 85(5).

19 See HC Deb., Vol. 675, 2 April 1963, col. 289.

20 The Commission remained in being until December 1965 but completed their executive work by the end of September 1965.

21 Sir Harold Emmerson, the chairman, was a former permanent secretary of the Ministry of Labour; Lord Geddes of Epsom, a former general secretary of the Union of Post Office Workers; and Lord Hemingford, alderman (since 1959) and chairman (since 1961) of the Huntingdon and Peterborough County Council.

22 HC Deb., Vol. 675, 2 April 1963, col. 287.

23 London Government Staff Commission *Report* (HMSO 1966) paras 10 and 11.

24 LGSC *Report*, paras 7–8.

25 The Commission could not be formally appointed until August, after the London Government Bill had been passed.

26 For example, in inner London the MBSJC reports were not available to the joint committees before November 1963.

27 LGSC *Report*, para. 172.

28 Ministry of Housing and Local Government Circular 6/63: Staff Commission Circular of 23 August, 1963.

29 Staff Commission memo. 6 March 1964.

30 Staff Commission Circular Letter 8 October 1964: the categories included junior, clerical and typing staff; newly qualified architects and planners; and manual workers.

31 LGSC *Report*, para. 109.

32 See Ministry of Housing and Local Government Circular No. 5/64 (13 February 1964): Ministry of Education Circular Letter, 23 March 1964.

33 British Medical Association memorandum 'Proposed Transitional Medical Establishment for a London Borough' (no date).

34 LGSC *Report*, para. 53.

35 Circular Letter LA (GEN) /D/L64/11 of 8 April 1964.

36 Circular Letter, para. 5 (iii).

37 Not simply the borough area since the existing child care service was not organized in this way; 7 areas were identified (eg LCC area for the 12 inner London Boroughs, Surrey and Croydon for the 'Surrey Boroughs' etc) See Appendix to HO Circular 114/1964, 14 May, 1964.

38 Estimates of 500–1,000 appeals had been made in advance but there were in fact only 38. (Report, para. 165).

39 Only 172 officers were declared redundant, 72 being chief officers or deputies; of the 172 more than half were over 60 and therefore close to retirement. (Report, para. 182).

40 LGSC *Report*, para. 15.

41 National and Local Government Officers' Association, Statement of Evidence on the Structure of Local Government in England (October 1966), paras. 37–9.

42 For example, the question of determining which of the county officers of Essex, Hertfordshire, Kent and Surrey were affected by the reorganization and therefore eligible for posts with the new authorities (Report, paras 100–103).

43 LGSC *Report*, para. 125.

44 There is no doubt that in a number of cases tacit understandings had been reached by joint committees, particularly over the appointment of clerks, which were simply accepted by the new authorities.

45 It has to be recalled that the borough elections took place only on 7 May.

46 Middlesex CC had no comparable posts, except for the licensing department.

47 GLC Minutes 9 June 1964, pp. 49–51.

48 GLC Minutes, 21 July 1964, p. 82.

49 The appointment of a medical adviser was not however made until 10 November 1964; this raised special problems as it was a joint appointment with the ILEA.

50 See MHLG Circular 23/64 of 3 June 1964.

51 See *Surrey Comet*, 13 June and 20 June 1964.

52 See *Hendon and Finchley Times*, 16 October 1964. Also, *Guardian*, 8 October 1964; the hint of political bias in these appointments (Willesden was Labour, Wembley Conservative) was vigorously denied by the Brent Council.

53 *Tottenham & Edmonton Weekly Herald*, 7 August 1964.

54 eg *Surrey Comet*, 27 June 1964.

55 *Richmond & Twickenham Times*, 25 July and 1 August 1964.

56 See above, p. 192.

57 eg Battersea Metropolitan Borough upgraded 97% of their staff at a cost of nearly £26,000 and were criticized by the district auditor for doing so, (*Guardian*, 23 February 1965).

58   The implication is that for years Middlesex staff had been under-paid; in which case upgrading would have to be regarded not as an adverse consequence of reorganization but a belated measure of justice.

59   At a later stage the GLC reviewed all its initial salary scales.

60   cf the article by Wilfred Whittle 'London Boroughs' staffing may set the pattern for the future' (*Guardian*, 1 February 1965).

61   The normal date because it coincides with the beginning of the financial year.

62   A small example is recorded in the *Municipal Review* for August 1968 on the occasion of the completion of the third swimming-bath in Bexley LB within 18 months. 'This will complete the pro-gramme which the previous authorities . . . embarked on.' (p. 328). One wonders if the new borough would have felt the need for three new baths.

63   In two other boroughs Labour was the largest single party before the election of aldermen (Havering: Lab. 27, Cons. 16, Ind. 12: Merton: Lab. 26, Con. 24, Ind. 4).

64   Of the 64 GLC Labour councillors elected in 1964, 31 had previ-ously served on the LCC including such prominent figures as Mr (now Lord) Fiske, who became Leader of the GLC, Mrs (now Lady) Serota and Mrs McIntosh.

65   *The Economist*, 18 January 1964.

66   Hugh Berrington, 'Local Elections' in *Aspect*, January 1964, p. 13.

67   Each borough area returned either all Conservative or all Labour members; single-member constituencies would almost certainly have resulted in fewer Labour members being returned.

68   See above, p. 169.

69   CHN/62/4/20.

70   See *London Teacher*, July 1965.

71   HC Deb., Vol. 736, 23 November 1966, Cols. 1419–86.

72   HL Deb., Vol. 281, 4 April 1967, col. 852.

73   HL Deb., Vol. 281 4 April 1967, col. 863.

74   Local Government (Termination of Reviews) Act, 1967, section 2

CHAPTER 12

1 This would have been even more so if, as is likely, the conversion of the largest Middlesex Boroughs into County Boroughs had led to the amalgamation of the remaining Middlesex authorities to form units of a size suitable in their turn for conversion into County Boroughs, on the grounds that Middlesex without the large boroughs would not make sense as a local government unit.

2 Royal Commission on Local Government in England 1966–1969.

3 See above, p. 12.

4 *Areas and Status of Local Authorities in England and Wales* (Cmd 9831).

5 Cmnd 1562

6 W.J.M. Mackenzie, *Theories of Local Government* (Greater London Paper No 2, London School of Economics 1961), pp 5–7

7 Mackenzie, *Theories of Local Government*, page 15.

8 Smallwood, *Greater London*, p. 79

9 Smallwood, *Greater London*, p. 8.

10 Peter Self reviewing Smallwood, *Greater London* in *Public Administration*, Vol. 44, Winter 1966, p. 485.

11 It is likely that Dame Evelyn Sharp, who became Permanent Secretary of the Ministry of Housing and Local Government in 1955, had a greater awareness of the problems of London government than her predecessor and that her advice carried considerable influence with Mr Brooke.

12 HC Deb., 29 July 1957. Vol. 574, col. 917.

13 HC Deb., 20 February 1962. Vol. 654. col. 245.

14 Elizabeth Stockwell 'London's New Order' (*Spectator*, 14 December 1962).

15 Smallwood, *Greater London*, p. 230.

16 Above, p. 187.

17 These measures were announced by Mr Selwyn Lloyd, Chancellor of the Exchequer, on 25 July.

Index